From a Chair in the Sun

From a Chair in the Sun

The Life of Ethel Turner

A. T. Yarwood

VIKING

Viking
Penguin Books Australia Ltd
487 Maroondah Highway, PO Box 257
Ringwood, Victoria, 3134, Australia
Penguin Books Ltd
Harmondsworth, Middlesex, England
Viking Penguin, A Division of Penguin Books USA Inc.
375 Hudson Street, New York, New York 10014, USA
Penguin Books Canada Limited
10 Alcorn Avenue, Toronto, Ontario, Canada, M4V 3B2
Penguin Books (N.Z.) Ltd
182 – 190 Wairau Road, Auckland 10, New Zealand

First published by Viking Australia, 1994
10 9 8 7 6 5 4 3 2 1
Copyright © A. T. Yarwood, 1994

Typeset in 12/14½ Caslon by Midland Typsetters Pty. Ltd.
Made and printed in Australia by Australian Print Group

National Library of Australia
Cataloguing-in-Publication data:

Yarwood, A. T. (Alexander Turnbull), 1927 –   .
From a chair in the sun: the life of Ethel Turner.

Includes index.
ISBN 0 670 83717 2.

1. Turner, Ethel, 1872 – 1958 – Biography. 2. Authors
Australian – 20th century – Biography. 3, Women authors,
Australian – 20th century – Biography. I. Title.

A823.2

To my family, whose belief in me
seems inexhaustible.

'From a Chair in the Sun' was the title of Ethel Turner's opening editorial in the first issue of 'Sunbeams' in the Sunday *Sun* of 9 October 1921.

Contents

Prologue

'I do want Fame – plenty of it. Today I feel I want it almost more than anything, nothing else can quite satisfy me. If a fairy came and offered me Love or Fame of course I should choose Love. No, I don't see why I shouldn't have both. I don't want to be married though for a long time, a little time ago I thought I did but I want to have a tilt with Fame first. Conceited little ape, you want your ears boxing.'

Ethel Turner was 23, and secretly engaged to Herbert Raine Curlewis, when she made this entry in her diary. A little over a week later she noted, 'Night started a new story that I shall call "Seven Little Australians". I don't think I'll let it go in the *Illustrated*, if I can do without it there I'll see if I can get it published in book form.'

Ten months later, the manuscript was welcomed by an English publisher as marking the appearance of the Louisa Alcott of Australia.

Many times in the course of published interviews and articles Ethel Turner addressed the broader question of why she had become a writer, telling of the impulse to journalism that made her the editor of the *Iris*, in competition with Louise Mack's official school magazine at Sydney Girls' High. Remarkable as it seems, looking back to the circumstances of an aspiring young female writer a century ago, she suggested that on leaving school it was no more than a natural progression to found and edit a literary magazine, the *Parthenon*, to write for the *Bulletin*, and establish a children's page in the *Illustrated Sydney News*.

All of this combined to offer a basic source of income for several decades. The desire for fame – and with it, absolute financial security – remained constant throughout her long career as a public figure. Repeatedly her diary, commenced in 1889 and continued almost all her life, shows how gratified she was by the recognition and respect she was universally accorded. Never more, perhaps, than when a Maori guide in Rotorua, on hearing her name, gathered her in her arms and declared that she too was the mother of seven ... 'Seven Little Maoris' ... from which Ethel concluded, 'now are my doubts set at rest, I am a truly celebrated person'.

Ethel's time in New Zealand in 1926 preceded a crisis in the family which culminated in the death of her daughter Jean in 1930. Yet she was able to rise above her anxieties and welcome the formation of the Junior Literary Society of Sydney, very like the organization to which she had belonged in the early 1890s. The later body had been formed through the involvement of former Sunbeamers, some of whom had been stimulated to aim for careers as professional writers. She was at first the founding vice-president and the patron, in which capacity she wrote an open letter published in the first issue of the Journal in June 1927.

On that occasion Ethel advised her readers: 'Do not be too easily content. Go higher and higher. Follow after Beauty.'[1] This injunction expressed a central conviction in her life, informing her approach to every aspect of literature, art and music. It was pre-eminent in her love of poetry and important to her appreciation of architecture and furniture.

When the *Town and Country Journal* closed in 1919 Ethel wrote to the Sydney *Sun* hoping to persuade the directors to appoint her as editor of a children's newspaper. Two years later this materialized as a colour supplement, 'Sunbeams', including a section for would-be writers – and of course, a comic strip which gave life to the immortal Ginger Meggs. Much credit has been given to the imagination of young Jimmy Bancks, the cartoonist, but Ethel Turner's part in devising the template to which he addressed his skills as an artist has been unrecognised until this time. Ginger was an amalgam of several of Ethel's own characters of which the 'Little Larrikin' was supreme, though in the last resort Bancks's contribution was decisive as Ethel immediately recognised.

While this book was in progress I received a vital article from Lesley Heath linking Ethel with the Junior Literary Society and demonstrating her long commitment to children's literature.[2] Forty years earlier Ethel and her sister Lilian had written the opening editorial of the *Parthenon*, a literary magazine they founded three months after Ethel had left school in October 1888.

There are very, very few Australian magazines devoted to literature only, they might easily be counted on the fingers of one hand, and yet they are very little encouraged ... Too often it has been said that high literature and high education is a mistake in Australia, that Australians cannot appreciate such things, and still worse, make no effort to appreciate them. We will say no more on the subject, except to express a hope that in the bright growing future that is opening to Australia, literature will play a very prominent part.[3]

Long after Ethel began editing children's pages for the *Parthenon*, Ruth Park worked on the *Auckland Star* children's supplement. As Ruth wrote in her autobiography the experience served her well: '[It] taught me what children like to read; often it resembles in no way what adults think they enjoy.'[4]

Ethel wrote one of her most illuminating articles for the *Lone Hand* in 1913, 'The Books that I Remember'. After giving details of her adventures as a reader, which were 'like a mouse [nibbling] on the edge of a thousand things', she returns to consider the needs of young people:

Did you ever find a child in an apple tree or curled up in an old arm-chair with hot cheeks and misty eyes tearing the heart out of a book, and discover that book to be classic, handsomely bound in suede ... price twenty-four shillings?

You know that you have always found the book to be a tattered sixpenny with a coloured picture of a boy hanging on to an aeroplane in high air, while pirates, from whom he has just escaped, are taking aim at him from earth with many guns.

They must cut their teeth on what they genuinely like, these young people, and you must leave them pretty much alone for a time. Let them establish the habit of swift and eager reading, spontaneous reading in almost any way they will.

Ethel Turner often sighed for recognition as an author of adult books but in the last resort she probably gained from the fact that she remained virtually free from the need to compete for adult readers. In September 1904 she was warned by her English publisher, George Lock:

I note your remarks about wishing to appear not as a writer *for* children but *about* children, and regret to say that in our opinion if you take [*sic*] on that standpoint your sales would drop to tens, where it is now thousands.

Ethel maintained her appeal for children for many years, combining elements of realism and fantasy in equal proportions. Brenda Niall, writing about *Seven Little Australians*, comments: 'As the first author of any talent to discard the outback adventure story and write about ordinary children in a Sydney suburban setting, Ethel Turner was in herself a revolution.'[5]

At the close of Ethel's career, Zora Cross wrote in the *Sydney Morning Herald* to summarize her influence:

Ethel Turner, from the moment she opened the door of an Australian house and showed the world what we were really like, has been a guiding star for the rest.[6]

*E*arly in her career as a writer Ethel Turner published an autobiographical novel entitled *Three Little Maids* which has an interesting balance of fact and fiction. Some matters raised in the first chapter about the relationship between the two elder Turner sisters endured for their entire lives. Ethel (represented in the book by the younger sister Dorothy) had always been charged by her mother with the responsibility of looking after her frail elder sister Lilian (represented by Phyl). In *Three Little Maids* the girls venture out into the freshly fallen snow at midnight to rescue the dolls which had been left in the garden. On their return both the dolls and themselves were wet and cold:

Dorothy was feeling still disturbed, for had she not promised her mother to help to look after this delicate Phyl and keep her from danger? She slipped out of bed once more, and went to the mantelpiece where stood the bottle of cod-liver oil, with which they had built Phyl up after her last attack.[1]

Ethel describes how the fictional Widow Conway had tried to keep her husband's textile factory going with funds settled on the elder girls by her first husband, at the same time sending his children to live with various relatives, dismissing the servants and drastically reducing her life style. All to no avail. With only 400 pounds left and a sickly eldest daughter whose chest put her life in constant jeopardy during the English winter the Widow Conway is advised by her doctor to remove her family to a kinder climate. The three daughters, who represented Lilian, Ethel and Rose, prepare to leave 'the big house' and emigrate to Australia. Much is made of the library, of which only a few special treasures are to accompany the family to the new country.

Sarah Shaw, Ethel's mother, was born on 16 December 1843. Her father was William Shaw, a professor of music and her mother was Rebecca (formerly Hall); they lived at St Marks in Lincoln and the family prospered to the extent of buying a well-equipped stationery shop in The Strait in Lincoln. William Shaw later went into business as a jeweller.

Sarah's eldest daughter, Lilian Wattnall Burwell, was born on 21 August 1867 at Gresham Street, Lincoln, but it is not certain that Sarah and Lilian's father were married; his name was Bennett George Burwell and he was described as a commercial traveller. By the time Ethel was born on 24 January 1870 the family had moved to Doncaster near York, where they occupied a small terrace house in West Terrace, in Queen Street, Balby. If anything the family was at a lower ebb since leaving Lincoln. At the census of 1871 Jane Burwell was recorded as the wife (Sarah's second name was Jane), while Burwell was described as a commercial traveller and was said to be abroad; Sarah's age was stated to be 25 years (it was 28). Lilian appears as 3 years and Ethel as 1 and the family was completed by a domestic servant (15 years old) named Harriett Bywater.

Family tradition has it that Burwell died in France but no record has been found. Sarah lost no time in remarrying. On 21 August 1872 she wed Henry Turner, aged 39, a widower with a family of his own. He was described as a factory manager, whose residence (and also Sarah's) at the time was

Simpsons Temperance Hotel in Yarmouth in Norfolk. Almost a year later a daughter Jeanie Rose was born (1 August 1873) when the family was living in Wellington Villas, Amberstone Road, Leicester, about 40 km north of Nuneaton.

Henry possessed an ornate clock which his daughter Lucy carried with her to Australia in 1880: 'Presented to Henry Turner Jnr as a mark of esteem and respect by the employees of Messrs H. Turner & Son, Brunswick Street Mills, Leicester, Dec 24 1869'. But the 1870s were the nadir of manufacturing in the area and a few years later Henry Turner was dead. His widow Sarah decided to seek a better life in Australia.

Many years later Sarah wrote to her daughter Jeanie Rose, for whom she had a special affinity, to tell her about the final illness of her father and the decline of his prosperity:[2]

I am so glad you asked about him' ... 'above all he was a good man, true, honourable, just in all dealings, cheery, genial, loving-hearted – always joking and as full of pranks as a schoolboy' ... 'we were rather a mad pair sometimes, altho' he was an invalid. I remember once how he dressed me up in one of the boy's suits and we went out together as Father and Son – and over the dressing up we went almost into fits of laughter. We had worlds of sorrow and trouble but we never let it crush us and frequently had the maddest, merriest times. Yes dear, it was heartbreakingly sad that he should die so young ... He is buried in Coventry cemetery with not a stone to mark his resting place.

About three months before they left England (24 September 1879), Sarah wrote from her home in Lincoln to 'My most precious Ethel', thanking her for her 'funny little letter' and expressing concern that she and her sisters had experienced a nice journey in the care of a Mrs Drewery. Even then Sarah cautioned Ethel to be 'very kind and forbearing to [Rosie] when she is self willed'. It appears that Sarah had been making preparations for the journey to Australia. Lucy Turner (aged 14) is intended to accompany Sarah and a further young person named Annie is named in this connection, so there was a group of five children going with Sarah rather than the 'three little maids' of Ethel's novel.

The actual date of Ethel Turner's birth remained a family secret throughout her life, a secret apparently known only to mother and daughters. It would seem that her widowed mother Sarah had altered the ages of her two eldest daughters, Lilian and Ethel, by two years in order to obtain fare concessions when the family emigrated to Australia from England in 1879.

The Turner party sailed on the steamship *Durham*, which arrived in Sydney on 24 March 1880. Their ages were recorded as follows in the ship's papers: Mrs Turner 38; Miss Turner 14 [Lucy]; Miss Turner 7 [Lilian]; Miss Turner 5 [Ethel]; Miss Turner 4 [Rose]; Miss Turner 3 [Annie]. As Philippa Poole writes in the *The Diaries of Ethel Turner*, 'Strangely enough none of the three girls were ever known by their descendants to talk about their life in England or the voyage on board ship . . . ' Presumably, the fear that their misstatement of ages might be exposed helped to drive the girls inwards to the security of their own company.

Having once gained a reduction in the fare by fraud, however, Sarah Turner and her daughters were bound to stick to the false ages throughout the long voyage, lest an incautious word to a fellow passenger should find its way to the captain, unleashing perhaps some nasty retribution. Uncertainties and fears on this score inevitably accompanied every phase of the journey and it can be imagined that Mrs Turner constantly reminded the girls of the need to guard their conversations. On their arrival in Australia that vigilance was still needed, because of the fear that a change in the story might be exposed by an observant fellow passenger, making them liable perhaps to serious legal consequences. The Australian colonies were very particular about migrants' vital statistics as they had been from the beginning of convict transportation. Once having reiterated the false statements upon arrival the family felt obliged to preserve consistency with the initial story. No doubt they felt on countless occasions that it had been a most unlucky departure from the truth. The deception was maintained in the cases of the 'three little maids' for the rest of their lives and in ways that must have caused considerable disquiet. From the time Ethel began keeping a diary in 1889 she did not waver in giving allegiance to the spurious date, notably in proclaiming 'I am 21 today, an infant no longer'.

Little is known of the family's activities from the time of the arrival of the *Durham* until Sarah married Charles Cope at St Peter's Church of England at Woolloomooloo (now Darlinghurst) on the last day of 1880. In the circumstances of the time a handsome woman like Sarah urgently needed a protector to provide comfort and support for her family. Charles Cope, then a clerk in the Lands Department in his eighth year of employment on an annual salary of 200 pounds, was a younger son of a grazier whose widow lived at 'The Dingle', one of the historic homes at Kirribilli overlooking Milson's Point. The family had extensive landed interests including 'Calala' in New South Wales and 'Dagworth' in Queensland. This background helps to explain why a modestly paid clerk should have been on the visiting list at Government House; and it also explains why Charles and Sarah Cope saw very little of their Australian relations. No matter how handsome Sarah appeared she had no prospects, and as well there was the matter of the children.

Three Little Maids makes no reference to the fourth and fifth members of the party who sailed to Sydney with Sarah Turner. Her older step-daughter, Lucy Turner, was living with the family both before and after the voyage; indeed, she was still important enough to the family to appear as a witness when Sarah married Charles Cope. To a large extent Lucy tends to disappear from sight, possibly because she herself married Thomas Board in 1884 and in any case the Copes had their own problems of readjustment.

Soon after being married the Copes went to live in Stanley Street near the church and then in Elizabeth Street within a stone's throw of Paddington Public School, where Ethel was a student until October 1883. That school, now one of the most lovingly restored in the heart of old Sydney, remembers Ethel's time as a student by offering each year the Ethel Turner Prize for Literature.

chapter

Two

*O*ur first clear image of Ethel Turner in Australia shows her, a tiny blonde girl of 11 years, entering the side door of Paddington Public School early in 1881. The school, a model primary built in 1856 on the south side of Oxford Street to meet the needs generated by the population of soldiers at the Victoria Barracks, was then a single-storeyed brick structure. An enclosed courtyard shielded its pupils and teachers from the noise and bustle of the stream trams that clattered and whistled down Oxford Street towards the city of Sydney, about two kilometres away to the west.

Ethel had an easy walk to school, for her family lived two hundred metres further out from the city on the same side of Oxford Street, just a block below the newly constructed gates at the entrance to Centennial Park. 'Erang' was the name of their home, which still stands a century later. It was one of a pair of two-storeyed semi-detached brick houses that perched uncomfortably between the ornate Byzantine grandeur of the Roman Catholic Church of St Francis and spartan severity of St Matthias's Church of England. The latter church was experiencing its final years under the founding rector, the Reverend Dr Zachary Barry, an Ulsterman of uncompromising anti-Papist principles who was famous for his powerful extempore sermons and a great favourite of

Ethel Turner and her family. Charles Cope was elected church warden in 1888 and Lilian and Ethel were to teach at the Sunday School.

In October 1883, Ethel and Lilian were part of the first intake of pupils at Sydney Girls' High, situated then in Elizabeth Street at the present site of David Jones, opposite Hyde Park. The building itself was said to have been designed by Francis Greenaway for Governor Macquarie, who laid the foundation stone of the red brick two-storeyed Georgian structure in 1820. Its life as a school began in 1824 under the Church and Schools Corporation and in 1867 it became a denominational school, remaining as such till the legislation of 1880 provided for the establishment of high schools that would prepare male and female pupils for entrance to the University of Sydney. At first both boys and girls used the school, the former occupying the lower floor and entering from Castlereagh Street and the latter the upper storey, which had access from Elizabeth Street, an arrangement that continued until the boys moved into temporary quarters at the Technical College at Ultimo in 1892.[1]

Admission of the first intake of thirty-nine girls on 7 October 1883 was by examination; scholarships were awarded to the first six placegetters irrespective of parental income and Ethel Turner was one of that select group, which also included her lifelong friend, Ethel Maynard. Ethel Turner was pupil number 35 in the chronological list; significantly, there is an erasure and correction in the column for 'Pupil's Age', and it appears that a 13 was written initially (her correct age) though it was altered to 12. Her name was given as E. Mary Turner, for all three girls took the name of Sarah's second husband (by the time Ethel was being published she used Sybil as her second name); Lilian's name appears next as number 36 and her age is given at 15 years, though she was over 16. We are reminded of the cynical observation that people who tamper with the truth need good memories.

After school the girls were inspected by a teacher on their departure through the gate to ensure they were wearing gloves. Many then repaired to the corner fruit shop to buy watermelons, which were consumed in Hyde Park. At lunch time on Fridays, if they had been well behaved, they were permitted to dance in the large school room; perhaps this is when Ethel learned an accomplishment that was to give her much pleasure. Not that there was much room for outdoor activities; the space was so limited that organised sport and physical culture remained unavailable, this despite the influence of such pioneering publicists as Louisa Lawson who thought women needed exercise as much as men, most of all because of the constricting modes of feminine dress.

For many years the girls did not use a uniform beyond having a hatband with the school's crest. They usually wore a blouse and skirt or frock, with a hemline varying from mid-calf for the youngest girls to ground length for the grown-up girls. The former wore their hair in long curls or a pigtail secured with a large bow though the latter 'put their hair self-consciously and proudly "up". Long black stockings, single strap shoes or buttoned boots, a straw boater, and gloves completed the outfit'.[2]

At Sydney High Ethel came under the influence of Miss Lucy Wheatley Walker, the founding headmistress, who stimulated girls to develop a love of scholarship which helped to produce some notable talents. For some years the school lacked a library but eventually Miss Walker put pressure on the Department of Public Instruction to match her own efforts at raising money. She was seen as a wonderful teacher and understood the need for students of literary subjects to receive marked assignments 'liberally corrected in red ink'. Girls were encouraged to take part in plays before the Christmas break.[3]

Miss Walker was seen as a 'bit of a snob'. Her special disapproval was reserved for, 'The vulgarity of dining out, in public eating places!' Yet as Ruth Bowmaker wrote, in Lilith Norman's engaging centenary history of the school:

None of her old pupils can think of her now without a thrill of pride and affection ... The head, Miss Lucy Wheatley Walker, by nature designed to be a Head, with her queenly air and her compelling glance. How terribly small one felt when sent to Miss Walker! One look and you knew!

Miss Walker taught us singing, and well, too. Of our part-singing we were particularly proud. We could never quite make up our minds whether by accident or design she started us on "Three Blind Mice" one day, just as three inspectors entered the room.[4]

Ruth Bowmaker began her studies at the age of 11 in January 1884, just three months after Miss Walker was appointed first headmistress at Sydney Girls' High, and went on to an honours degree at Sydney University. Whereas Ruth was obliged to abandon her career on marriage, when Miss Walker became Mrs Garvin in 1891 she was able to maintain her position for another twenty-seven years. It was suggested by George Reid in speaking about the initial appointment of Miss Wheatley Walker in 1883 that the influence of Professor Charles Badham was decisive. He was Professor of Classics at the University of Sydney and remained a steadfast friend of the school for decades.

Lilith Norman writes of the period when the school began as a time when women were preparing to take a big step forwards, 'It is hard to imagine today what it must have been like to be a lively, alert, intelligent girl a hundred years ago; a girl for whom a little French and drawing, the dates of the kings of England ... were not enough.' She visualises these women as having been held back by the lack of education and of constructive outlets for their energies. To them it was all a marvellous new adventure and there 'was a joy and a delight in being privileged to learn, in going to a proper school and learning proper subjects'.[5]

The school quickly established a magazine, the *Gazette*, under the editorship of Louise Mack, who entered the school in 1884. As Ethel later wrote, 'The editor of the school paper evidently considered the aspiring contributions I used to drop into her box as beneath contempt, so in a wrathful moment I rallied my particular friends around me and started a rival paper'.

This was the beginning of the *Iris* and gave Ethel an experience that set her on a lifetime track in journalism. Lilian was a member of the editorial staff as were girls whose names recur for many years in the diary, including Marcia Cox, Ethel Maynard and Nina Hague-Smith.

Commenting on the rivalry between the two editors, Lilith Norman suggests that Ethel's product was the 'livelier magazine'. The *Iris* was smaller and carried front page advertisements costing a guinea a time, and ran to social notes and reporting day to day events. However, neither magazine survived the departure of its editor and Ethel, being unsupported by school funds, was obliged to turn to her mother for help in paying an overdue printer's account. What was remarkable about the incident was the rarity of Ethel's making a mistake in a matter of business.

The tiny upstairs room at 'Erang' in which Ethel and Lilian began their careers as editors may still be seen at 485 Oxford Street, now a doctor's surgery. From its little western window one can look out, as the girls did over a century ago, on the Church of St Francis next door. Ethel describes it in her chapter, 'The Writing Room', in *Three Little Maids*.

The room was about seven feet square, so there was space for no furniture beyond a little table and a chair each. The chairs stood back to back, touching each other, so that if one writer in the throes of an idea that would not reduce itself to words, moved restlessly, the other was forced to protest. On the walls, hanging bookshelves held every volume the girls possessed: and like most of the shelves that depend from a cord, these had an irritating knack of occasionally tilting forward, or sloping sideways, and showering their contents on the owners' heads.

Photographs, little pictures, and nick-nacks filled every available corner; under each table a tiny ink-bottle and fancy pen ... a vase of flowers, sixpenny statuettes of Milton and Shakespeare, a photograph or two, a penwiper, a stamp-sponge, a doll's saucer filled with paper fasteners.

Sydney Girls' High was not one of those schools that offered 'softer' options for study by females, intending them for graceful accomplishments rather than scholarship. The University of Sydney had been opened to women in 1882, and the new school was designed to enable them to take advantage of the new opportunity. At her Junior Examination Ethel achieved A standard in English History, Latin, Geography and Geology and Bs in French, Arithmetic and English. She sat also for examinations in Algebra, Euclid, German, European History, Greek, Plane Geometry and Perspective, Bible History, Music and Painting. By the time of the Senior Examinations in June 1888 she is shown as coming second in the year; her rival editor and later bosom friend, Louise Mack, came sixth. Ethel left school at the end of September 1888, a year after Lilian.[6]

Amongst the decisive experiences that had already shaped her life were the loss of two fathers before she was ten and the observation of her mother battling to keep the family afloat in seas made perilous by financial disaster and chronic ill health. At least five homes had been abandoned and the family uprooted and moved to the furthest point in the globe. Insecurity and danger had been her constant companions and after the family's arrival in Australia, her mother was married a third time, to a man with a violent temper and a disposition to tyranny. Small wonder that Ethel's strongest impulse was to seek security by using her talents as a writer productively and profitably, sometimes turning out potboilers in order to maintain the flow of royalties and continuing with the editing of repetitive children's pages which returned a stable income when her spirit cried out for more satisfying intellectual stimulus.

But no study of Ethel's life can afford to neglect the steady contribution made by her mother, whose influence was the prime reason for her daughter's emerging from the most hazardous childhood with a remarkably serene mind and a capacity for enduring and selfless friendships.

chapter
Three

On the last day of September 1888 Ethel said farewell to her friends and teachers at Sydney Girls'
High and joined her sister Lilian at home. The
Cope family was still living at 'Erang', on the north-western
side of Oxford Street, little more than a hundred metres from
the boundary of Centennial Park, which had been dedicated
on Anniversary Day in January 1888 to commemorate a
hundred years of British settlement in Australia. Lord Carrington, the aristocratic young governor of 'liberal views and
winning ways', had conceived the park as providing an
equestrian track like London's Rotten Row and the ageing
Sir Henry Parkes, then in his fourth term as premier, quickly
adopted the idea. Both men welcomed the chance of con-
verting the wastes of the Lachlan Swamps, bordering Oxford
Street as it marched east to Bondi Beach, into a resource to
be enjoyed for all time by the people of Sydney.[1]

Yet it would be mistaken to imagine Ethel and her siblings
enjoying the ambience of Centennial Park as we know it
today. A contemporary photograph shows an 'almost treeless
waste' on the hill sloping north from Oxford Street only
months before the dedication ceremony. From Ethel's 1889
diary it seems clear that the sisters seldom ventured into the
park, perhaps because their long dresses would have suffered
from the raw state of the new roads and sandy lawns. With

the two elder sisters now at home, it became necessary at the end of the year for a search to be made for more ample accommodation. Lilian was now 21, Ethel 18, Rose 15 and Rex Cope, their half-brother, was 7.

Though tiny, the three sisters were charmingly pretty in peaches and cream fashion with masses of soft blonde curls. In a contemporary photograph Ethel regards the camera with her blue eyes in a steady gaze, her face showing classic and regular features and the upper part of her body marked by strong athletic shoulders, a trim bosom and a firm shapely neck. Both the set of her shoulders and the resolute mouth and chin suggest those qualities of determination that had carried her through many crises.

Ethel had not yet begun the habit of keeping a daily diary, which, once it started in April 1889, continued without a major break till 1951. If she had we might then have known why on leaving school she did not enrol as an undergraduate at the University of Sydney or embark on some other formal career path. Certainly her achievements in June at the school's Senior Examination, being graded second in a distinguished year, indicated a capacity for disciplined study. The most likely explanation was her eagerness 'to grow independent early', to use the phrase Ethel applied to her daughter Jean at the same stage of *her* life. Financial security was her overwhelming desire and it was to be sought neither in a continuing dependence on her stepfather nor in exchanging the family roof for the protection offered by some aspiring husband. Until that basic need had been satisfied there would be no question of a conventional courtship or marriage. To Ethel's mind, marriage seemed the riskiest venture a woman could embark on, associated with disaster rather than security.

As head of a family that commonly accepted invitations to vice-regal functions, Charles Cope would hardly have considered it appropriate for either of his stepdaughters to work in a shop, no matter how refined its clientele. His explosive response to Ethel's later suggestion of becoming a governess gives a clue to his feelings on such matters. Not so clear is the reason for rejecting the university's claims, except that study for a degree would have reduced her productivity as a professional writer. Yet the university appealed to Ethel as a venue for social and sporting activity and as a stimulus for adventures of the mind. One of her earliest publications was a humorous poem that appeared in the university's new literary journal *Hermes* in December 1889.

If Charles Cope had the notion that his two elder stepdaughters would accept easily the limitations of a life of leisure he was speedily made aware of his error. Within three months of Ethel's leaving school, she and Lilian had taken over the little attic room that looked out on the Catholic church next door and prepared it as a base for a brave new literary venture. They became founders and joint editors of a magazine named the *Parthenon*, showing an awareness in the title, perhaps, of an English publication of the same name.

As the girls explained in the opening editorial published in January 1889 the title signified 'of the virgins'. Rather daringly, they went onto admit:

This, our '*Parthenon*', is not in both senses of the word a *maiden* effort. 'Of the virgins' it certainly is, as the old Greek word suggests, but we have guided a small rudder before, the rudder of a little bark with '*Iris*' for its name, and hope soon to guide this one better, as every day leaves us older and, we will suppose, wiser.

Although two years older than Ethel, Lilian had simply served on the *Iris* as a staff member, with her sister described as Editress. In their new venture they were joint editors though it fell to Ethel as the younger sister to take charge of the children's page. So began a literary apprenticeship that led on to her experience as editor of the children's pages on several Sydney papers, reaching a high point of originality and popularity in her work as Chief Sunbeamer for the Sydney *Sun* in the 1920s, the decade that produced Ginger Meggs, an authentic Australian boy created by Jim Bancks to a verbal template drawn up by Ethel Turner.

Several times in later years Ethel told the story of the *Parthenon*'s origins most persuasively in responding to an adventurous request from the editor of the Brisbane *Grammar School Magazine*. Writing to her in April 1900 when she was one of the most famous authors in Australia he sought advice for boys who hoped to make names for themselves in the world of letters. Answering almost by return mail she told him that:

The thought of schoolboys worrying over anything (except what pudding will be for dinner, what home lessons can most safely be 'scamped', and what holidays can be squeezed out of the quarter's tedium) is absolutely painful to me.

However she did tell the story of serious articles being ignored by newspaper editors and of her decision to set up with Lilian their own monthly magazine. It was kept going for three years, printed initially by W. C. Penfold & Co. at a cost of 25 pounds a month. That cost was recovered by the sale of advertisements to banks, insurance offices and big firms and from a circulation of 1500 subscribers who paid sixpence a copy or six shillings a year 'for the poor little sheet'. In good months as much as 15 pounds would be left over for the hard-working editors to share.

For we were hard-working; there was no money to pay contributors, and the result was we had occasionally to fill the magazine from cover to cover ourselves – poems, stories, editorials, erudite articles, popular articles, cookery, and answers to correspondents, signing each with a different nom-de-plume, to show the size of our staff.

One of the contributions to the maiden issue of 1 January 1889 was a six-stanza piece of rhyming verse acknowledged by the initials H.C., standing for Herbert Curlewis, a law student with a classical bent who lived with his parents at 'Hermsley' in Tupper Street, Marrickville, not far from the Warren Brickworks which his father managed. While studying for degrees in Arts and Law he was to figure in Ethel's life as one of a group of young people who lived in the inner city suburbs close to the university and increasingly as Ethel's secret suitor. He was a slim, athletic young man, with regular features and a moustache, a founder of the bicycling club at Newington and dux of the school in 1886.[2]

His literary interests brought him close to Ethel and his was one of the influences that helped to extend her reading while she was editing the *Parthenon*.

Unremarkable and fleeting as the *Parthenon* was in the literary firmament of Sydney it afforded a valuable experience of the realities of journalism, which was to give Ethel her basic income for forty years. The sisters' first task was to persuade businessmen to buy advertising space to defray the basic printing costs and then to persuade their friends to subscribe. As a young entrepreneur Ethel developed self-confidence and learned to keep accounts and pay bills, adopting regular habits which are attested by her Pen Money Book and Account Book. Studied in conjunction with the diaries they give a minute acquaintance with her published writings and earnings to a degree that is rare in the careers of journalists, novelists and poets.

The *Parthenon* was soon regarded seriously enough in the world of letters to attract contributions from Rolf Boldrewood and Kenneth Mackay, whose stories in the final issue for 1889 were favourably noticed in a review that appeared in the *Sydney Morning Herald*. Writing in the same issue under the *nom-de-plume* of 'Princess Ida', Ethel included 'A Christmas Song' of her own which the reviewer described as a 'pleasing piece of verse in the old *ballade* form'; altogether the 'young editresses' were congratulated for their 'taste and care'.[3]

The very first week of Ethel's diary shows something of the mechanics of the support system for the magazine. On Friday 5 April 1889 she went to town to buy prizes as mementoes of the *Parthenon* 'at home' that was planned for the afternoon. Mrs Cope and the entire staff, comprising her two elder daughters and the two secretaries, Annie Christian and Marcia Cox, received the visitors in their little terrace home in Oxford Street. The guests were so numerous there was no room to move. Next day the girls took a cab to the Newington sports day at Stanmore which was pronounced 'very poor'. Ethel walked a little with Mr Curlewis, who here makes his first appearance in the diary, also with Mr Curnow; the sisters then hurried off to catch the five o'clock train to Picton, where they were to stay for a holiday with the Daintreys, long standing friends of the Cope family through its pastoral connections.

Apart from holidays in later years in the Blue Mountains this was one of Ethel's rare country vacations in the sense of a stay with friends in a rural environment. For the Turner sisters, as recent migrants, there were no blood relations who could offer the chance of a stay on a farm, which has meant so much in the Australian experience of bush life. And the deficiency was not rectified by visits to the pastoral stations owned by Charles Cope's mother and elder brother, suggesting the possibility that his marriage to an impecunious widow with three daughters was hardly welcomed by Charles's propertied family. The diary reveals an almost complete absence of contact between Charles's wife and children and his mother and brother, who lived at Kirribilli in a fine old

home known as 'The Dingle'. Such a conclusion is strengthened by the fact that Cope's mother, who lived as a widow
for most of her life, did not mention Charles in her 1905 will,
though it is possible that substantial gifts had earlier come
his way. The ample prosperity of his life after 1895 is otherwise inexplicable.[4]

Brought up as town dwellers, deprived of viable links with
the land, neither Ethel nor Lilian tended to use farms as
locations for their novels and short stories. *Seven Little Australians* was an exception; in that story the almost irrepressible Judy meets her death on a farm as the victim of a falling
gum tree. For Ethel, unlike Mary Grant Bruce, the bush was
a mystery; Sydney and its suburbs offered the preferred
locale.

The first day at Picton might suggest one of the reasons
for this. Ethel's diary entry for Sunday 7 April runs simply,
'Poured with rain, it is so cold and dreary I wish I was
home.' In the bush one was at the mercy of the weather;
in town, especially in the heart of the city where the Copes
then lived, there was a variety of activity available, even
on wet days.

For the rest of the time with the Daintreys the girls joined
them in calls on neighbours, took part in a buggy picnic to
Douglas Park and attended their first country show. Pony
riding and mushroom gathering occupied some time during
the day while at night they played cards, though one evening
Ethel worked on a serial story for the magazine. Pressed with
more work to do for that taskmaster they left for Sydney on
16 April and were met at midday by Mrs Cope.

Like many of her friends, Ethel responded to the 'crazes'
that captured Sydney folk at various times. In 1889 it was
roller skating and ballroom dancing; ten years later it was
bicycle riding. Living in the heart of the city, the Turner
girls were able to share with young men and women a variety
of intellectual, social and outdoors activity. What strikes the

modern reader about Ethel's diaries is the imagination and energy she and her friends showed in entertaining themselves and the range of their interests. A diary kept throughout 1890 by Sophie Steffanoni, a contemporary of Ethel's at Sydney Girls' High, who became a highly successful artist in the 1890s, showed that she and her friends, though less affluent and constantly occupied in earning a living, had a similar capacity to obtain pleasure from the resources of the harbour and its beaches.[5]

On 29 May Ethel went to the home of her friend Nina Hague-Smith, at Marrickville, to play tennis all the afternoon and games all the evening, after which she stayed to sleep, as was far more common when middle-class houses had many more rooms than the efficient economy models of modern times. Much of the change can be attributed to the advent of the family car, but in 1889 that was forty or fifty years from realization. Three days later Ethel and Lilian went for the afternoon to the Darlinghurst Rink and collected their tickets for the season. Next day she went with her family to St Matthias's and taught in the Sunday School. Monday was taken up with making plans for a dance that was to be given for *Parthenon* subscribers by Annie Christian's mother at 'Westbourne', her home in Point Piper Road. Later she attended the establishment of Mr Needs, who regularly gave her dancing lessons, for in this as in other accomplishments and sports such as singing, drawing, tennis and later cycling, bridge and chess, Ethel was something of a perfectionist. For example after bathing at Bronte in December she decided to take some lessons, 'as I can't swim well and can't dive properly'. It was an apt viewpoint for the future mother of Adrian Curlewis.

Seventy-five people were invited to the *Parthenon* dance by formal letters posted on 6 June. Next day the girls ordered the lemonade – it would have been unthinkable to offer alcoholic drinks apart from claret cup. Pencils and programmes were also ordered, for custom still demanded that participants be issued with programmes listing the types of dances to be offered; on them, preferably early in the evening, the names of prospective partners would be entered, so that it was possible for Ethel to record in her diary how many dances she had with each of her beaus and what she thought of them. Much of this is described in Ethel's *Little Mother Meg*, though neither there nor in the diaries are we told how the all important music was produced. One guesses that a violinist and a pianist would have been hired for big occasions, while for others the skills of family and friends often sufficed.

For days before the *Parthenon* party the girls were busy preparing Annie Christian's home, first by throwing open the sliding doors that separated the dining and drawing rooms, removing the carpets and waxing the floor, which commonly produced as much fun as the dance itself. By 20 June the supper room had been decorated, the table laid and the claret cup concocted. This completed, the girls went home to dress, returning at seven with Lilian in a crepe dress, Ethel in pink and silver and Annie in blue liberty. Rose, the third of the Turner girls, came too but at 16 years of age she did not rate a detailed mention.

Ethel enjoyed herself immensely and recorded having liked fifteen of her partners. Amongst those favoured were Herbert Curlewis and his law student friend, Sid Mack, brother of her literary rival and later bosom friend, Louise. The elder Turners remained at Christians' to sleep the night, ready for clearing up the following day and the reward of more dancing in the afternoon.

One of Ethel's more time-consuming engagements in 1889 came from participation in a stall her mother managed for the Prince Alfred Hospital Bazaar and Village Fair held in the old barn of the Exhibition Building in Prince Alfred Park. It was opened on 12 September by the genial young governor, Lord Carrington, and ran for a fortnight. Assisting Mrs Cope were her elder daughters and ten other young women, many of them former school friends from Sydney Girls' High, for it was an institution whose claims of love and loyalty reached far into the lives of its old pupils. Ethel and her friends were turned out uniformly in blue serge dresses with white aprons and caps trimmed with turned-back collars and cuffs.

They sold a variety of things, ranging from aerated drinks and cream cakes to more substantial items; the governor himself came to chat with Mrs Cope, continuing the practice for which he was applauded during the centenary year of 1888 of going easily amongst the people. Mrs Cope, known within her family for skill in curing pork, persuaded him to buy two hams.

During her time on the stall Ethel had the opportunity of chatting to many friends including Miss Lucy Walker, her headmistress from Sydney Girls' High, with whom she remained in close touch during the remainder of her long service at the school. While in conversation, Ethel was forced to concede that the school would be unable to pay the debt still owing on the *Iris*. Eventually Mrs Cope paid what remained of the bill, drawing from Mr Penfold the remark that 'we had behaved very handsomely and honourably to him'. The conversation gave Miss Walker the chance of telling Ethel how much she liked the style of her Aunt Elgitha column in the *Parthenon*.

The other great project of 1889 was a theatrical night staged by the friends on 30 October to raise funds to cover the *Iris* debt. Early in August, after a morning of skating and an afternoon of dancing, Ethel and Lilian had a visit from Arthur Barry, son of the rector at St Matthias's. Together they planned a fund-raising entertainment and drew up what Ethel described as a 'list of *tableaux vivants*'. Rehearsals were usually held at Ethel's home and during the ten weeks of preparations there were frequent heart-burnings as people dropped out or failed to attend practices. Sid Mack was the most consistent offender and drew the angry comment of 18 October, 'if he does not [come] next time we'll get some one else. He is abominably rude'.

A final dress rehearsal late in the afternoon of 30 October was promisingly imperfect but that night the whole thing went off superbly. There were performances of *Pygmalion and Galatea*, *Sleeping Beauty* and *Uncle Tom's Cabin*, interspersed with a noisy and hilarious baby show and solos for voice and violin. After the play itself, *Allow me to apologise*, the cast were all praised for their acting but one of the chief objects of the show was unrealized because of the poor attendance, so that they did no more than clear expenses. Ethel crossly commented 'the girls did not sell their tickets'.

Sensitive as Ethel was about public appearances, she was encouraged by this exposure to embark on a new project for self-improvement. Intending to have her voice professionally trained she chose to take lessons from Madame Vera, an Italian-born student of Signor Garcia and a member of the Schubert Society. The money was to be saved by resolute personal economies including a determined effort at making her own dresses, starting immediately with a pale blue zephyr.

Some sacrifices, however, could not be contemplated. Just prior to the theatricals Ethel was invited to discuss with the editor of the Press Association an opportunity for her to act as fashion writer and warehouse noter, probably for the *Illustrated Sydney News*. Attractive as the salary of 60 pounds a year then seemed she refused because she did not like the prospect of going around to the places involved in the trade and taking notes, though the Copes might also have had a part in this rejection.

Towards the end of the year Ethel was encouraged to believe in her capacity to make a mark as a writer. She had offered the editor of *Hermes*, the university's new literary magazine, a humorous poem entitled 'The Altar of Examdomania'. The opening verse gives a fair sample of its character; it scans rather awkwardly and the humour is firmly undergraduate in style:

You must wake and call me early – call me early, mother dear;
For I must cram into this month the work of the past year.
The 16th is, of all the year, the darkest, gloomiest day,
For I feel within my heart, mother, I'll fall an easy prey.

The editor called to tell her that he and his associate (the famous Christopher Brennan) both liked the poem and intended to publish it in the December issue.

Ethel saw this poem in print on the same day as the *Herald* published its generous review of the *Parthenon*. The following day, 7 December, she had an interview with William Astley, who was soon to become well known to *Bulletin* readers as 'Price Warung', author of *Tales of the Convict System*. Of this meeting she wrote with girlish enthusiasm, 'He has engaged me for certain to write the Ladies Letter, at a guinea a letter, I am to write some political leaders too, & an Australian story. I'll be a millionairess soon.' Little came of these hopes, for although Ethel wrote several pieces for Astley, including leading articles and ladies' letters, she was still seeking payment from him in January 1892. As his biographer Barry Andrews makes clear, Astley had financial and health worries that made him an uncertain performer of promises.[6]

As we noticed, the first issue of the *Parthenon* included a poem by Herbert Curlewis. The association between him and Ethel developed only slowly in 1889: he appeared again in her diary on 4 September when she referred to a cranky letter from the young man, explaining, 'I suppose he has found out Socrates in "Stray Shots" is his beloved self and it has made him feel amiable to me. I don't know why he should like me, I always snub him unmercifully.'

Ethel's sense of humour ran often to teasing and to

practical jokes, from time-to-time involving two men who were inclined to take themselves rather seriously, her step-father Charles Cope and her soon-to-be-lover, Herbert Curlewis. On 4 October Ethel wrote to Cope a letter containing a formal proposal 'for my own hand'.

Picture the scene that ensued at the Copes' Paddington home the following day, a Saturday. Ethel had been busy with her proper tasks of tidying, arranging flowers and creating an atmosphere of sweetness and light, when . . .

Mr Cope came home at 1/2 p. 10 fuming about the letter – he thought it was real, I never saw him in such a state. I am sorry now I did it but it was only in joke. He declares he would rather bury me than see me married.

It was not a happy augury for the time when a real suitor would declare himself. But marriage was the last thing on Ethel's mind. She had a career to set in motion and in any case the quarrels of Charles and Sarah Cope discouraged emulation. Saturdays seemed to have the worst of it as the diary entry of 23 November suggests:

Mother & Mr Cope had a fearful row. He smashed her gold bangle to aggravate her and there was a terrible piece of work. Heigho, I wonder do all married people have rows? I wouldn't be married for *anything*.

For some time the family had been thinking of moving to a bigger house. On New Year's Eve 1889 Ethel and Rose went to see a house at Newtown which they liked so well that in the afternoon the senior Copes examined it too. It was number 20, L'Avenue, one of a batch of fifteen terraces that had been built that year on the southern side of King Street, looking east towards an attractive park. In its position, close to the university and to the city centre, the house appeared ideal, particularly to the older members of the family. For Ethel and Lilian with their literary and journalistic ambitions and active social lives, L'Avenue Newtown seemed a wonderful address.

L' Avenue, as it was grandly described in *Sands Directory*, was a product of the housing boom that hit Sydney in the late 1880s. When Ethel and Rose first saw the street the original group of eight terrace homes, running into Fitzroy Street, Newtown, was less than four years old. Another terrace of fifteen three-storeyed homes, numbered from 9 to 23 L'Avenue, was built before the end of 1889. All of them were erected on the initiative of George Sydney Brock, a developer whose office stood in the imposing home now described as 1 Warren Ball Avenue. They ran at right angles to the original eight, in what is now called Georgina Street, forming the western boundary of the newly gazetted Hollis Park, which still offers a splash of welcome green to the residents of this busy inner-city suburb.

Hollis Park possessed two features that were bound to interest active young people, a pair of tennis courts and a large timber ballroom, both of which were to be much used by Ethel and her sisters. Clearly the speculators who built the two groups of imposing terraces wanted to create an enclave close to the heart of the city with an atmosphere of relaxed and graceful living.

Unable to resist the urgings of their daughters, Charles and Sarah Cope inspected the vacant home at number 20, which today stands fourth from the end of the terraces in Georgina Street, and immediately loved it. Some of the houses in L'Avenue were three-storeyed, with fine castellated turrets, others were two-storeyed with sharp gables and fretted bargeboards reminiscent of Maori carvings. Common to all of the homes was the most delicate iron lace on the upstairs balconies; in the original eight was a front fence made up of heavy stone pillars and iron spiked railings, which appear as handsome today as they did a century ago. Number 20 bore the name of Leonidas, one of the heroes of ancient Greek history. It enjoyed an optimistic easterly aspect and looked across the road to Hollis Park and towards the morning sunshine with distant glimpses of the Pacific Ocean. The arterial road of King Street with its tramway to the city was about 200 metres to the north up a gentle slope. On the far side of King Street and several blocks to the west was the parish church of St Stephen's, one of Edmund Blacket's triumphs as an architect, built in 1872 in the grounds of an old cemetery containing the bones of pioneers, some the descendants of William Bligh, whose Camperdown grant had been a farewell gift from Governor King.

As a street name, L'Avenue aspired to upper middle-class tastes. It offered the Copes, who were on the visiting lists of both the governor and the mayor of Sydney, a move into a more elevated social sphere than they had known at Paddington, where most of their neighbours had been tradesmen. In the new home they had on either side William Weiss, a ship's captain, and Charles Hamburgher, an importer. Further along the street lived another captain, an insurance agent, a photographer, a merchant and a railway inspector. As one can imagine on seeing the street today it was solidly well-to-do if not wealthy.[1]

On 1 January 1890, the day after he and Sarah inspected 'Leonidas', Mr Cope 'pulled down' the girls' Parthenon room in the attic of the Paddington home. Next day the decision to rent the Newtown terrace home had been made 'for certain'. By then they could talk of nothing else, though the excitement did not prevent Ethel from completing her regular writing chores for the *Parthenon* and going into town with Lil to buy a new dress and see Mr Maclardy of Gordon and Gotch about binding the magazine's 1889 issues.

Ethel's optimistic mood continued into the following week in spite of her knowing that a libel suit brought against the *Parthenon* arising from a children's competition contained in the July 1889 issue was soon due for a hearing. Every day she practised piano and singing for about an hour and spent time packing books and clearing out cupboards in preparation for the move to Newtown. On 9 January she and Lil collected their cheque from Maclardy and Ethel spent some of the proceeds on a new hat. She also bought a purse and the all important Letts Diary for 1890.

The reality of the impending move was brought home for Ethel on 19 January when she used the family pew at St Matthias's in the morning. In the afternoon she gave little keepsakes to the girls in her Sunday School class; they were all sad to think of her going away and she too was touched by the parting. At night, church again, when Mr Olley, apparently a curate working with Dr Barry, delivered 'a splendid helpful sermon' and afterwards they all went into the parsonage opposite Centennial Park for an hour's fellowship 'in the old informal way'.

On the morning of the move Ethel went with her mother and her half-brother Rex to the new home 'which is all so beautifully fresh, & well fitted'. An attractively-tilted front verandah was partly enclosed by a low stone balustrade and led to a heavy front door and a tiled passage that gave access to the kitchen and to spacious drawing and dining rooms. Attached to the dining room was a fernery that created a feeling of the cool green outdoors. On the next two floors were the bedrooms and the 'special sanctum' the girls were to use for their writing, which was soon set up with a bookcase and a piano as well as little tables, chairs and a 'whatnot'. Down a steep flight of steps outside the kitchen was the laundry and a rear courtyard leading to a private lane which ran the length of the terrace.

Two days later Ethel celebrated her birthday, when according to the English birth certificate she was 20 years old. At 2.30 the girls and their mother went into the district court, where the libel action was to be heard against the publishers of the *Parthenon*, then Gordon & Gotch. Competitors had been invited to make up the largest possible number of words composed from letters in the given word, REGULATION. The libel, complained of by Mr Hugh McKenney on behalf of his daughter Elizabeth, was contained in the August issue. It was noted that she had made 687 words but in examining the list with dictionaries the editors sternly declared:

We much regret to find she had used quantities of words that she must herself have invented to make up a large score. She is disqualified. We hope this will be a warning to our young competitors.

McKenney had given the young editors ample opportunity to retract and avoid litigation but they stuck to their claim that the girl had cheated and remained determined to give no ground. In any case they thought the publicity would be useful to the magazine. Judge Fitzhardinge found in favour of the plaintiff, awarding damages of a farthing, as requested, and setting costs on the lower scale.

On her first Sunday at The Avenue, as she always described it in her diary, Ethel went with Rose to church at St Stephen's Newtown and they sat in the pew belonging to their neighbour Mr George Brock. The church itself they thought pretty but the minister lacked the depth of Dr Barry, 'he read his sermon which was on Socialism & only repeated badly what has been often said'. It was not only his depth that had made Zachary Barry's sermons memorable; his biographer, Ken Cable, describes him as a charismatic, if highly prejudiced, Irish protestant of the old school who scorned the use of detailed notes and spoke with vast eloquence. Four weeks later Ethel again tried the water at St Stephen's but only confirmed her first impression. The preacher was a Mr Free, apparently a visitor to the Sydney Diocese, of whom Ethel commented, 'I never disliked a minister as much ... he is so self-righteous & egotistical'. In the months that followed, she and her sisters shopped round for a church and minister with whom they could feel comfortable, trying out Christ Church at Stanmore and St John's at Glebe but finding apparently no satisfying replacement for St Matthias's. All six Copes celebrated Easter Sunday by going to their old church and sitting in the family pew but this did not become a regular thing. From this point of view the move from Paddington may be thought a turning point in Ethel's spiritual life though she was still a long way from abandoning the habit of church attendance. In late December, on learning that her friend William Weiss from next door was an atheist she commented, 'I am so sorry'.

Within days of arriving at The Avenue Ethel and Lilian were trying out the tennis courts in the park opposite their home. They were badly out of practice and some of their neighbours played 'awfully well' but they persisted in playing several times a week throughout their stay in 'Leonidas'. The courts provided residents with opportunities for regular exercise as well as a social focus that enabled the sisters to make friends with their neighbours. One of the ladies whom they liked was Miss Alexander, but her brother was a different matter, for 'he is far too familiar, or rather, tries to be'.

Tennis soon offered the girls a link with people at the University of Sydney, notably with St Paul's College students, whose tennis courts had been built a few years earlier between the Warden's Lodge and the college. This was a time, fortunately for the Turner girls, when Paul's was becoming more active socially.

More significant in the long run were two young men, Sid Mack and Herbert Curlewis, who though not resident at Paul's had close associations with the college that brought them into touch with Ethel. On 21 March 'Mr Curlewis' was mentioned in the diary as having been a fellow passenger to the city. He lived at Stanmore, a kilometre or so to the west on the same tram route and went to say hello to Lil and Ethel when they boarded the tram at Newtown. Chance and propinquity are attentive servants of human relationships and Herbert took the opportunity of promising a ticket to the university Commemoration celebrations which were to be held a fortnight later.

Herbert Raine Curlewis was born in August 1869 at Bondi, son of Frederick Charles Curlewis and his wife, Georgiana Sophia, formerly O'Brien. Herbert's paternal grandfather had come to Australia in 1824 and played an important role in the pastoral industry with runs in both New South Wales and Victoria. On his mother's side he was descended from Edward Smith Hall, a famous newspaper editor and grazier, who had migrated to the colony in 1811. Frederick Curlewis had a short time working in a bank but had been attracted by the call of the Queensland frontier. He subsequently owned a coal mine at Newcastle, which explains the continuing interest Herbert had in the Hunter region, and became for the final thirty years of his life a brick manufacturer at Alexandria. By 1889 the family lived at Upper Tupper Street, Marrickville (or Stanmore) in a house named 'Hermsley', which no longer exists. It was from here that Herbert made the short walk to the westward to attend Newington College, where he left a considerable mark as a Greek scholar and as founder of a cycling club which went for long rides to places of beauty on the coast.

A photograph taken of Herbert at the time of his admission to the Bar in 1892 shows a tall athletic frame, a steady and almost severe gaze from well-spaced eyes and a moustache above a firm mouth and strong chin. Below his barrister's wig was a high forehead and dark brown hair inclined to be curly.

When Herbert began his association with Ethel in January 1889 as a contributor to the *Parthenon* he had completed an Arts degree at the University of Sydney. His journeys by tram, either to the university or to the Law School in the city involved a ride along Stanmore Road to Newtown and then down King Street, which took him within two hundred metres of 'Leonidas', giving him opportunities of seeing Ethel that he was quick to grasp.

In April Herbert accompanied Ethel to the Commemoration Day celebration, when she thought he looked very nice in his BA gown. Sid Mack was also a member of the party and together they enjoyed the spectacle of the floats and horseplay, which Ethel thought 'awfully wild' but 'a good deal of fun'.

Next day the girls put on a dance in the wooden ballroom at Hollis Park opposite their new home. All morning they were cooking and in the afternoon cleaning out the ballroom and laying the supper table. With the evening came severe storms which kept the majority of guests away, in those days before the motor car. Only about twenty took part; Ethel herself provided a good deal of the music by playing waltzes, still seen a century ago as offering an exciting degree of legitimate physical contact between men and women. Her friend Ethel Maynard from schooldays was a prized guest as were Sid Mack and Herbert Curlewis. Ethel danced with Mr Alexander, whom she hated and with Curlewis 'whom I liked very much'. One surprise guest was Charles Cope's brother, William, of the legal firm of Cope and King, who had briefed counsel for the *Parthenon* libel case in January. On that evening, when he was making a rare visit to his brother's family, Ethel thought him 'so very nice'.

Ethel's was a varied and active life, not yet strong intellectually or in terms of a satisfying output of published writing, but offering a range of experiences that enabled her to become more secure in her emotions and capacities. Her admission that she liked Mr Curlewis 'very much' in April marks the beginning of a special friendship.

Ten days after the dance at L'Avenue Herbert called at number 20 to collect Ethel and Rose to take them to watch a university boat race on the harbour. Ethel wore a white muslin dress and a black lace hat and 'hardly ever enjoyed myself more'. She was introduced to a number of Herbert's friends who accompanied her home on their way back to St Paul's College, when Herbert pressed her to come to a tennis party that was to be held at the college a month later. Yet when Herbert called on the girls to accompany them Ethel was out of temper with him, later remarking in her diary, 'Mr Curlewis came to call for us, like his impertinence, – we were vexed. I'm getting so tired of him. He saw we were vexed'. It seems that Ethel resented actions which assumed a familiarity or closeness for which she was not yet ready. Certainly the effect on Herbert of her inconsistency of action was puzzling and unnerving but it kept him in thrall.

By this time Ethel was friendly with Mrs Weiss from number 19 and her son William and daughter Ada. As a seafarer, Captain Weiss was seldom home, making a friendship with Ethel and Lilian the more desirable. It was with Mrs Weiss's help that a new type of entertainment was planned for 3 June, a nocturnal walking party. On the 'most glorious moonlight night imaginable' a group of thirteen men and fifteen women, including three chaperones, met at Circular Quay where they caught a ferry to Mosman's Bay and walked to Middle Head. There they consumed the food that had been prepared in the morning and returned to the wharf, just missing a ferry, which meant waiting for the last one at 11.40

p.m. and walking home from the Quay. Ethel slept in for a midday breakfast.

Her chief walking companion had been Curlewis, who came the following night to offer some pieces for the *Parthenon* which were 'very acceptable' and lend her two books. Another friend who turned up that day to wild delight was the family dog Rover. The 'dear old fellow' had been missing for several days, during which he had been seen scratching at the gate of 'Erang', their former home in Paddington.

Towards the end of June Ethel and Herbert spent evenings together from time to time, sitting in front of the fire on a winter's night, discussing poetry and chatting. In spite of this deepening of their association there was ample room for misunderstandings and doubts. In August, when Ethel was feeling relieved by having at last paid the expenses of the *Parthenon* libel case, she was told of something Curlewis had said, 'or was said to have said' and so called off a date with him. Next night he came to sit beside her at a performance of the University Dramatic Society but she said not a word to him, 'I was in such a temper'.

The estrangement lasted until mid-August, when Rose and Ethel went to Morning Prayer at Glebe and in the afternoon Curlewis came up and we 'made friends again'. Ada Weiss and some friends from St Paul's College joined them for a chat on the verandah and Curlewis stayed for tea and the evening.

While excluded from Ethel's society Herbert composed a poem entitled 'There is none like her, none', which was published in the September issue of *Parthenon*, drawing upon its editor some amused comments from friends who were aware of the author's devotion. The first verse gives a sample of the sort of pedestal on which he placed his love:

Long time ago God made the world then made He
  The lights of Heaven. His task to perfect make

Fairest of all His works He sent my lady
  And kindly views the world for her sweet sake.

In spite of the rebuff, Herbert called for Ethel to take her to
a dance given by the Hague-Smiths. Though the rooms were
crowded it was lovely in the grounds, where, Ethel told her
diary in the strictest confidence, 'Mr Curlewis told me
something, ... I could never like him in that way though but
I am sorry, so sorry it has come to this. He wants me still to
be his friend, but I know it is not wise.'

Herbert was going through hell during this time and after
the next upset was noticed by a mutual friend standing
outside 'Leonidas' late at night gazing at Ethel's bedroom.
For her part Ethel revealed to her diary not the slightest hint
of disquiet, for it was still a most unequal relationship. There
were occasional and brief meetings with Herbert, when Ethel
reaffirmed the intention always to be 'good friends'.

On 3 September came a bombshell. Some friends called in
and let fall the news that gossips were saying that Ethel and
Herbert were engaged to be married. Ethel's response was to
decide, 'I must never be seen with him again, that is *very*
certain' so she wrote next day to terminate the association and
cancel a date to accompany him to the boat race on the harbour
between University and Mercantile crews. In the launch following the race she hardly exchanged a word with him and
was escorted home by a young medical student from St Paul's,
Mr Millard, who appears frequently in the diary.

Although the temptations afforded by spring in Sydney
were sternly resisted for several weeks, with Herbert showing
the wisdom to give his loved one some breathing space, on
the last day of September 1890 they were included in a party
that went by the 5.30 tram from Erskineville to Lady Robin-
son's Beach on the harbour for a Gipsy Tea by moonlight.
They went for a long row, where Herbert showed to advantage, and they walked a good deal together.

Common literary interests had an important place in this friendship from the beginning and at this stage it was Herbert who made most of the running. On 26 October when Ethel came back from the evening service at St Stephen's Newtown she found Herbert waiting for her at home with a present. He had copied out half of Swinburne's poems for her to read, 'a sort of expurgated edition because Mother won't let me have the book complete' but even so, his *Poems and Ballads* were irresistibly suggestive. His swinging rhythms were hypnotic in their repetitions of patterns of sound which help to convey the reader beyond language itself. Ethel's diary on the following day reported that Swinburne was 'glorious' – a special word in her vocabulary of enthusiastic praise, used much in later years to describe a really sparkling morning in the surf at Manly or Palm Beach. She went on, 'The Triumph of Time carries one away. Tennyson's loves seem quite feeble after this man's'.

That same night, after doing some business with a publisher and playing tennis in The Avenue, she read the poems again and sat out in the moonlight on the verandah before going to bed early 'to have a good think'. Some weeks later Ethel noted in her diary, 'Got a very excited letter – a love letter I suppose – from C. I couldn't help laughing & yet – oh I don't ... '

Real sorrow was waiting to engulf the family. For months there had been a hint of impending tragedy in every reference to Annie Christian, the family's long-time friend and secretary on the *Parthenon*. On 15 November Mr Cope had gone to see her for she was thought to have a clot of blood or an abscess on the brain and one side of her body was paralysed. The doctors advised an operation but the family declined to allow it. Next day the diary recorded:

Annie is dead.
Mr Cope went out by 6 o'clock & she expressed a wish to see

him, he went in & while he was there they thought she died ...
Lil and I went out at 3. The poor, poor father & Willy & Mark
and the Mother and Ruby, oh their grief is terrible. So small &
still & white she looked – O God, it seems too awful.

The whole Cope family went into mourning. Herbert told
Ethel he would write some copy for the forthcoming issue
of the *Parthenon* as he knew the girls would not feel inclined
to do so.

Five days before the death of Annie Christian devastated
Ethel and her family she received a note from Louise Mack,
to whom she had written a letter of sympathy on the death
of her father, the Rev. Hans Mack, a well known Methodist
preacher. She 'asked me to be friends again & forget the past.
I wrote to her, dear little thing. It is nearly 2 years since we
"fell out".'

The diary entry of New Year's Eve 1890 demands extensive quotation. It began in a sad strain with a reference to
Annie's death and the continuing sense of grief. Then she
wrote, showing a notable seriousness of purpose and a strong
sense of social position and class relationships:

I haven't a thing to show for this year, no new language or science
started. I've gone back in my studies except English, it's been a
profitless frittered away year. It's very easy to make new resolutions for the new year but I don't suppose for a minute I shall
keep them, – I do want to keep 3, – i. To be a better home
daughter, ii. not to be caddish if people are below me, iii. and the
chief one, to be 'larger', – I do hate pettiness, littleness of all kinds,
iv. then be noble and singlehearted, dare to be all that is good and
womarly and – Christlike.

Though 1890 had not been a great year for Ethel's literary
output it produced some interesting results. Her disposition
to make plans and discipline mind and body is well exhibited

by the schedule that appears at the front of the 1890 diary, where she writes a detailed programme of the activities she intended to follow every day, rising at 6 a.m., studying briefly before seeing to the breakfast table, then doing housework for half an hour before practising singing and piano. Tennis was included in the regime and details of the classical works she was to learn. A formidable list of studies was set out, including French, Latin, German and English literature, though mathematics and geology and the history of the Bible were not neglected. Added to the demands of this pro-gramme was the commitment Ethel had been given to teach her 14-year-old sister Rose, who had been withdrawn from her previous school because the headmaster Dr Murtagh had been involved in a 'disgraceful lawsuit'.

September had brought to Ethel a new and lifelong com-mitment when she became a junior member of the Women's Literary Association. On the first of the month she had her first taste of the group's activities, in the company of Ada Weiss from next door, when they heard several papers on *Macbeth*. It was not long before Ethel was making her own contributions.

At odd times during the year Ethel referred to minor writing projects apart from the *Parthenon* but on 12 Septem-ber she began a commitment that really launched her career as a journalist working for employers on newspapers and magazines. On that day she wrote her first weekly letter for the *Tasmanian Mail*, a task she was to share with Lil for 5 pounds a quarter.

The year 1891 began for the people of The Avenue with great promise and sense of neighbourliness. On New Year's Day there was a little dance in the communal ballroom that Ethel found 'rather nice', then two days later she was included in a tennis match in which the Avenuers were 'beaten shamefully' by a team of mixed visitors whose ladies played at intercolonial level. Next day, a Sunday, Mrs Cope and Mrs Davis from number 23 started a Sunday School for the Avenue children in the ballroom, for which Ethel took the head class comprising five boys and a girl. It was a task that continued until the family moved to Lindfield.

For Ethel the new year was made notable by a deepening of personal relationships, especially with Louie Mack, whose father had recently died, and Herbert, and a maturing of her craft as a writer. The Mack family had taken a cottage at Manly for a month, which became a centre of merry resort for young men and women. On 10 January Ethel arrived on the 4.30 ferry from the Quay to begin a week's holiday and immediately liked Mrs Mack and her numerous sons and daughters. So much, indeed that the experience was embedded in Ethel's memory: Louie's mother was to reappear in 1919 as the plump and hospitable Mrs North of *Laughing Water*, one of the most sympathetic and authentic characters of her later novels.

One of the first arrivals from town was Ernest O'Brien, a cousin of Herbert's on his mother's side, who was nicknamed 'Wild Dog' because of his good-tempered ways. When Herbert came down he took Ethel and Louie for a stroll on the Corso and a long chat on the sand, which became an occasion for whispered confidences when Louie dozed off to sleep. 'I believe I like him a little better', she wrote cautiously.

Twice during his daily visits to Manly Herbert distinguished himself in little emergencies. Louie fainted in the heat and needed to be revived, so he collected water in his hat and bought brandy at a nearby hotel. A more dramatic need for his services occurred on 14 January when they were returning to Manly in rough weather after a picnic on the harbour. One of the boats was swamped and it was Herbert's cool decisiveness that saved it from being swept onto the rocks. When she caught the ferry home with Lilian, Ethel felt it had been a most delightful week, made the more satisfying by Louie's remark that 'everyone down in Manly that I knew liked me'.

A new element was about to be introduced to the social equation. On 29 January Ethel met Herbert coming from tennis at the university and he told her of a young law student named John Creed, freshly arrived from England, who was boarding at The Avenue and seemed lonely. She was asked to show him any possible kindness.

It was not always easy for Ethel to treat Herbert with similar consideration. On 14 February Curlewis and Sid Mack gave a boating party on the harbour. Always a bit of a daredevil on the water, Ethel was drenched to the skin by a big wave hitting the bow of her boat. Going home through the Domain Ethel walked with Herbert, 'I was horrid to him, when he said he loved me I told him I detested him with all my heart, – & so I did, I don't like him an atom.'

Three days later there was a dance to round off an evening in which Ethel had starred in a play and Herbert insisted on having words with her. 'He is getting awful,' she complained to her diary. 'I do like him, but not in that way an atom. He says it is driving him mad. I wanted to tell him to go away & never see me again but I simply couldn't, he seemed to feel it so.'

Instead of sending Herbert away Ethel packed her portmanteau next day and caught the late afternoon train to Picton with Lil to holiday again with their friends the Daintreys. There were horses to canter on, country shows to visit with the Jarvisfield Antills, and a Crimean War veteran to charm. During a dance at Jarvisfield Ethel was taken into the garden by Captain Jack Thompson who gave her a rose and promised to send around a fine horse of his own for her to ride. 'I like him very much,' she mused, 'but I'm sure he's an awful flirt.'

While at Picton Ethel and Lil received a letter from the

editor of the *Tasmanian Mail*, who told them their social letter was falling off in quality and he would replace them at the end of the quarter. 'That's cause we scribbled off so,' she confessed.

During the fortnight away there was also an exchange of letters with Curlewis. Ethel wrote firmly insisting that they should have nothing more to do with each other as it only made people talk and was of no use. At the same Herbert had written suggesting a year's delay after which he might ask her again about her feelings. He thought better of this offer hearing of his dismissal and wrote 'such a dear letter, so manly' advising that he would return all Ethel's letters by way of Mr Creed. 'You must not ask me ever to see you again,' he wrote on 5 March ... 'my pain is now greater than I can bear and I could not trust myself to increase it.' A parcel containing the correspondence was delivered on 6 March together with 'two withered roses & the little verse book & card I sent at Xmas to him. – And there endeth the last chapter'.

On 7 March she wrote at the top of the diary entry:

'I have put my days & dreams out of mind
Days that are over, dreams that are done'.

She then went on to write the *Tasmanian* letter, taking it more seriously now it was perhaps too late. Next day she read Annie Besant's *Golden Butterfly*, took her class at Sunday School in the ballroom at L'Avenue and went to church at night with Lil. A new young man offered to walk the sisters home.

On 9 March Ethel wrote an essay on Friendship for her Literary Class, went in the afternoon to the Macks and talked with Louie, who lent her copies of Keats and Poe. At night she talked literature with John Creed who lent her a volume of Dante Gabriel Rossetti's poetry after making her promise to read only the marked verses. There was an encouraging letter from Mr Stead, editor of the *Review of Reviews*, to whom she sent a copy of the February *Parthenon*. And she wrote to John Le Gay Brereton thanking him for the poems he had offered for publication. The young man was later to become Challis professor of English at Sydney University and a durable friend and fellow resident of Mosman. On 10 March she read Rossetti and Poe, started a new short story and played tennis. Wednesday she 'Idled & read poetry' and lay on the floor trying to see how many poems she could say from memory. There were, 'Tears, the Oblation, The Forsaken Garden, Indian Serenade and Arnold's Self-dependency.'

This intellectual idyll ended on Thursday when the washerwoman failed to turn up, confronting the family with an unfamiliar task. 'The clothes were all in oak, we did not know what to do, – at last we set to and did a copper full, – Mother washed, we rinsed and pegged out. My first washing! ... Afternoon had a fearful headache.'

A month passed. Herbert sent Ethel a note to say he would never give her up. He had been made to promise he would trouble her no more but Ethel felt unmoved. 'I have a voice in the matter,' she reminded herself, 'and I shall never change.' There was a brief flirtation with the idea of engaging as a governess, evoking Mr Cope's angry promise that he would have her tracked down by a detective because she was under age, which was certainly incorrect. On 25 March she and a mixed party of friends and chaperones, began a camping holiday on an island in the Hawkesbury. There was sailing by day down to Peat's Ferry, music and dancing by night, spiced with short-sheeting of the boys' beds and scary reprisals involving huge toads.

On the return to Sydney there was a reprieve from the editor of the *Tasmanian Mail*, who was better satisfied by the girls' later efforts. A normally vigorous social and intellectual life continued and then out of the blue on Saturday 18 April, after doing the *Tasmanian* letter, Ethel wrote in her diary:

Idled & day dreamed a good deal, C. figured in those dreams very much I am ashamed to say. Someway I can't help thinking of him. Read a stupid story. Evening dreamed again, – I want shaking.

Imagine if Herbert had been aware of this! But in any case events were slowly moving in his favour. There were unavoidable meetings, one of them at a picnic on the Lane Cove River at which a happy crowd played rounders and had tea in the pavilion. Ethel had seen a good deal of John Creed, whom she found witty and charming, 'but he is effeminate I am afraid'. She then talked to Herbert and decided there was no harm in their being friends. Next day Louie stayed the night at 'Leonidas' and the girls talked until 5 a.m. Curlewis had confided in Louie after the conversation at Lane Cove and had suddenly broken down, crying with great dry sobs. He'd always had a hard life, as Louie remarked, prompting her friend to reflect, 'it does seem too bad of me.'

They met next at Mack's home in Neutral Bay when Herbert and Sid and Pickburn came back for tea after a day of sailing on the harbour. Ethel hardly said a word to Herbert but:

'I had to let him bring me home though & – I can't write it down. Lay awake nearly all night. I am frightened at what I have done, & yet so happy, – I never really thought I cared for him till tonight'.

Reading this startling entry we might think momentarily of *Tess of the D'Urbervilles*, however Ethel had simply agreed that night to a secret engagement. On 18 May she missed the weekly meeting of the Literary Society, commenting to her diary, 'I don't seem to care for anything just now but *that*'.

The two lovers now seized every chance of being together and Herbert commonly walked with Ethel to her singing lesson and waited so as to accompany her home again. She reflected on 22 May, 'I'm getting downright wicked but I do like being with him & after all there's no harm we're going to tell Mother soon, I'm dreading it'. Together again at a tea party given by the O'Briens at 'Ravenscourt', their gracious old riverside home at Fivedock, they watched fireworks being let off and strolled in the garden, where Herbert made Ethel promise unconditionally, 'what I had half promised before'. Unable to be open with her family – in particular her stepfather – Ethel wore a bracelet as the secret token of her engagement.

Having secured Ethel's commitment Herbert became so protective in his ardour as to lose all sense of proportion for a time. Ethel twisted her knee in a fall and was sent to bed for a brief rest; when she wrote to tell Herbert of the mishap he sent a remarkably intemperate response:

June 4th 1891
My own sweet Ethel
    Your note only reached me ten minutes ago as I have been out sailing all day and am only just home. It has made me more anxious than I ever felt in my life. I shall not know what to do with myself till I hear the doctor has seen you. My own darling some day when it will not matter who knows that you are mine no harm shall come to my lady ever again.[2]

A few days later Ethel was able to take the tram to Fivedock with Lil to have tea with the O'Briens, who sent their buggy to the tram to collect the visitors. On the same tram was Mrs Curlewis, who had written to Ethel 'a sweet, motherly sort of letter' which made the young woman eager to meet her. Yet after doing so, Ethel was overcome for a time by fears that her family would not welcome a close association with the Curlewises.

I have felt perfectly miserable all day about it [she wrote], I knew Lil was taking stock, & oh, I don't know what Mother & Mr Cope would say to her. She's educated & all that, I'm sure, but she was frightfully dressed & seems worn out & unmindful of herself with drudging after all her boys ... I do hope C. is good to her. There was a hobbledehoy schoolboy brother of his too, Dolly is alright & Rex a dear little lad. Lilly seems perfectly aghast & says I'm doing a nice kind of thing. I can't help feeling miserable about it, though I suppose it is caddish of me & after all *he's* the same, & can't help his family.

In July 1891 Ethel missed another meeting of the Literary Society in order to get together with old friends from Sydney Girls' High at the Women's Common Room in the university to arrange for a present to give their former headmistress, Miss Lucy Walker, who had just married a Mr Garvin. The following Friday night Ethel slept in Louie Mack's bed after watching a boat race and the girls exchanged confidences, Ethel speaking of her love for Herbert and Louie of John Creed, though she admitted her anxiety about the young man's drinking problem. Next Monday night she went to see Sarah Bernhardt as Cleopatra and fell in love with Marc Anthony, wishing Herbert was just like him. Again she felt concerned about her feelings for the young man, 'I do wish I could feel wildly in love with him. I only feel affection, I'm afraid for I simply could *not* let him kiss my lips ever.' At the end of the week she saw Louie off in the train for a governessing job at Quirindi, thinking as the train pulled out of how fearfully she would miss her friend.

In some important ways the two young women were radically different, as Nancy Phelan makes plain in her sensitive biography of Louie, who was capable of outrageous and unconventional behaviour. Ethel, for all her quiet strength, which became more and more apparent as she became involved in public issues, was essentially conservative and conformist. When she next attended the Women's Literary Society for a discussion of 'The Influence of Women's Suffrage on Politics' she commented later:

It's horrid to see the way some of them go on about their rights & wrongs, it's old fashioned of me I suppose but I do think it would take from the womanliness of a woman to be in Parliament.

After only a year and a half at L'Avenue, the Copes had to consider moving house again. Ethel expressed alarm at the state of her mother's health, and there was increasingly serious discussion of a move to Ryde or some other more countrified suburb where the atmosphere would be healthier. In between bouts of sickness Mrs Cope was house hunting, eventually finding the very place she wanted to rent on the North Shore at Lindfield, standing in several hectares close to the railway line but a kilometre or so south of the nearest station at Gordon. To Ethel's mind it posed the danger of 'being buried alive' after the bustle and excitement of town life.

So the girls found themselves writing invitations for their friends to come to a final dance in the ballroom at L'Avenue on 18 September. One of those who received an invitation, written on charming notepaper showing a waltzing couple, was Dowell O'Reilly, an up-and-coming man of letters, with a fine and sensitive Irish charm, who had contributed verses to the *Parthenon* and was to become one of Ethel's most faithful friends.[3]

Herbert was back in early spring from a fortnight's camping holiday spent at Jervis Bay with Sid Mack and other university friends. He had written copious letters to Ethel while away, describing their efforts to astonish and impress the 'bucolic mind', for example by going to church wearing flannels and sporting 'Varsity crosses', whatever they were. Instead of feeling delighted to see her lover after such a break, as she had expected, Ethel found herself repelled by the roughness of his appearance and by the stink of tobacco on his coat. But next night at the Wolstenholme's dance she liked him better, admitting her changeability in small ways but assuring her diary that she wouldn't break her word to Herbert now even if she wanted to.

The farewell dance in the ballroom at Hollis Park, for which Lil and Ethel paid from their own pockets, attracted forty to fifty people. 'Everyone seemed to enjoy themselves & said they were awfully sorry we are going away'. But there was a promise to arrange walking parties from the university to visit the girls and plans were soon in train to have a 'Leonidas Dance' in October.

Dowell O'Reilly, who had evoked special attention in Ethel's reflections on the farewell party, came to say goodbye to her among the packing cases on the eve of the move to Lindfield. That night, Lil and Ethel ran down to the summerhouse for a brief farewell to Herbert, who gave his love a little book of Austin Dobson's poems, *At the Sign of the Lyre*. In the morning of 29 September the elder girls watched their household goods being loaded into carts, bade adieu to the Weisses and lunched at the Fresh Food and Ice restaurant in the city on the way to Lindfield by tram, ferry and train.

chapter
Five

The fear of being 'buried alive' at Lindfield did not last long. At first sight Ethel decided that she liked 'Inglewood' 'awfully' well, describing it in late September 1891 as a 'pretty, square house with a long balcony and verandah, honeysuckle and white roses creeping up'. Both upstairs and down, leadlight coloured glass was strategically placed to catch the sun at doorways and hall windows. Though there were two fewer bedrooms than the six at 'Leonidas' they were much larger and the public rooms downstairs more spacious, especially the drawing room to the left of the big front door, which was a nice long room with four windows and pale blue walls. Ethel was to sleep together with Rose and she and Lil had immediate plans to paper a little downstairs room and transform it into their new sanctum.

Driveway and garden had been much neglected, for when the house was completed in 1887 the woman for whom it was built declined to live 'so far out in the bush' and the husband, George Braham, a gentlemen's outfitter of King Street, sold it in 1890 to George Munro, a Sydney merchant. Quite possibly when the Copes began to rent this house in September 1891 it had been unoccupied for some years. At that time it was set well back from an unmade road and stood in four acres with an orchard and ample room for running a few pigs, fowls, ducks and a cow. Ethel's diary regularly recorded the slaughter of a pig and Mrs Cope's hectic involvement in the kitchen making sausages and pork pies, using culinary skills acquired in Lincolnshire. Since the roses badly needed pruning Ethel quickly took up the challenge and dealt vigorously with an infestation of aphids. From this time dates the enthusiasm for gardening both at Mosman and in the Blue Mountains, which lasted for the remainder of her life.[1]

In those first weeks at Lindfield Lil and Ethel tried out the quality of their shoe leather on the unmade roads, walking to Gordon, then the closest station on the North Shore railway from St Leonards to Hornsby, where they collected and posted mail every day or so. It was to the public school at Gordon that Rex Cope went for his lessons because he was too young to go away by train to a private school. And it was to the 'funny little church' at Gordon the family went to worship, finding the Rev. Mr Cresford a very good preacher and enjoying the company of their neighbours, the Pockleys. During a 'tremendous walk' in October Lil and Ethel explored the vicinity, calling at cottages about fowls and other livestock and being made much of by the occupants, who told them their life histories and troubles. Poor Mrs Nash had a sick husband and a lot of children, evoking from Ethel the reminder in her diary, 'Memo, send Mrs Nash old books, old clothes.'

One effect on Ethel of her removal from the bustling Newtown scene was to give her more time for contemplation. She and her sisters were fairly regular attenders at the little parish church at Gordon and one Sunday late in October they sat out on the lawn with Mrs Cope discussing theology:

I wonder [*she asked herself later*] what I should be called if I had to be classified in some religious sect. Free thinker I suppose though like many others I go to church of England. God I believe in &

trust with all my heart. God is good & I think man is man & master of his fate. As to heaven, I don't think it is just a place for good people. But just God the great essence of Life & all life, after death, merges in him.

In describing herself as a free thinker, Ethel identified as a person who refused to submit reason to the control of authority in matters of religious belief. Herbert at this time was rarely to be found in church and when they had children, declined to have them baptised. Yet when he wrote to Ethel he acknowledged the power of prayer, saying 'I feel that when I pray my prayers are heard for your sake and that I could never do an unworthy action now that I have the love of such a pure and sweet woman'.[2]

The servant problem was a matter that regularly agitated Mrs Cope after the move to Lindfield and Ethel herself when she became mistress of her own house. The diaries record a constant struggle to find and retain reliable servants, interspersed with harrowing stories of surreptitious departures and hurried journeys to a registry office to engage new ones. Ethel went on such an errand on the first and third of December, on the second occasion to be bullied by a 'half drunken woman. I was awfully frightened', she wrote.

Mere anxieties about servants gave way to high drama when Alice, their pretty new maid of about seventeen went off at night with her lover, Alec Ferguson. A police constable came to the house and told Mrs Cope Alec had been put in prison but it was arranged that the couple would be married in court and he would be released, with the idea that the Copes would start them with housekeeping requirements in a little cottage. Against the advice of 'everyone here' Mrs Cope was determined to allow Alice to come back rather than see her put in 'one of those horrid Reformatories for 3 or 4 years'. 'Oh it *is* a shame', Ethel reflected. 'She has had no chance, no good home or friends & she is pretty & of course has not had the help of education'.

One observation that is suggested by the constancy of the problem is that Mrs Cope and her daughters came to Australia with English expectations about how servants should work and behave, expectations that had become anachronistic and unattainable in a society which had deliberately turned away from English class traditions and values. And increasingly, young women in Australia were attracted to employment in shops and factories where they were paid at least as well as in domestic service and enjoyed the immense advantage of having jobs in which conditions and hours of work were well defined.[3]

The fact that the Copes now had servants reveals a growing prosperity that matches the progression of their residences from rented homes at Paddington, Newtown and Lindfield and eventually to 'Bukyangi' at Killara, which they built in 1895 – a situation that is not explained by Charles's position in the Lands Department. His salary as a clerk did not vary much from the 200 pounds per annum he received at the time of his marriage to Sarah Jane Turner in 1880 till his retirement in 1913. Almost certainly the improvement in the family's material circumstances and in their ability to afford indoor and outdoor servants resulted from Charles's eventually receiving money from the estate of his grazier father, Joseph, who at his death in 1862 had left a substantial part of his property in trust to his wife, Mary Anne, for distribution among their children when they attained their majorities.[4]

The girls had barely begun the process of 'redding up' the house, hanging pictures and whitewashing the kitchen, when they received invitations in the post for 'The Leonidas Dance' their friends in town were planning in honour of 'the 3 little Miss T's', to be held in the ballroom at L'Avenue on 16 October. Into town the three of them journeyed, by foot to Gordon station, train to St Leonards, horse drawn omnibus to Milson's Point, ferry to Circular Quay and tram to Newtown, arriving at Ada Weiss's in time to change for the party. 'It was a divine dance, everyone was so nice & made such pretty speeches to us, it is lovely to have so many friends.' Ethel recorded dancing with several partners and three or four times with Curlewis. Though they had exchanged a few letters during the weeks of separation she felt shy with him at first but that feeling was submerged by the glow of happiness at being back among lively and interesting companions. The girls remained in town for several days, staying with the Weisses and the Hague-Smiths and catching up on gossip.

That shyness with Herbert was still evident six days later when he came by train to spend some hours with Ethel, choosing a Thursday when Mr Cope would be at work. He brought a book by William Morris for her to read and they went for a long walk, eating chocolates and succeeding in getting quite lost, so that it was two o'clock before they returned to 'Inglewood' for lunch. 'I believe', she wrote, 'I am just beginning to be really & truly in love' and she concluded that 'Life is very beautiful.' Yet she was aware that something was troubling Herbert; pressed to tell her about it he declined, saying he only wished to think of pleasant things that day. Only much later did it emerge that he had been injured in a sailing accident on the harbour and would need surgery to deal with an internal injury.

A charming letter from Mrs Curlewis to Ethel in late November encouraged Ethel to arrange a stay with the Mack family, who lived not far from 'Hermsley', while Herbert recuperated at home from the surgery. After the salutation, 'My dear little Pet', Mrs Curlewis asked Ethel to imagine how difficult it would be to keep Herbert in good humour during this time as a prisoner and implored her to 'take pity on me and come and see us as often as possible until the dreadful fortnight is over'.

As the period came to an end Ethel reflected on the 'lovely hours' they had been together, spent partly in one of the most loving and tender activities available to human beings, with Ethel reading aloud to her frail friend, from Kipling. On the final day she realised the parting would be as painful for her as for him.

While staying with the Macks, Ethel, Louie and John Creed had used the opportunity to be together at 'Hermsley', the Curlewis home, though Mrs Mack asked Ethel to use her influence to discourage Louie's association with Creed. At first Ethel declined to do so but on 4 December when she saw her friend confronted by an angry mother she decided to plan such meetings no more since she was certain Creed would not make her friend happy. And she added, 'Herbert and I know of something dishonourable he has done, as well he drinks, – Oh I am so disappointed. I used to like him so much.'

The Irish-born Creed, a lawyer, was six or seven years older than the crowd of young people who met regularly under the hospitable roof of the widow Mack in George Street, Redfern and later in Neutral Bay. Herbert, who had introduced him to the group, called him 'The Admiral' and Ethel wrote of how he 'takes off his hat with such a sweep one could fancy him living in days of three-cornered hats which were flourished off & put under the arm'.[5] He was clever and well read with a fine sense of humour, a man who had seen much of the great world of which Ethel and Louie dreamed together when they shared beds and confidences. No wonder Louise was attracted for she had a strong Bohemian impulse that responded to Creed's tales of the Left Bank at the very time when artists' camps were being set up at Mosman Bay and Sirius Cove. Against her mother's wishes, Louie was to marry Creed in January 1896.

Returning to 'Inglewood' for Christmas, Ethel spent a quiet few days at home, enjoying a long letter from Herbert and reading the 'loveliest edition' of Browning he had sent her. On Boxing Day she wrote a new story, 'Jerry', which she planned to offer to the *Bulletin* and at year's end reflected on the books she had read in 1891. The list is impressively catholic and lengthy, even though it seems to cover only a few months. In February, for example, she had read Mrs Ward's *Robert Elsmere* for the second time, Phillip Marston's *Poems*, Ibsen's *An Enemy of Society*, Swinburne's *Forsaken Garden*, Sharp's *Life of D.G. Rossetti* and Matthew Arnold's *Function of Criticism at Present*. March was even busier, with seventeen titles, including *Progress and Poverty*, by Henry George, who had recently been on a visit to Australia, a *Life of Goethe*, Ruskin's *Sesame and Lilies* and books of poetry by Arnold and Poe. It is no surprise to find Ethel writing, after tidying up her books and adding another shelf, 'I think I like books better than anything on earth'. So she promised to forego some chiffon and buy more books.

Early in January 1892 Ethel was surprised to hear from William Astley, expressing interest in the *Parthenon* and mentioning his indebtedness for some articles she had written at his request for the Press Association. Payment, he suggested, might be effected by his contributing a story to the *Parthenon* in lieu of money. She replied:

At any time hitherto I should have done so unhesitatingly for I am one of 'Price Warung's' most interested readers, but the *Parthenon* affairs are very unsettled at present, – in all probability it will not be continued much longer & the mss. we have in hand together with our own scribblings will suffice either until it dies or has a resurrection. Therefore – I hope it does not sound very mercenary – if you think what I sent you is worth some trifling consideration – I will choose the former alternative.[6]

Although Astley's promised cheque did not eventuate he made interesting suggestions about the future of the magazine. On 29 January Ethel went in with her mother to meet

Astley at Quong Tart's elegant and popular tea shop in the Queen Victoria Building where he told her he represented journalists from the *Bulletin* and elsewhere who admired the magazine and wished to buy and operate it, though on a more commercial basis than the girls.

The following Tuesday a long letter came from Astley, again without the promised cheque for three guineas, but with fulsome praise for the manuscript of 'That Young Rebel' which she had given him to read and virtually promising that his principals would publish it as a book when negotiations for the *Parthenon* had been concluded. Ethel and Lilian would retain their positions as editors on a fixed salary. Mrs Cope, meanwhile, had been making enquiries about Astley's reliability, with unpromising results. In what seems to be the final phase of the association, Ethel wrote to Astley suggesting he contribute a story to the Australian Annual, *Gum Leaves*, which she and Lilian were planning to publish.

A far more pleasing correspondent at this time was Dowell O'Reilly, last seen saying farewell to Ethel among the packing cases on the eve of the move to Lindfield. Ethel had written to him accepting a little story he had submitted, for publication in the December issue of *Parthenon*, though declining the poem 'Life' which had accompanied it. She liked also the roundel he had sent, adding the gracious comment:

Do you not think it is a dainty, pretty form? Not suited for a big subject of course but just fitted for trifles light as air or pretty conceits. They make a pleasant variety I think in our reading as 'some to church repair, not for the doctrine but the music there'.[7]

Negotiations with possible buyers having failed, Ethel noted on 7 March that the *Parthenon* would probably publish its own funeral number that month and asking herself, 'what will the Turners do then, poor things?' Once again she considered becoming a governess, like Louie, for she could not face the thought of letting Mr Cope keep her after she'd been independent for over three years.

One of the people who wrote to comment on the demise of the magazine was O'Reilly, whose letter was one neither of sympathy nor of congratulations. (Unfortunately this letter, like much of Ethel's incoming personal correspondence, was a casualty of her need regularly to toss out the mountains of mail she received during her long career as editor of children's pages for various newspapers.) Her reply told O'Reilly that she and Lilian were now able to follow their own bent, 'with gardening, tennis, painting & unlimited reading, – anything but writing'. She invited O'Reilly to come for lunch whenever he could face the hour's journey from Circular Quay.[8]

Disappointment at the ending of the *Parthenon* was slightly compensated for by a warm reference to Ethel's article 'The Hidden Meaning of Pagan Myths' in the February issue of the *Review of Reviews*. Such praise did not contribute, however, to living expenses, so the coming months are marked by a zealous search for new sources of income, since the only regular fees came at that time from the *Tasmanian*, which paid only 10 pounds a year for Ethel's Sydney letter. On 25 March a Mrs Montgomery called on Ethel and Lilian at 'Inglewood' to discuss the education of her two girls, Florrie and Alme. A fee of three guineas a quarter was settled on and when the girls arrived for their first lessons Ethel pronounced them to be 'nice little children'. All those painting lessons of earlier years were also turned to good account in the second half of 1892, when a Miss Archibald began taking instruction from Ethel at a fee of two guineas a quarter.'

By February of 1892, Herbert was preparing for his final examinations in Law when, he told Ethel, he must inform Mr Cope at once of their engagement; it was dishonourable to keep it a secret any longer and put him in a false position, for right actions must come even before love.

Ethel's refusal had a good deal to do with her lingering concern to retain independence, a feeling that she was not yet ready for a full commitment, so she asked him to wait a further six months. 'I feel it would choke me, I must be free a little longer. All my life I shall be bound & I will have 6 more months.' Herbert accused her of not loving him properly and there followed a painful comparison between her love for Mrs Cope and the family and the feeling she had for Herbert. Four hours they 'were at it' ... '& the result is we have completely parted, for ever & for ever'. There was talk of burning all Herbert's letters and returning his books but before such drastic steps could be taken (for the second time) an exchange of letters occurred. Herbert wrote first admitting he was wrong and handsomely offering to give Ethel the six months she sought. 'Oh I am a hateful thing to have hurt him so much,' she confessed to her diary and she wrote to tell him so. On reflection, though, she regretted giving him the impression she would go back 'the second he likes', so she wrote again assuring Herbert, 'everything must be completely over'.

For a day or so Ethel remained adamant. She then spoke to Louie, who told her what a heartless creature she was and made her promise to think seriously about it for a further night. Then there was a further reconsideration, as the diary reveals:

I couldn't do it. Oh I have been proud & horrid, I seemed to see it all in the night. I got up & wrote him a note – he had asked me to forgive him, I asked him to forgive me, which was far more as it should be. I dreaded the thought of him going out sailing in the rough wind without knowing so I got up early & went out to Stanmore at 5 to 9 ... And just as I got to the street who should come up but he himself ... Everything is alright, we had the Mack's study to ourselves all the morning, & part of the afternoon.

I shall never doubt again that I love him & I will never hurt him again by saying things, I didn't think I hurt him so much.

Inevitably, the confrontation with Charles Cope could no longer be deferred. It was the news of Herbert's success in his final law exams, which he passed with third class honours, that precipitated action. He came up to 'Inglewood' for a picnic lunch with Ethel on the top of the nearby hill, when they suddenly decided to tell Cope of their engagement as soon as he came home from work. Never lacking in moral courage, Herbert walked down to meet the train but Cope refused to hear a word and snapped his fingers at him. Arriving home in a white heat he gave two notes to his stepdaughter, one utterly refusing to sanction an engagement, the other supposing that on reaching the age of 21 she could do as she liked.

This was the beginning of a time of great strain at 'Inglewood', involving not only Ethel and Mr Cope but also spilling over into relationships with her mother and elder sister. Lilian seems to have been troubled, very simply, by jealousy. 'She is perfectly hateful today & always is throwing Herbert & Louie at me cause she knows it vexes me most,' Ethel wrote on 30 March. At the end of a session of nagging from Lilian she threw at her sister a canvas she'd been working on but it missed the mark and fell on the carpet, ruining the picture.

Several weeks later the diary recorded another 'fearful scene' with Mr Cope. Ethel had been away in town for two days, attending a garden party at Government House, then staying for the night with Mrs Weiss from L'Avenue and going to the university on the Saturday to see Herbert graduate BA, LLB. Curlewis accompanied her to St Leonards station 'as usual' and she travelled home with their neighbours, the Pockleys. For the next two days Cope struggled to contain his anger and frustration, exploding several times with the threat that he would force Ethel to prove her age by law before permitting her to marry. Ironically, on the evidence of the English birth certificate, Ethel had turned 21 fifteen months earlier on 24 January 1891. We cannot help wondering exactly who, apart from Mrs Cope, knew the truth about the ages of the three sisters. Both Lilian and Mrs Cope came into the quarrel, the elder sister taunting Ethel with having no time for anyone but Herbert and the mother also becoming very frosty and assuring Ethel it would be a relief if she carried out her promise of going away as a governess. For someone as tender-hearted as Ethel the situation was barely endurable. 'Everything is wretched wretched wretched,' she concluded.

But by the end of May Mr Cope was changing his tack, acting towards Herbert with the utmost graciousness although taking care that the lovers were not left alone together for a moment. One Sunday in June the two men worked together all day, in what was becoming a typical pattern, making stiles over the fences and chatting for hours at night over their pipes as if Ethel did not exist.

Soon after, there was a long letter from Herbert urging Ethel to become reconciled with Cope. Conscious as she was of her fondness for her stepfather, she wrote asking him to forgive her ... for what, one can hardly imagine ... and to be friends. The answer is recorded in the diary. 'He says he would far rather bury me than give me to any man, that after Mother he always loved me better than anyone on earth ... he should have the same feeling of abhorrence to any man.'

This time of extreme strain produced a diary entry, on 18 September 1892, which uses one of Ethel's sharpest and most evocative metaphors: 'Herbert & I sat out in the sunshine on the tennis court most of the day, – chaperoned by all the windows of course.'

In August it was Ethel's turn to reject an overture of peace, slight as it was:

There was a great crisis this morning, [*she wrote on the 25th*]. Mr Cope had been as horrid as he could for these 5 months & then this morning he suddenly stooped down & brushed my face with his beard. I couldn't be hypocrite enough to turn & kiss him thankfully for his tardy forgiveness especially when I have done nothing to be forgiven for. I turned my head away instinctively, it was all over & done in less than a second, he declares he won't speak to me again this side of the grave.

For a while now Ethel was in disgrace on all sides and Mrs Cope spoke of her going away as soon as the engagement to teach the Montgomery girls had come to an end in September. All that remained to complete the emotional shambles was for Herbert to fall out with Cope. This happened easily enough in late October, after Ethel had spent two days in town, largely with Herbert, going to a performance of Congreve's *Love for Love* by the University Dramatic Society and actually spending the night at 'Hermsley'. When Herbert visited on the Saturday Cope told him he was not to give presents to members of his family. Asked to explain this ban, Cope 'flew in a fearful rage & called him some dreadful names, a – liar with an epithet was one ... he says H shall never enter his doors again.'

Applied to a man as proud and sensitive as Herbert such treatment produced a stiff resolve to do exactly what his foe had commanded. So the lovers were substantially removed from surveillance and able to spend far more time in each other's company, sometimes at 'Hermsley' or at the Mack's home, often in yachts on the harbour, for many of their friends were keen on sailing.

The spring of 1892, confused as it was emotionally, brought Ethel to a time of high productivity as a writer. Even more importantly she began to find publishers interested in her work. On 20 September, though wretchedly ill with the Russian influenza, complete with a maddening headache, sore throat, fever and pains in the limbs, she had the pleasure of seeing her story, 'A Little Maid Errant' appear in the *Mail*. A week later her poem, 'Footsteps' came out in the *Tasmanian* and the following day, well recovered from the 'Russian', she began writing one of her most important short stories, 'The Little Duchess', which established her with the Sydney *Bulletin*, the most sought after and influential of all Australian magazines in the 1890s.

This story, which was completed on 28 September and copied out by hand, occupied the best part of a page in the *Bulletin*'s Christmas number of 1892, sharing space with Banjo Paterson's poem 'The Two Devines'. It told of a young clerk who fell hopelessly in love with a blonde salesgirl, who looks for all the world like Ethel, and goes to prison for two years when he draws suspicion on himself in saving his 'Little Duchess' from prosecution for theft.

Jules Archibald, proprietor of the *Bulletin*, wrote to Ethel at the end of 1892 complimenting her on 'a neat little story, very naturally told' enclosing a cheque for 2 pounds and promising to keep the manuscript for a special occasion. A week earlier, Herbert had passed on the substance of this news to Ethel, who wrote on Christmas Eve in understandable excitement, 'My first thing in Bulletin! I believe I shall be successful in the literary line after all. I *will* be'.

Contributing to this growing confidence was the beginning of a steady new commitment to write for the *Illustrated Sydney News* in its final year or so of publication. Ethel had sent the editor, Mr Spooner, some stories, one of which, 'A Mutable Maiden', was published in the *News* on 13 August. It was a romantic story, set in the goldfields of Lambing Flat at the time of the riots of 1861. Early in October she had the idea of writing some social paragraphs entitled 'Between Ourselves' and sent them on spec to Mr Spooner. A letter soon came from Spooner saying how well he liked the material and commissioning her to write a similar column every week, for half a guinea a time. Publication began on 22 October and took the form of a letter from Yum Yum, a Sydney girl, to her dearest friend in the bush.

Something of the style of 'Between Ourselves' and a measure of the distance Sydney has travelled socially in the past century may be gathered from taking a sample of the columns Ethel wrote for an issue in February 1893. The big news was the unexpected announcement that the Governor and his wife, Lord and Lady Jersey, were soon to return to Britain, just when they had succeeded so well in filling the gap left by the departure of the popular Carringtons.

Who were loved the best? [*Yum Yum asked*] I suppose the crucial test ... will be on the day of departure. Do you remember the day Lord and Lady Carrington left? All Sydney seemed gone mad. Government House was mobbed, women wept and fought each other for a last handshake, men cheered themselves hoarse ... and all along the drive and down Macquarie Street thousands of flowers were rained down before the carriages.

Other paragraphs addressed the acute problem of the dearth of servants and urged the abandonment of the practice of deep mourning at funeral processions, which Yum Yum thought one of the most unpleasant spectacles to be seen in an Australian city on a hot day.[9]

Spooner liked Ethel's work so well that he had asked her in November to do an extra column of 'Between Ourselves' and to take charge of the Children's Page. 'The Childrens Corner' had its first airing under Ethel on 26 November 1892, beginning with the first chapter of 'Laddie', the story of a mischievous, curly-headed boy and his 'young, bright-faced mother', which ran for many months. In the same issue we meet Ethel in the persona of 'Dame Durden' and encounter her 'Post Office', which offered young children a mixture of ideas for simple, sticky recipes, party games and competitions. She was paid thirty shillings a week for her efforts, 'abominably little' as she understandably complained to her diary, but at least it offered independence and solvency. An era had begun in Ethel's life that was to continue with only short breaks for nearly forty years, going on from the *Illustrated Sydney News* to the *Town and Country Journal* and at length to the Sydney *Sunday Sun*.

Ethel's Christmas of 1892 was considerably brightened by the news that the *Bulletin* was to publish 'The Little Duchess'. Herbert was still excluded from 'Inglewood', partly by his own sense of pride, and there was strain all round, which only lifted when the lovers met elsewhere. One such opportunity was provided at the cottage the Macks took on the road fronting the ocean beach at Manly for the holidays. Ethel went there by ferry on 30 December and stayed for a week during which Herbert came down for daily visits or else stayed at a local hotel so as to meet Mr Cope's objections to his living in the same house. They went for walks on the rocks, with Ethel revelling in the stormy weather. In what soon became a regular aspect of her craft as a writer, she sat down before leaving Manly and began writing a story, 'At the Manly Rocks – a sweet small tragedy', which was posted on spec to the *Illustrated Sydney News* and soon accepted for publication.

In her end-of-year assessment Ethel felt fairly satisfied by additions to her library and by having 10 pounds in the bank. For the following year she wanted to have 50 pounds in the bank, and, significantly, to have published a children's book and written several short stories for the *Bulletin* and other papers as well as completing her regular work.

A gradual improvement had been taking place since Christmas in Herbert's situation at 'Inglewood'. Mr Cope had actually shaken him by the hand in what Ethel described 'as a Xmas treat' and in January a new regime began, with the young man invited to stay for Saturday dinner. Lilian declined to shake hands with him and 'only addressed feeding remarks to him at the table' but a further advance occurred when Cope told Herbert to stay the night as the weather was so threatening – if he did not mind sleeping on the sofa in the drawing room.

A couple of days later after a brief time with Herbert on the way home from the city, Ethel decided there wasn't anything to be compared with love, 'Fame would be a Dead Sea apple if one hadn't love too' and the fame she sought was largely to make her lover more proud of her.

On 24 January 1893, Ethel's birthday, Herbert went up to 'Inglewood' and the lovers enjoyed a tête-à-tête lunch in the summerhouse. 'I am 21 today,' she wrote later, 'an infant no longer. I shall have to stop Herbert calling me "Baby" as he always does.' In the margin there were the words, 'Seven L Aust – Sketched it out.'

She had begun a project that would soon deliver the fame she so wanted. On 27 January she wrote in her diary, 'Night started a new story that I shall call "Seven Little Australians". I don't think I'll let it go in the *Illustrated*, if I can do without it there I'll see if I can get it published in book form.'

chapter
Six

$\mathscr{E}$thel herself told of the circumstances in which she wrote her best known novel. One account is from a facetious piece, scribbled down in later years with many corrections and second thoughts, apparently as notes for an informal article. It makes a good deal of how she had been affected by removal from the bustle of Newtown to the serenity of Lindfield. At that time there were only four train services to the city each day, and before the opening of the railway extension from St Leonards to Milsons Point on 29 April 1893, office workers from the North Shore caught the 7.40 a.m. train from Hornsby which arrived at St Leonards at 8.15 a.m. and linked with a horse omnibus that took passengers to the Point for the ferry ride to Circular Quay. So, instead of Ethel's riding into the city from L'Avenue on a steam tram that ran along King Street only a few minutes walk away, the journey to town from Lindfield was a matter for serious decision. For the same reason friends were far less likely to call in and pass an hour in conversation or tennis or arranging an outing.

It had an effect, [*Ethel wrote*], like adding half a dozen hours or so to days that since leaving school had been filled to the very brim ... red lonely roads running up hill & down dale, silent bushland everywhere filled with towering gums & wattles, & the songs & flittings of birds; sunrises & sunsets uninterrupted by houses – of course one wrote a book![1]

At the same time, Ethel was writing weekly contributions for the *Tasmanian Mail* and the *Illustrated Sydney News*, aiming further stories in the direction of the *Bulletin* and putting ideas together for an Australian Annual to which John Le Gay Brereton was contributing some poetry.

Promising as this year had seemed to Ethel in its opening gestures to her as a writer, it soon presented her with health problems – her own and Herbert's. Her diary for 10 February records a visit to Dr Quaife, a fellow pew holder at the family's old church of St Matthias at Paddington, whom she consulted about some deafness in her right ear. He syringed and poked at it and told her to come again for further treatment. A week later Ethel returned to Dr Quaife who sent her on to see his brother, the ear specialist. There ensued 'rather a rough time', at this stage not described in harrowing detail, with the promise of worse to follow.

Herbert seemed often to be in poor health and Ethel passed on Dr McAllister's comment, 'he doesn't have enough to eat, – that's the wretched state their house is in, no management or anything. It makes my blood boil.' Ethel's earlier uneasiness about the family's household affairs was being reinforced.

Her diary in 1893 shows the beginning of an awareness of Herbert's financial problems as he confronted the costs and uncertainties of striking out into the world as a young barrister, problems that were magnified by his father's anxieties as a brick manufacturer during a time of stagnation in the building market. A general economic crisis was approaching and many businesses were beginning to fail. Of immediate concern to the couple was the sum of 25 pounds which Herbert had lent to his mother but which she had no chance of repaying, just when he needed it to furnish his chambers, evoking Ethel's comment:

I have £15 already & shall have £10 more in a week or two & shall *make* him borrow it from me ... I'll never forgive him if he doesn't, I should love him to have it from me.

Within another week the matter was resolved by Ethel's threatening to give the money instead to the Queensland Flood Appeal.

For Ethel this was to be the beginning of a contribution to Herbert's legal career that combined tenderness and commonsense. He was admitted to the Bar on 17 March in the presence of the Full Court, 'H. R. Curlewis B.A. LLB, Barrister-at-law, it takes quite a lot of ink to write,' she commented. Six days later the diary records, 'H. 1st brief. Brown v Minister for Works, Want QC Hanbury Davis & Curlewis V Sir Julian Salomons, Pilchers & CB Stephen.' Only a week elapsed before the new barrister shared in his first victory and was rewarded with a tip of 5 pounds from the grateful Mr Brown in addition to his fees. He too was on his way. His immediate desire was to be married on the proceeds 'right away'.

With their relationship on more secure ground Ethel now determined to take Herbert and his family in hand, '26 February. Night wrote to H, a very personal letter – told him he was terribly careless about his appearance.' This was promptly followed by another note telling him not to open the first. But it was too late:

1 March 1893. H came for day. He said he was *pleased* about the letter! Because it showed I would say anything to him & more, it was nice to feel someone took some interest in him. He *did* look nice, he had a high collar, white pique tie, new hat, altogether I have never seen him look so nice.

Encouraged by this success Ethel then turned her attention

to the redecoration of the Curlewis home at Stanmore, starting with the dining room, 'which is comfortless in the extreme'. A fortnight later she began on the drawing room, moving the piano to a corner with its back to the room and draping it with green art muslin caught back with coral pink, displaying some family photographs on two draped easels and tossing about some frilled cushions. The place was 'transformed'. Gaining confidence, she moved to remodel Herbert's bedroom. As far as the Curlewis family was concerned, marriage was no longer in question, it was now only a matter of when the young couple would feel ready for it; for Charles Cope, however, it was to be another matter entirely.

By April 1893, the worries expressed by Ethel for Herbert and his family had given way to the feeling that she was observing the onset of social disaster. Her thickest ink was used to note that the E. S. & A. Bank had stopped payment and that with the likely winding up of the Brick Company Mr Curlewis would be out of employ. Next day the London Chartered Bank followed suit, touching Ethel's own pocket. 'The distress in Sydney is getting terrible', she wrote, '1000 bank clerks are out of employ.'

The Maritime Strike involving about 50,000 unionists had broken out in August 1890 and soon disorganised communications and trade throughout Australia. Violent confrontations took place between militant unionists and unemployed workers who had been brought in by shipowners to break the strike. The trial of strength between capital and labour had, predictably, been won by capital, which received crucial assistance from the State and its armed forces. It was that defeat and their estimation of the reasons for it, which convinced trade unionists in New South Wales and other colonies of the need to form their own political parties in the hope of exercising power directly at the heart of the State's executive authority.

This industrial convulsion, which rapidly transformed the

Australian political scene, had had few reverberations in Ethel's diary until 1893, by which time she was touched by the economic dislocation of her society. The depression of the 1890s saw the classic Australian conjunction of low wool prices, a decline of British investment, the cessation of a building boom, banks being forced to close their doors by a sudden withdrawal of deposits, and massive unemployment, as manufacturers shed workers and battened down for the duration. Accompanying this urban tragedy was a rural crisis that had been touched off by low export prices and brought home to every farmer and pastoralist by a prolonged drought that penalised landholders who had overstocked during the earlier time of prosperity and high rainfall.

For many Australians of literary bent it was the poems of Henry Lawson, sent west by Jules Archibald of the *Bulletin* to 'collect material and atmosphere for sketches, stories and poems', that revealed the dimensions of the human tragedy being played out between the bronze skies and baked earth at the back of Bourke. Ten years later, by which time a friendship had developed between Henry Lawson and Ethel Turner (Lawson had been touched to receive a letter from Ethel responding to his problems as a writer), she had been enabled by her brilliant but impecunious colleague to feel some of what Manning Clark calls the 'haunting sympathy' that Lawson aroused in his countrymen for the sufferers from yet another bush crisis.[2]

Retrenchments were now so general that Ethel's income from journalism was bound to suffer. On 16 May she received the news from the *Tasmanian Mail* that the Sydney letter would have to go, reducing by 20 pounds the annual payment received by the girls, so Ethel passed the whole of it to Lilian. Two days later on a visit to the office of the *Illustrated Sydney News*, she was told by the editor that her chatty column, 'Between Ourselves', would be cut out, reducing her income by 55 pounds. Yet Mr Spooner introduced her to

Walter Jeffery, who was then editing the *Town and Country Journal* and he took away some of her stories to assess the possibility of her writing for him. By the end of the year he had published her story of the goldfields, 'A Modern Achilles', in the *Journal*'s Christmas number and when the *Illustrated Sydney News* ceased publication in February 1894, 'Dame Durden' and her Children's Page were taken over in the *Town and Country Journal* almost immediately. The friendship and esteem of Walter Jeffery was to prove as important to Ethel as the steady income from this new source.

In the autumn of 1893 Ethel's younger sister had an experience that was soon to furnish an idea and a location for the story of 'Seven Little Australians', already quietly brewing in the author's mind. Rose Turner, then in her twentieth year, was sent to complete her education at Mrs Laby's boarding school at Bowral. At the end of March, when the family was expecting her home for the Easter holidays, they learned that she was prevented from travelling by an injured knee, so Ethel spent a busy day clearing her desk of journalistic tasks and packed her bag for the journey to the highlands to keep her sister company. It was the sort of gesture she made throughout her life, from the time she had been deputed by Sarah Turner to watch over her frail elder sister.

Not that the task at Bowral was performed with the sombre air of a martyr. When Ethel's ten days with Rose came to an end Mrs Dixson and all of the girls remaining at school over Easter came to the station to see her off. She had an unaffected love for people of every age and rejoiced artlessly in their admiration, which she commonly reflected on with fresh wonder at her good fortune. As she put it, 'I am really fond of the girls, they are very nice, – I think they reciprocate it too. They quarrel for the last kiss from me at night, who is to sit next to me'.

To provide exercise and recreation during the chilly days

at Bowral Ethel organised some long walks and hired a dray with a team of four horses that took the girls on a picnic to Fitzroy Falls, a round trip of nearly fifty kilometres. There they enjoyed the spectacular scenery and 'much climbing down ladders & places warned to be unsafe'. At night there were party games, of which Ethel had a professional knowledge in her capacity as Dame Durden of the Children's Corner. At other times she cast a skilled and appreciative eye over Rose's sewing, music and painting, deciding that boarding school had been very good for the development of her sister's feminine accomplishments, though in the end there was to be disappointment at her failure to matriculate.

Predictably, Herbert became impatient for his lover's return and wired her two days earlier to ask why she had not yet come back. He was waiting on the platform to meet the train and took her home to dine at 'Hermsley', where they were joined by Jack Creed and Louie.

One of Ethel's milestones in 1893 was recorded in her diary on 24 June, a Saturday, when her story of low life in the back streets, 'Wilkes of Waterloo', was published in the *Daily Telegraph*. The satisfaction of seeing her work in the pages of a major metropolitan newspaper was heightened by the suddenness of the achievement, for she had only sent the manuscript to the editor twenty-four hours earlier. Wilkes was a herculean wife beater who saw it as his duty to lay it on with a heavy strap he kept on the kitchen dresser when his missus stepped out of line. 'You're my wife, Em'ly girl,' he said quietly, 'an' when you won't do things fer askin', I've got to learn you.' Encouraged by a neighbour to rebel, she offended again by staying out late and Wilkes was taken by a strong party of police when he administered the usual punishment. What is outstanding about the story is its understanding of human behaviour, as in the slap on the face given by Emily to the neighbour when she rejoices in Wilkes's imprisonment. At the end of the seven days Emily was waiting for her husband with two tram tickets and a readiness to accept a return to the old regime, though in the final scene he tells her to burn the strap in the fire. Also natural and easy is the author's handling of back street dialogue; like the children's stories that soon followed, it showed a keen and perceptive ear.

Contrary to the expectations aroused by her diary entry of 27 January Ethel turned aside from the manuscript of her first novel until July. Then she came across three chapters that had gathered dust for months while she had worked at a 'turgid novel in the vein of George Meredith', and decided to make friends again with Judy and Bunty. At the same time she had a visit from Louie Mack to whom she proudly showed the 'Great Work', a serious novel, in which she was then investing her hopes, only to learn that it was 'melodramatic and artificial and quite fourteen other hateful things'. Instead, picking up the crumpled chapters of 'Seven Little Australians', Louie asked, 'Why don't you go on with this tale about all the children. It really isn't half bad.' Ethel suggested, coldly, that if Louie hurried, and did not talk so much, she might catch her train. All the same, Ethel's diary records several fresh chapters of 'all those children' during the same month.

Yet there was a long period while progress came to a halt, when Ethel became hopeful of making a fortune from her first play, 'The Wig', a one-act legal farce, which she completed on 17 June. The following day, a Sunday, with the Cope family seated around the fire on an early winter's night at 'Inglewood':

Read it to my skeptical family at night. Lily has been laughing at my cheek in attempting a play. They all think it is really good. They laughed in the right places & were really a pleasant audience. I *am* excited. Sat very late over the fire & built hundreds of divine castles in the coals of the things I'd do if ever I 'struck oil' with a play.

Like Ethel's early ambition to write a major novel for adults, this hope was unrealized despite several attempts. 'The Wig' itself was given to the dramatic entrepreneur M. Bouiecault but returned unread. In spite of this disappointment Ethel saw it performed a year later by the University Dramatic Society but it drew crushing reviews.

August and September were productive months. 'The tale about the children' continued at a steady pace and after copying out chapter 7 Ethel breathed a deep sigh and remarked 'it's a big undertaking writing a book'.

Seven Little Australians, which briefly had the working title of 'Six Pickles', was very much the product of Ethel's life as a member of a mixed family. The Woolcots in the novel were broadly modelled on the Copes, except that it was Captain Woolcot and not Esther, his child bride, who brought a quiver full of children into the marriage. A good deal of the tension Ethel observed in her stepfather's house, from which no one in the family seemed exempt, was reflected in the friction and sense of impending calamity that marks life at 'Misrule', as the Woolcots' home was called. Both step-fathers, fictional and real, were angry and insecure men given too readily to bullying their gentle wives and ruling their families by fear.

Rex, the child of Cope's marriage to Sarah Turner, born in 1881, was another casualty of the climate of tension and the absence of candour at 'Inglewood'. Ethel writes in June of an incident involving her half-brother which was soon to be used as a pattern for Bunty's behaviour in *Seven Little Australians*:

Rex said a very wicked word, swearing & I overheard. Then he vowed & swore before heaven he didn't say it & said it was Frank [*possibly a gardener*]. Then he confessed it. I feel utterly miserable about it, the child is being ruined by never being punished & all of us are responsible. We are not going to tell Mother about it till morning.

Bunty's fibs and more broadly his failure to take responsibility for his actions become important ingredients of *Seven Little Australians* and other early novels. For Ethel, prevarication was seen essentially as a male trait and it is not without significance that she uses Bunty's weakness as a foil for Judy's strength:

By nature Bunty was the most arrant little story-teller ever born, and it was only Judy's fearless honesty that had kept him moderately truthful. But Judy was miles away, and could not possibly wither him up with her look of utter contempt.

Yet it was Bunty who had found Judy in the loft of the old stable where she had hidden, sick and weary, after running away from Miss Burton's boarding school at Mount Victoria. In an impressive reversal of form he had stolen food from the pantry to feed his starving sister and had suffered a beating from the captain's riding whip rather than break Judy's confidence.

During October, Ethel moved quickly to complete her story; on the 18th, as she put it in her diary, she 'killed Judy to slow music'. All that remained was to copy out some chapters and go and 'hunt for a publisher'. A week later she called on Mr Jeffery, who gave her a note, 'a very complimentary one', introducing her to Mr Steele, the Melbourne manager of the English firm of Ward, Lock & Bowden. It was to prove most useful.

'2 November. 'Walked up to post & sent "7 Australians" to Ward & Lock, Melbourne. It took 18 stamps.' In the same post she sent a new story to the *Daily Telegraph*. There was in her head, as well, an idea for a new book, 'The Story of a Baby', intended for an adult audience. Quite a day.

Precisely a week after posting her manuscript to Ward, Lock & Bowden, Ethel was amazed to have a reply:

They say they have read my mss & conclude I wish to negotiate for the immediate publication of it. That owing to the terrible depression they are using their power of selection very sparingly but if I will tell them what value I place upon the work they will write me further. Not at all a bad letter to get from my first publisher & within a week. I can't think what value I place on it, I must get advice.

Next day, 10 November, Ethel spoke to Mr Archibald at the *Bulletin* office and was told to ask for 20 pounds plus a royalty. So she wrote to Melbourne and said 30 pounds plus royalty! But she had the grace to tell her diary, 'I am *living* for an answer.' Perhaps significantly, two days later she went to church for the first time in ages, only to find after walking several kilometres through a rainstorm that there was no service.

Replying on 20 November Steele told Ethel he considered *Seven Little Australians* a 'bright juvenile tale of considerable merit' and offered to pay 10 pounds on publication for the copyright, with royalties of a penny for each copy sold at less than 2 shillings and twopence for copies sold at a higher price. Under pressure from Ethel, Steele lifted his offer, on 30 November, to the sum of 15 pounds for copyright and a royalty of 12 per cent on sales above two shillings and sixpence. The book, he promised, would be well bound and illustrated by a first class artist, 'they say they are "very glad indeed to be associated with the Louisa Alcott of Australia".'[3]

Ethel responded readily and gratefully to the new offer from Steele, who until this point was acting entirely on his own initiative, rather underlining the confidence inspired in him by the prospect of his new author. She now embarked on a long and mutually valuable association with him that proved as important to her literary career as her friendship with Walter Jeffery, editor of *Town and Country*. Ward, Lock and Bowden – the last mentioned was managing director in 1893 but later left the firm, when it became Ward, Lock & Company – published most of Ethel's books. With their expertise and strong representation in Australasia and the United States in addition to Great Britain, they contributed greatly to her early and sustained success as a writer of novels and stories for children.

Steele's letter to Ethel of 4 December offered a nicely judged mixture of the praise, encouragement and practical advice she needed. He was about to send the manuscript off to London and trusted his principal would be pleased with his judgement:

With the ability you possess in writing young people's tales, there should be a very bright future for you. As indicated in my previous letter, strive to develop the pathetic and touching phases in your stories. I am a man of 40 and pretty tough as business men go, but I do not hesitate to confess that your death of Little Judy very much impressed and affected me.[4]

It was apt that William Steele should have fastened so readily and positively on the element in Ethel's story that has proved most appealing to readers of every age during the century the book has been continuously in print. Not all critics approved Judy's death, some regretting that the story's brightest spark should be unavailable for a sequel. The *Sydney Morning Herald* reviewer, while complimenting Miss Turner on the book's healthy, gay and innocent tone, regretted that her 'sympathetic mind' should not have discerned that Judy's death was 'too heavily charged with sentiment and the human tragedy for children'. A family tradition has it that the sudden death of the girl had been suggested to Ethel by her mother when she was seeking Mrs Cope's advice about how to devise some suitable climax to crown Judy's contribution to the story. Rather than use the conventional solution of having the rebel reform, she adopted the more dramatic and novel expedient of killing her with a falling gum tree.

The most effective answer to the critics is the consistent support the public has given *Seven Little Australians*, buying, it is said, two million copies in a hundred years, keeping it constantly in print and prompting its translation into a score of languages, starting with the Swedish edition of 1895. It thus became the first Australian children's book to earn in a foreign currency. From the beginning of its sales, Ethel became one of the outstanding figures of the literary scene, sought not only for the official table at writers' functions but also constantly called on to attend speech days at Sydney Girls' High, her own school, and at Hornsby Girls' High.

Ada Cambridge, a novelist in her own right, and a more worldly woman than Ethel, wrote an important piece about *Seven Little Australians* and its sequel, *The Family at Misrule*, in the *Review of Reviews*. She begins by stressing that they are 'authentic literature' and that the characters are alive, 'each clearly individualised'. She views Captain Woolcot 'as one of but few recognisably real men in the realm of fiction'.

The little general, [*she goes on*], is the *only* real small infant of my acquaintance in that thickly-populated world. The account of his journey by the ferry-boat from the barracks to his home, with his father's iron grasp on the back of his woolly pelisse, forbidding him to slither off the seat to see where the puffing noise came from, is, of course, drawn from nature.

Ada Cambridge placed the 'General' first 'as a work of art', but Bunty, 'fat and lazy, greedy and cowardly', she sees as the most original character in the book.

In dealing with the death scene, she writes, 'Her pathos is unforced; there is scarcely a touch of the mawkish sentimentalism which has become almost a conventional necessity in a novelist's treatment of the subject, travestying and desecrating the deep tragedies of life.' She then quotes the simple words that evoke the world in which Judy passed her final moments:

Greyer grew the shadows round the little hut, the bullocks' outlines had faded, and only an indistinct mass of soft black loomed across the light. Behind the trees the fire was going out; here and there were yellow, vivid streaks yet, but the flaming sun had dipped beyond the world, and the purple, delicate veil was dropping down. A curlew's note broke the silence'.

Summing up the achievement, Cambridge reminds us that Ethel was a beginner, making the excellence of her work the more remarkable. 'She is not a great writer yet; she is only so good that she is bound to become a great one if she goes on as she has begun.' On the question of her breaking free from children's books and entering 'the higher walks of literary life', the reviewer felt that 'anything is possible in the case of one with her equipment'. Concluding her review, Cambridge noticed briefly the quality of *The Story of a Baby*, a novel not about a baby but a young couple, and felt confirmed in the view that Ethel would succeed with any subject she took in hand.

Ethel Turner's mother lived as a child at The Strait in Lincoln. Courtesy of Peter Radford and the Lincoln Central Library

Sarah Jane Shaw, Ethel's mother, as a
young woman

Ethel's class at Sydney Girls' High School, 1888. Front row sitting: the Misses F. Johnson, Ethel Turner, Louise Mack and Ethel Maynard. Second row sitting: the Misses Elmina Sutherland, Marion Bolton, Henrietta Orr, Lily Jones, Dora Elphinstone. Back row: the Misses Maud McPhee, Ruth Bowmaker, Lily Grace, Evelyn Green and Florence Delohery

Sydney Girls' High School, Elizabeth Street c.1900. Courtesy of the Mitchell Library

Sydney Girls' High School staff, 1890. Back row: Mr Holmes (Classics and English), Mr Anderson (Mathematics). Middle row from left: Miss Grossman (afterwards Headmistress, Newcastle), Miss Whitfeld, Miss Wheatley Walker (Headmistress), Miss Thompson. Front row: Miss Artlett, Miss Bruce. Courtesy of the Mitchell Library

Ethel and Lilian's study

The first issue of the *Parthenon*, 1 January
1889

'The Three Little Maids', Rose (16), Lilian (22) and Ethel (20), photographed by Kerry & Jones

L' Avenue, Newtown c.1905, now Warren Ball Street. The Copes' house, 'Leonidas', was to the left, facing Hollis Park

The University of Sydney as Ethel knew it. Courtesy of the Sydney Water Board

'Young Herbert', as a graduate in Arts and
Law, April 1892

Georgiana Sophia Curlewis (née O'Brien),
Herbert's mother, commonly known as
'Marmee'

Frederick Charles Curlewis, Herbert's father

A boating picnic including Ethel, Herbert and Lilian

*E*thel's 'Red Letter Day' which brought Ward, Lock & Bowden's offer of a contract to publish *Seven Little Australians* was a Saturday in November 1893. Not unusually for the start of a weekend, Charles Cope was in a prickly mood and Ethel wrote of a bad row between her mother and stepfather. She determined at once to use the advance from the publishers to take Sarah on a holiday to Tasmania early in the new year.

If there had been any doubts about Mrs Cope's need for such a break they were resolved on the following Monday by another domestic storm, which required Ethel's best efforts as a mediator:

Mother was bent on going away from him, at any rate for a time. She really is a good woman, my idea of a good woman. Not religious outwardly but just doing her best for everyone always. She deserves to be well treated.

Coincidentally, Ethel was working that day on chapter 4 of her adult novel about violent domestic discord, *The Story of a Baby*. We should not wonder, perhaps, at the frequency with which, in Brenda Niall's words, Ethel used women in her novels as sources of 'moral power' on whom her men all too often depended to support their stumbling progress.[1]

Not only at home but also in her wider life it was an emotionally exhausting time. In December Ethel took part in a cruise on the harbour in the Electric Launch which had been hired for the day by an eccentric young man called Mr Tucker who had been admiring her from afar for the past year. The party, which included their friends the Pockleys but not Herbert, landed at Clontarf for a meal that would have done no discredit to Kenneth Grahame's Ratty and after tea she walked with her host along the beach and sat with him at the end of an old pier. Here, after talking of many things, Tucker suddenly declared his love for Ethel, forcing her to reveal for the first time she was secretly engaged to Herbert. 'He was so white and strange looking,' she wrote. 'Coming back he sat at the end of the boat alone, I had to talk to some wretched man Ginnes who never stopped'. Perhaps she would have preferred to have been able to administer comfort to the disappointed lover. Next day Herbert came up to 'Inglewood' and attempted to win permission to accompany the two women on the ship to Hobart, returning to Sydney immediately, but Mrs Cope was not prepared for the inevitable conflict with her husband.

On Christmas Eve the family and Herbert exchanged presents and all but Mr Cope went to the little Anglican Church of St John at Gordon and sang carols. Herbert slept the night at 'Inglewood', went back to 'Hermsley' for dinner with his own family and returned on Boxing Day for, as it proved, some heartfelt words with Ethel of which she wrote:

I have been in horrid moods lately, – felt as if I had absolutely no capacity for feeling & as if my heart had gone to sleep. It has made me cold & careless to H. till tonight & then he told me how it was hurting him, – he was nearly heart-broken at the thought of losing my love. I'm a beast.

It was a time of reflection and assessment. Her end of the

year summary recalled that she had promised herself a year earlier to have 50 pounds in the bank and to have completed a prodigious amount of sewing, as well as lessons in piano and singing. In fact she *had* saved 50 pounds though half was about to be spent on the Tasmanian holiday. The sewing was a failure in spite of some rush jobs in readiness for the trip and in the music department there was only a quarter's singing to her credit.

Writing was another matter. She had finished 'Tekel' for Cassell's competition (it was unsuccessful there and was never published) and had written a children's book that was to appear in October. A weekly children's page had been done for the *Illustrated Sydney News* as well as a 'Between Ourselves' column. In the first half of the year she had a weekly column in the *Tasmanian Mail* and had written twelve short stories which had been accepted, four for the *Bulletin*, two for the *Daily Telegraph*, four for the *Illustrated* and two for the *Town and Country Journal*. Not counting the money that was to come as an advance from Ward & Lock she had made 100 pounds by her pen. Writing, clearly, would be a viable profession.

With departure of the *Oonah* planned for 6 January the preceding days were crammed with shopping and sewing, especially the latter. A few days earlier she wrote, 'Sewed hard all day, scarcely lifted my head from the needle. I'd rather break stones than be a seamstress perpetually.' As was to be a feature of her holidays until 1931 Ethel had to prepare her children's pages in advance for the period of absence but there was consolation in the cheque from Mr Spooner of the *Illustrated* and the promise of more from Walter Jeffery for two stories in the Christmas number of *Town and Country*.

The day before departure Herbert came to 'Inglewood' to say goodbye and was permitted to stay the night, so the lovers enjoyed the balmy air of the summerhouse until the mosquitoes drove them inside, when Ethel admitted, 'It's

impossible to write about Love in a Diary, love like ours.'
Next morning Herbert was excluded by Mr Cope from the
family party to farewell Sarah and Ethel; it would have been
a further wound if he had realized that Ethel had as a fellow
passenger a young doctor, R. J. Millard, who had figured in
Ethel's diaries in the most approving way since the days at
L'Avenue. But from 10 o'clock that night, having decided to
forego dinner, she was so troubled by seasickness as to be
safe from any entanglement.

Approaching Tasmania Ethel and her mother 'lay limp &
unlovely' in their berths till late afternoon when they crawled
up on deck to have a biscuit and watch the grand coastal
scenery, 'only we were past nature'. On arrival in Hobart they
were thankful beyond words to be met by a friend, Mr
George Taylor, who saw to their luggage and engaged rooms
for them at Waterloo House in Davey Street.

Much of the time in Hobart was spent in the company of
Taylor and his married brother, the city librarian. Ethel also
met the editor of the *Tasmanian Mail*, 'such a nice man,
running over with fun'. From the first day they ate huge
quantities of the delicious red currants, raspberries and straw-
berries that were in season and 'marvellously cheap'. After a
trip across the harbour to Bellerive Ethel wrote a long letter
to Herbert, feeling the traveller's sudden ache for a lover at
the end of a journey and confiding to her diary, 'I never
wanted him so much in my life'. She reflected on her recent
unkindness, and his remarkable patience with her 'quips &
cranks' and impulsively sent him a cable to assure him of her
love.

A visit to the home of Taylor's married brother, on a hill
above Hobart, revealed another form of colonial cuisine, raspberry vinegar, prompting Ethel next day to start her story
'To the City of Raspberry Jam' while she lay in bed recovering from over-indulgence. Soon after, the rain came down
so heavily that a planned trip to the Strawberry Feast at Fern

Tree Bower was cancelled, giving their stomachs a rest from fruit. When it did take place they travelled in the box seat of a brake up the Huon Road 'with the great blue mountain before us & the great blue bays behind'. The feast followed, of fruit spread on white-clothed tables and they pressed on to the Silver Fall 'a perfect forest of magnificent tree ferns ... Then the drive back, the rapid motion through the cold air the sharp mountain rain in our faces & the blue harbour & river in front'. Conscious of their glowing cheeks and noses they were struck by the contrast with Sydney in January, for the letters from home spoke of temperatures over 100 degrees Fahrenheit.

Many of the letters from home were of course from Herbert. There was a difference in the keenness with which the two partners required reassurance about the strength of the other's love. From the beginning Herbert had been the more needy and the feeling was acute when they were parted. Initially Ethel had been wary of his intensity but by the time of the Tasmanian holiday she was much better attuned. On their last Saturday in Hobart, instead of going with her mother to tea at the Taylors' home she went to the post to collect an expected letter, 'such a letter, he is so wretched – my last letter was cold. He implored me to send an immediate answer, so I just got one in before the post went'. The following Monday she wrote:

Read, idled, packed. I am glad we are going home. I have enjoyed myself immensely but I want to get home to that poor boy without any further delay, he is fairly eating his heart out for me, he did not let me know before and I never dreamed he would miss me so dreadfully. He says he can't sleep or eat or do anything rational & is counting & crossing off the time on his calendar.

On their return journey Ethel and Sarah fared more easily with the sea and berthed early on 2 February to find Herbert (looking 'fearfully thin') and Mr Cope waiting; they had risen at 2 a.m. and walked from Lindfield to catch a ferry to the Quay.

Herbert must have found it difficult to share Ethel with the family, for Rex and the girls were waiting for the travellers at the station and 'Everybody talked at once for hours of course'. Several days later Ethel received a letter from him:

he is not quite happy yet, feels I am thinking regretfully of past pleasures & am not glad to be back. He seems to think I am a little tired of him & that I am cold & it has made him so miserable again. I seem always to be hurting him & I never mean to.

Such problems could not long divert Ethel from thoughts about career and income, not least because the expenses of the trip had made her 'nearly penniless'. It was a letter from Mr Spooner of the *Illustrated Sydney News* that had elicited this reaction; he told her the paper was about to stop publication, a casualty of the depression and the fall in advertising revenue, so removing a major source of Ethel's income.

A trip to town next day did much to reassure her. She had called on Mr Archibald at the *Bulletin* office and answered his queries about her literary progress, then saw Steele – 'My publisher!' – as she proudly reminded herself. He was most encouraging about her prospects. From there a call on Louie Mack for lunch at Neutral Bay and a chat until late afternoon when Herbert joined the girls for tea and then accompanied Ethel on the train home, walking with her through the leafy roads all the way to the stile at the back fence of 'Inglewood'.

As so often happened in Ethel's life when one door closed another opened. Going on 9 February to the office shared by several magazines she was met by Walter Jeffery who asked if she would write the Children's Page for the *Town and Country Journal*. 'My ill luck did not last long, I am safe once more, it is a great relief,' she exulted. And she was to have a free hand. Her mood again optimistic she had lunch at the Gladstone, then called at 'Hermsley' to have tea with Herbert and his family. After tea Herbert took her to visit Mrs Raine, an old family friend at Ashfield, 'such a dear old lady' who had long wished to meet her. Later, Herbert told her how satisfying it was at such a time to be recognised as Ethel's husband-to-be, whereas at 'Inglewood' ... 'he has to behave like a chidden child & before other people pretend to have no connection with me'. They had both been reproved by Mrs Cope for the warmth of affection they had displayed when reunited after Ethel's absence in Tasmania; small wonder that Herbert had felt so disheartened.

On 12 February Ethel wrote her first Children's Page for the *Town and Country*, which was to be published a fortnight later and would earn her a regular guinea a week. Always a loyal and zealous friend, after staying for the night at Neutral Bay she took Louie to talk with Mr Jeffery about the possibility of his publishing some of Louie's stories. Afterwards the girls had lunch at the Shamrock, a tea shop started in the city by Jack Creed's sisters and Ethel caught the 3.25 train home from Milson's Point feeling exhausted, for her insomnia seemed to be recurring and had no doubt been exacerbated by the tendency of the two friends to chatter far into the night. Sleeplessness did not go well with creative writing; Herbert on the other hand was busy 'taking the world by the horns' as Ethel put it, collaborating with William McIntyre in writing a monograph comparing English and colonial statute law.

Ethel's decades of editing children's pages may have had the valuable effect of providing a basic and reliable source of income but it was soon evident that a heavy price was involved. On 16 March she recorded with an exclamation that there had been 92 incoming letters for Dame Durden to deal with; a fortnight later there were 290 for the week. 'It's getting alarming,' she wrote and settled in next day for hours of solid work, relieved only by needing to help the family search for Daphne the cow, which had gone off to have a calf.

Professionally April 1894 was a busy and significant month. On the ninth Steele tried to buy from Ethel the complete rights to *Seven Little Australians*, offering 50 pounds in cash in return for her surrender of royalties. She quickly decided to refuse, believing the story would earn more than that sum and enjoying the prospect of a continuing income no matter how trifling. Her judgement was vindicated by the immediate and lasting popularity of the book and offers an illuminating contrast with Louie Mack's decision a little later to accept a lump sum of 10 pounds from Mr Robertson in lieu of royalties when Angus & Robertson ventured into novel publishing with her highly successful *Teens*.[2]

On 11 April Ethel completed the sequel to *Seven Little Australians* called for by the contract with Ward, Lock & Bowden and reflected with satisfaction that it had been done in the two months since the Tasmanian holiday. She had intended calling it *Growing Up* but was obliged to look for another title, settling on *Family at Misrule*, referring to the home on the Parramatta River of the Woolcot family. The burst of intense concentration, during which she had also been writing 'The Story of a Baby', exacted an anxious price in the form of strained eyes. No more reading for a few days, she told herself, realising she had depended too long on the flickering light of a candle and resolving to use a kerosene reading lamp in future, for it would be years before gas or electricity became available on the upper North Shore.

In June the English connection improved wonderfully with an inquiry from Ward, Lock & Bowden about the fee Ethel would require for the serial rights to *Seven Little Australians*. On advice from Messrs Jeffery, Archibald and Roydhouse she asked for half of what the publisher received. On 2 June an acceptance came from Cassell's for her story, 'The Great Third Wave', her first with an English magazine. Four days later, there was a flush of girlish enthusiasm:

A lovely letter from Ward Lock & a perfectly delightful notice. I must get a scrap book & some stickfast. It speaks of me with Miss Alcott & Mrs Hodgson Burnett & says 'Judy' is likely to become as famous a character in fiction as Topsy of Uncle Tom's Cabin. Mr Steele says Mr Bowden was 'quite enthusiastic about the new book' & thinks it will be a big success. And they want my photograph & a sketch of my 'literary career' for the Queen or some other big English paper. And they want to see all my other writings at once. Oh I am so happy. All life seems rose coloured, fame seems coming to me & money too. I will make such good use of the money.

This did not prevent Ethel from soliciting interest from other publishers, even before her first book appeared. She sent 'The Story of a Baby' to Fisher & Unwin and Heinemann, prompting an immediate response from Steele, who wrote to reprove her for sampling other firms and asking her to send the manuscript to him at once. His letter of 11 June made a point that was to be urged many times in the next twenty years:

I am sorry you have offered the tale past us, as I frankly tell you, that while we are doing all we can to make you known and your first book a success, we should naturally not like another house to have the benefit of our introductory exertions for the publication of a further work from your pen, unless we failed to come to terms with you on such a book.[3]

Steele was a zealous and effective promoter, whose contribution to her success was not fully appreciated by Ethel until she tried other firms. The first potent demonstration of this was given when Ethel's book, *The Wonder-Child*, was published by the Religious Tract Society, with disappointing results. Ironically, the head of that firm was now James Bowden, former managing director of Ward Lock, who knew well what a treasure his old firm possessed in having Steele as the Australasian manager. Writing to Ethel in October 1902 to explain *The Wonder-Child*'s poor performance, he said:

I know that Mr Steele has worked your books splendidly in the Colonies, and has been many years working up a sale for them, so that we cannot hope to do as well with a *single* volume of yours.[4]

Steele's wife had also taken part, being on the spot in London when illustrations were commissioned for *Seven Little Australians*. Writing to Ethel on 15 June 1894 he had quoted Mrs Steele's description of the laughable misconceptions of the English artist, who made all his men look like bushrangers, from the style of their dress. In correcting such a potentially damaging error the Steeles contributed significantly to the books' immediate success in Australia. And the point was not lost on Ethel, who tried consistently to have a say in decisions about the presentation and illustration of her work, showing a thorough professionalism that was perhaps her outstanding quality as a writer.[5]

Yet another opportunity arose when Ethel had an interview with Mr Armand Jerome, a French American who had started an illustrated magazine, *Cosmos*, and asked her to write a story for him and take the post of women's editor. Though somewhat repelled by the unctuous flattery of the man she accepted the offer and kept at it until February 1895, recording a modest ten shillings a week from this source in her 'Pen Money Book'. She had four pages of chatty material in the second issue of 20 October 1894. It begins with two pages on literary subjects, especially women writers, composed in a fresh, lightly humorous style and moves on to look at political subjects, fashion and food. Louie Mack had a poem in the same issue.

A new and important project began in July 1895. Ethel started work on her third novel for the year, *The Little Larrikin*, which she decided would be 'very much drawn from life' with Billy Curlewis as the model for the larrikin, Herbert as Roger and 'other people real too'. Many of those people are in the sub-plot, which tells the love story of Roger Carruthers, a young barrister who is struggling to bring up three orphaned brothers, and Linley Middleton, an artistic young woman who lives in Boyd's Road, a more affluent part of the same suburb.

That sub-plot reflects much of what was currently happening to Herbert and Ethel themselves. Both men are caught in 'genteel poverty' and weighed down with family responsibilities, living for the day when they can afford to marry. Roger is just as dependent emotionally on Linley as Herbert is on Ethel. Consider the ecstasy he shows on seeing her unexpectedly in his own shabby living room:

'Linley!' he said. There were almost tears in his eyes ... He gave a long breath and caught her in his arms in passionate, unspeakable thankfulness.

The colour came into her cheeks a little, she felt she could never get used to that part of an engagement.[6]

Linley, like Ethel, resists her lover's pressure for a formal engagement, telling Roger, 'I should hate to be publicly branded like a reserved railway-carriage'. Roger feels that whereas his work means little more to him than providing the wherewithal for marriage, Linley's painting absorbs her to the exclusion of other interests, 'on my life, my darling, I can't help it. I am jealous of your work'. By the time *Larrikin* was published this conversation cut very close to the bone, for Ethel and Herbert had been married at last and there really was some tension between them in reconciling Ethel's literary and romantic interests.

Lol Carruthers, the little larrikin, was of course the central character, and a highly original creation. A six-year-old imp with an angelic face, he had lost his mother two years before and his father a year earlier. The family doctor persuaded Roger that Lol should defer attendance at school until freedom and exercise had corrected a constitutional delicacy. So Lol became the head of a 'push' of small boys who were the 'frequent terror and permanent mortification of the whole neighbourhood'. His exploits were so outrageous as to cause A. G. Stephens, the literary critic of the *Bulletin*, to reprove Ethel for a lack of realism but she assured him that Lol was based solidly on her own half-brother, Rex Cope.

Larrikin is the first of Ethel's books to ventilate her ideas on the great issues of the day, including questions of social justice, privilege and poverty. In the chapter 'Washing up in Balcombe Street', the boys are revealed in earnest conversation about the pinching and scraping to which they are reduced by poverty. Clem, a 'great, growing lad' had launched into an attack on the social system, saying:

'There oughtn't to be such a thing as charity ... it is the wretchedest thing in the world ... There oughtn't to be a Boyd's Road and a Canning Street; it all ought to be Balcombe Street' ... 'All the world ought to be respectably comfortable'.

He waxed fiercer and fiercer.

'Why should half the race work like horses and die like unsatisfied dogs, so that the other half can have carriages and *culchaw*?' he said. 'I don't ask for luxuries, but every one ought to have *enough*'.[7]

Kerry White has written of Ethel's 'dual plot' formula which allowed her to write about issues that were normally outside of children's fiction but kept her novels within that classification, so that in the one book there were two strands, one aimed at children, the other at mature readers. The compromise enabled her to satisfy a need to participate in the major league of adult fiction, virtually by the back door.[8]

The Little Larrikin contributed much to Ethel's literary impact, reinforcing a growing perception of the nature of the larrikin in urban Australia. She saw them as 'comic figures, rather as C. J. Dennis was later to present them, rough, aimlessly destructive, but scarcely evil'. In dedicating her new story she suggested that the word 'larrikin' had originated with an Irish police constable who in charging some youths had inadvertently coined a new word which meant '"one who just larks about," heedless of whether his larking disturbs his graver-minded fellow citizens or not. He is the foe of all policemen, Chinamen, and dumb animals, and hates the shadow of the Education Department'.[9]

With *The Little Larrikin* Ethel introduced a strongly regional note to her stories, which were set increasingly in the sparkling harbourside suburbs of the lower North Shore stretching from Neutral Bay to Mosman and Manly. She knew them first as the locale for boating picnics and moonlit walks, then as the home of her friend Louie Mack and finally as the place where she lived with Herbert Curlewis and raised their children, Adrian and Jean. Much of her authenticity and popularity came from this basic identification, giving her work a 'local habitation and a name'.

By July 1894 the Copes were busy clearing part of the two hectares of bush land they had bought at Gordon. Care was taken in the selection of the native trees that were to be retained, before clearing began. The house they built was named 'Bukyangi', a solid, early Federation bungalow named after one of Joseph Cope's properties on the Macquarie River. Largely single storeyed, it had big attic rooms in the centre and broad verandahs facing an extensive buffalo lawn and stood in Powell Street, Killara.

Continuing problems with hearing took Ethel back in July to Dr Brady, an ear specialist who 'thought it would do the other ear good to be cauterized again so he did my throat about 7 times again – without cocaine. Horribly painful. We got to be very friendly however, I like him very much'.

Soon the University Dramatic Society was rehearsing Ethel's legal farce, 'The Wig', which was the occasion of a quarrel with Herbert. He wanted to attend the full dress rehearsal but she insisted on keeping him away, fearing his presence would inhibit her. It was staged on 24 July at the Royal Standard Theatre with Herbert and his brother Claude joining the Copes and Flo Pockley. At the final curtain there were shouts for the author and when Ethel appeared she received three bouquets; later the cast and friends had coffee and cakes and enjoyed a spot of dancing.

Returning to 'Hermsley' to sleep they found Louie there with Creed, surprisingly absent from the performance even though she was joint author of a little comedy that concluded the evening. Next morning the *Herald*'s critic did not share the enthusiasm of the friendly audience, pointing out that the author 'had not tried to be funny and succeeded very well' and slating two young barristers for appalling lapses in speech. He went on, 'A sketch of this sort depends ... wholly upon the wit and drollery of the dialogue – qualities in the present instance conspicuous by their absence'.[10] Ethel was realistic enough to trust the opinions of professional critics before those of friends, 'I have a slightly mangled feeling,' she wrote, adding philosophically, 'I can't expect success in each thing though probably this will be good for me & serve as a tonic or conceit extractor'.

Compensating for this disappointment was a visit from Mr Steele who came to dine at 'Inglewood' and talk 'shop'. He got on well with the family, assuring them that a great deal of money would be made by Ethel's work. The realization of this prediction seemed to be on the way the next month when she received a cheque for 50 pounds, half as an advance on royalties for *Seven Little Australians* and half for the sequel.

During these months Herbert dreamed of several schemes which had as a common element the aim of enabling them to marry immediately. In March he had spoken of applying for a classical lectureship, worth 400 pounds a year, that was being offered at Melbourne University but Ethel thought that a dreadful idea. Late in August there was a 'wild plan' to seek his fortune at the Bar in South Africa, where he had close relatives who could offer a 'brilliant opening'. As he put it to Ethel the possibility of winning her so soon made him 'feel faint with a mad delight'. There had been a quarrel between them a week earlier over the question of a formal and public engagement but they were reconciled so deliciously it 'made us both glad we had quarrelled'.

The first day of spring brought the news that Lilian had won first prize in Cassell's competition for her novel *Lights o' Sydney*. 'The first,' Ethel exulted. 'It is splendid ... it is the first bit of real success.' So the girls went into town a few days later to do some celebratory shopping and lunched at the Fresh Food and Ice Restaurant with their former neighbour from L'Avenue, Ada Weiss. Transport problems ensured that Ethel and her friends rarely dined out at night except at friends' houses; lunches were the occasions for visiting restaurants and cafés.

Ethel and Lilian depended much at this time on the hack work, as they saw it, which they did for magazines. In September they saw Walter Jeffery who offered the weekly social pages to Lil for 1 pound and the fashion page to Ethel in addition to her children's page for a total of 1 pound 10 shillings. 'We feel it is *infra dig* to do such work but we want money badly for the tennis court & furnishing so are going to take it & tell no one.' As befitted a fashion editor Ethel had a care to her own wardrobe; she soon mentioned a dress made for her by a Miss Williams, a brown check skirt and zouave jacket to wear with blouses – 'immense gigot sleeves fit to fly with'.

Then came the 'happiest minute' of Ethel's life. The arrival of the post on 21 September brought an advance copy of *Seven Little Australians*:

It is in an art green cover with Judy running across it, a quaint little gilt figure in top corner, & Bunty taking bread & butter at back. Lovely altogether, beautiful type & thick paper. Made lunch of it & read all the way down in train, the illustrations are excellent.

The book began selling at Angus & Roberston's on 10 October: a portrait of Ethel was published a week later in the *Bulletin* together with a 'perfectly lovely' notice. The reviewer thought it to be a 'clever and charming narrative'.

Miss Turner appears to have chosen, in the humour and pathos of child life, a subject with which she is in thorough mental sympathy ... In scope and treatment the book is a little above children, a little below most grown-ups, and it will hardly be acceptable to boys at any age; but to girls between the lights, fluttering a new and timorous soul at the meeting of the brook and the river, and a brief and tremulous gown at the meeting of the calf and ankle, 'Seven Little Australians' should prove at once an oracle and an ecstasy.[11]

The critical reception of *Seven Little Australians* began famously with the review in the *Herald* on 6 October and so continued in other papers. A letter from William Steele enclosed splendid reviews from Victoria and South Australia while from Angus & Robertson's came the news that the book was selling strongly; by November a rumour was being circulated that it had been sold out in Sydney. In the *Daily*

Telegraph John Farrel gave the story 'almost unreserved praise' and assured its author of success on account of her literary grace and originality as a 'teller of delightful tales' about 'real children'. Somewhat remarkably this piece coincided with a favourable review of Herbert's joint monograph comparing English and New South Wales law. The timing was welcome for Herbert had been showing resentment for what he saw as Ethel's preoccupation with her writing.[12]

In *Review of Reviews*, 20 November 1894, the work was seen as being 'of the same literary class as "Little Lord Fauntleroy," "Little Women", &c., and with much of the dainty literary grace of the first, and something also of the humour and pure moral tone of the latter'.

Jealousy had an evident bearing on the tensions surfacing among the three sisters at this time, stimulated probably by Ethel's fame as a writer and her engagement. She had angered Rose by reporting to Mrs Cope her younger sister's misbehaviour at a picnic when she had gone off alone with Harold Pockley for several hours. In doing this, Ethel revealed an undue readiness to intervene in her sibling's affairs, forgetting her own little subterfuges with Herbert and ignoring the fact that Rose was really 21. Rose responded by asserting that she too was secretly engaged and swore to have vengeance. On 17 November Ethel's diary showed that the tensions had generated an explosion:

Lily, Rose & I had a great quarrel. I am utterly *tired* of Lily's exasperating interference & remarks about H & I. Today I got at the end of my patience & in such a temper I let the nail brush fly at her like a washerwoman might have. Of course it went yards over her head, she picked up my favourite blue vase & smashed it. Recriminations on both sides followed, Rose siding with Lily. An edifying spectacle Mother & Mr Cope interfered, Rose made mischief & had a separate quarrel with Mother & we all three declared we were going from home. Altogether a lovely day.

For some months the whole family had been following the progress of the builders in erecting their new home at Gordon. By November it was sufficiently advanced for Ethel to be able to settle where she wanted the cupboards and shelves built in her room, the first she had to herself, in an attic looking out on a buffalo lawn that Herbert had helped plant. The move was effected on 19 December amidst scenes of 'wild confusion', for after weeks of dry weather the rain pelted down and wet much of the bedding, making this the most tedious and anxious removal of the many they had experienced in fourteen years. At the end of it Ethel went to sleep on the floor, bone tired and feeling really ill; when she woke Herbert was there with the welcome offer to help Mr Cope get the fences ready for the cattle before going off to help his friend Moors sail the *Eula* to Port Hacking.

Christmas Day found the family more settled and peaceful, exchanging presents and feeling a quiet pride in the achievements of the elder girls, for Ethel had major stories in the Christmas numbers of the *Bulletin* and the *Town and Country Journal*, while Lilian also had a story, 'Young Lochinvar', in the latter magazine. At the end of December Ethel recorded having finished *Miss Bobbie*, which was to be published in 1896 and estimated her total income for the year from writing at 159 pounds, 60 per cent up on 1893.

An early price paid by Ethel for her meteoric success was to attract letters from women seeking help in their intended literary careers. Some sought criticism, others needed help in finding a publisher and some made the most bizarre requests. We can imagine her chuckling as she described a 'wildly dear' letter from a girl 'in the backblocks of Queensland' who had struggled unavailingly to get her writing accepted:

So she calmly asks me if I would have one of her books published under my name to give her a start! I am sorry for her & will write her a nice letter about publishers & other advice, but that proposal is a little too beautiful.

Partly in response to Louie Mack's urgings Ethel took her mother in March for a holiday to the Blue Mountains, where they stayed for three weeks at the Ivanhoe Hotel at Blackheath. On arrival she pronounced it 'the nicest hotel I have ever stayed at' and after a rapturous walk to Govett's Leap with Louie they took their appetites back to the hotel. A letter from Herbert was waiting together with a bottle of chloride of lime which he had sent up to help deal with the snakes which he was sure were 'all over Blackheath'. There had been a snake scare at 'Bukyangi' a week or so earlier; it had the useful effect of suggesting an idea for a story aimed at the *Bulletin* entitled 'As it fell out', which had the express object of helping pay for the holiday. It was completed before nightfall the same day and judged 'rather good ... for a potboiler'.

In the midst of athletic and culinary adventures in the mountains Ethel received 'the loveliest of lovely letters' from Coulson Kernahan, literary advisor to Ward, Lock & Bowden. He grudged William Steele the honour of having discovered her and wrote of the 'hot tears' brought to his eyes by the death of Judy. He'd spoken of it to Conan Doyle and Zangwill and planned to give it to Swinburne and Frances Hodgson Burnett, the creator of Little Lord Fauntleroy. Her head a little turned by this praise Ethel wrote 'I must do something better', implying, almost certainly, something for adult readers.

A week later, after a drive to Sublime Point and Katoomba Falls which became tiresome when one of the horses pulling their waggon became lame, Ethel relaxed in a hot bath and read letters from overseas. From the Sheffield *Weekly Telegraph* came a request for permission to reprint her *Bulletin* story, 'The Little Duchess', and asking her to send other stories for their consideration. On the other hand there was a rejection by Warne & Company of *The Story of a Baby* which prompted the candid self-appraisal, 'It must certainly be a poor story, – I am half sorry I accepted Ward & Lock's offer, I think I should have published it in the fireplace.' To this opinion one can only assent for the story illustrates all too well her difficulty in creating authentic adult characters and developing them at novel length. Steele had written to her in November 1894 renewing his firm's readiness to publish the manuscript but making the point that it was far below her first book in quality and seriously deficient in length, the latter being a recurring problem for Ethel.[13]

After weeks among the gum trees the city beckoned and on 9 April Ethel went to see Walter Jeffery at the *Town and Country Journal*. He had greatly enjoyed her long letter with its skits about the fellow guests at the Ivanhoe Hotel and had some ideas for her to work on. One of the artists had drawn some 'startling illustrations' of a future century and he wanted her to write a story to fit them for the Christmas number. The outcome was her imaginative essay in science fiction 'A Story of Strange Sights', which gives some glimpses of her thoughts about modernization, the natural environment and the emancipation of women. As to the last, there is a conversation between two newspapermen who have files of sketches recording the shape of the future in which the chief expresses hostility to the 'new woman' and his idealization of the 'happiness and perfection of its private home life' as the foundation of a nation's strength:

when I see women trying to be men; when I hear of the 'shrieking sisterhood', and 'revolting daughters', the greatest temptation of my life ... is to ... take out two sketches of her, a twentieth century one in all its hatefulness, this one in all its utter lovableness, and publish them prematurely'.[14]

Shortly after coming back from the mountains Ethel had promised to marry Herbert 'before very long even if we have nothing'. On 9 May she went with her mother to hear Dr Emily Ryder lecture on marriage, remarking later:

I have always had a shrinking from physiology but really every girl ought to know certain things. Ignorance is not innocence, I should be a great deal stronger woman today if I had known the importance of taking care of myself before instead of being reckless as I have been.

At the end of May there was, at last, a commitment to be married in the following March and a desultory start was made at house hunting. Ethel was in the last stages of writing the much altered *Little Larrikin* at this time but felt far more like 'making pretty trousseau things & little mats for the little dream house'.

This was a time for Ethel to redefine her relationship with William Steele. Within a week she had received two letters that made conflicting impressions on her mind. The first was from George Meredith – 'there is no one in the whole world I would rather have had a letter from' – acknowledging his pleasure in reading the book, which had:

introduced him to an ideal nursery of real children, whose humours, characteristics & chatter are as redolent of their stage of life as breath of the nodding meadow flowers. This claims my gratitude & I render it warmly; with the certainty that you will not fail when you try it upon larger themes, as you will; for evidently you have the literary gift.[15]

Steele on the other hand had written to censure Ethel for offering her new manuscript, *Miss Bobbie*, to Cassell's, after sending it initially to his firm. Ward Lock, though 'very disappointed' with the story, had made an offer which Ethel frankly sought to improve upon. She had become convinced that authors generally got a raw deal from publishers and had sent Steele a copy of *The Methods of Publishing* (which he described as 'unfair, prejudiced, and altogether mis-leading') to prove her point. He returned to the oft-repeated claim that his firm's expenses in launching her outweighed receipts so far and that it would be unfair for a competitor to 'get the value of all our preliminary work'.[16]

A fortnight earlier Steele had passed on the substance of James Bowden's letter, expressing surprise that *Seven Little Australians* 'had not taken better with the English Public', only 800 having been bought there by 18 Janaury compared with two Australian editions totalling over 6 000. The firm had advertised widely in England (and America), even 'sending out copies with suitable letters to the children of note, thus bringing the book into Royal and influential circles', including Prince Alexander of Battenberg and the Duchess of Albany.[17]

Ethel reacted hotly to Steele's rebuke:

Night wrote a long letter to Steele & a sharp one. I told him I really must rebel at being so perpetually reminded of all he had done for me etc. That I consider things are equal, my business is to write as good a book as I can, his, to engineer it as well as he can. Sent him Kernahan's letter to read & a copy of Meredith's.

Soon there came a peace offering from Steele in the shape of a *de luxe* edition of Meredith's *Tale of Chloe and other Stories*. By the end of July the friendship had been sufficiently restored for Steele to offer Ethel and Lilian a dinner at the Hotel Australia followed by an orchestral concert, saying 'I think we are entitled to celebrate the success of "The Seven".' Soon after he wrote from his Sydney hotel saying, '"The Larrikin" is in my possession. I shall be like a child with a new toy for the next few days.'[18]

Since moving to 'Bukyangi' at Gordon Ethel had seen rather more of the inside of St John's and had engaged the Reverend King in a theological debate which spilled over from verbal discussion to correspondence. The subject gets only brief mention in the diaries including one rather startled comment on 11 February, 'Morning went to church, the sermon was straight at me & all about our discussion'. From this point there is a falling off in her church attendance and one Sunday in May, during a weekend when Herbert was a guest, she wrote crisply, 'Played tennis in morning, we are going to play on Sundays despite the horror of the Pockleys & Kings. It keeps Rex out of worse mischief & does no one any harm in this quiet place.'

With success coming so amply to Ethel it was as well that Herbert's career was buoyant. He came up to 'Bukyangi' on 15 June to stay for the weekend 'quite knocked up, from his exertions on the previous day as defence counsel in a 'stiff brief' against Mr Rolin. Against the advice of Judge Windeyer to settle he carried on and got the verdict after a 'splendid defence'. On the Sunday they had a fire in the study and spent much of the day talking about ways and means and budgets. 'We shall be very poor,' Ethel wrote. 'But we shall be together & that is everything in the world.' The expectation of poverty comes as a surprise when we read in her 'Pen Money Book' that her income from writing was 159 pounds in 1894 and 377 pounds in 1895, a year that finished on an optimistic note with a cheque from Steele for 210 pounds, being advance royalties on *Seven Little Australians* (30 pounds), *The Family at Misrule* (30 pounds), *The Story of a Baby* (15 pounds), *The Little Duchess* (25 pounds), *Bobbie* (50 pounds) and *The Little Larrikin* (60 pounds). Putting the matter another way we can estimate that her actual and anticipated sales of books by the end of 1895 amounted to about 43 000, assuming an average royalty of three pence a copy.

These figures, perhaps, assisted Charles Cope's decision,

noted in Ethel's diary on 26 August, to accept his stepdaughter's impending marriage, even to the point of agreeing to give her away. One person who was not so pleased was William Steele. He wrote on 25 September entreating her to postpone her wedding so as to go to England to be 'put in touch with English readers and English taste', arguing that, 'If you are to make money as a writer to any extent, it must be by having many readers among the English millions.' And, he continued:

a little English experience would help to (excuse me so putting it) correct the free and easy, somewhat rowdy associations, due to atmosphere, climate, environment and the influence of The Bulletin ... To ensure your complete success, the English people must be reckoned with, and that is why I advocate your staying for a time in their midst.[19]

What this advice neglected to consider was that Ethel's appeal came from her distinctively Australian flavour and that a compromise aimed at English taste might have destroyed her essential local market. Perhaps Ethel realized this intuitively; in any case her response was clear and direct. She knew that such a delay would have destroyed Herbert and she was now very ready for marriage. Early in August she had been taken to task by 'Sappho Smith', who wrote a splendidly satirical women's column for the *Bulletin* and urged her to abandon any thought of marriage. 'Why don't you stick to literature, you can't do both,' she was told. 'I said I fancied I could.' And she did, with remarkable success in both.

The lovers had the unusual experience that winter of spending nine weeks sleeping under the same roof at 'Hermsley' and no doubt learning a good deal of each other. Their reason for doing so was the Copes' need to conserve their tank water at 'Bukyangi' during one of Sydney's worst droughts; all three girls were packed off to stay with friends until it broke. Then, in a wonderful conjunction of Christian prayer and divine action, the colony observed a Day of Prayer and Humiliation on Sunday 15 September and next day, as Ethel gratefully recorded, 'It rained, actually rained.'

Contributing to the optimism with which Ethel finished her last year as a spinster was the surprisingly warm reception given to *The Story of a Baby* in October and November in all the major newspapers and notably by A.G. Stephens of the *Bulletin*. Just as reassuring were congratulatory letters she received from Frances Hodgson Burnett and Marcus Clarke. The former had been given a copy of *Seven Little Australians* by Coulson Kernahan; she wrote saying:

It is a dear story and it is beautiful that at twenty you can write a thing so full of real sweetness and pathos ... Believe in yourself. Have great courage & be very happy.[20]

Ethel began 1896 by taking communion for the first time in two years and having word from Steele that the Christmas sales of her books had been very strong. Even more thrilling was the news that both *Seven Little Australians* and *The Family at Misrule* had been translated into Dutch. In the absence of a copyright agreement between England and Holland there would be no immediate hope of royalties but even so there was enormous satisfaction at this development, which was eventually to see Ethel's books published in a score of languages.

An early taste of the public adulation that was to follow Ethel throughout her life came at the prize-giving ceremony at Sydney Girls' High held in the old school in Elizabeth Street on 7 February 1896. Mrs Garvin introduced her to the Minister for Education as 'her very distinguished old pupil' and when they went on the stage the girls clapped for five minutes, Ethel little dreaming it was for her. The point was made that Ethel's books were frequently chosen as prizes, which reinforced Steele's argument that she must avoid coarse or slangy expressions which might give offence, especially in the lucrative Sunday School prize market. As he had put it to her earlier, 'Let some of the Ministers and Teachers only get an idea that there are objectionable phrases in your books and this important outlet may be closed to us.'[21]

This was a problem for which Ethel had no easy solution. As she had announced in the opening page of her first book, the little Australians for whom she wrote were neither model children nor paragons of virtue. 'There is a lurking sparkle of joyousness and rebellion and mischief in nature here, and therefore in children.' Concerned to achieve realism in character and incident, she ran the risk of employing language or depicting situations that prompted editorial intervention or else hostility from parents and other guardians of juvenile morals.

Steele wrote a further letter to Ethel on the subject in August 1901, pleased at having been assured that it was her intention 'to avoid using words and expressions which might cause offence to some'. Confirming the need for such caution he enclosed a letter he had received from a friend who said that:

on looking through a book by Miss Ethel Turner which had been given to a child of his he was shocked to find such language in it as led him to tear it up leaf by leaf and burn it and forbid any books by the same author to enter the house again.

Steele, like his friend, thought it a pity if Ethel, after 'having made a name for writing pure stories of Australian childhood' should 'spoil herself by an unnecessary realism'.[22]

Louise Mack and Jack Creed were married in January 1896 at the Mack's family home at Neutral Bay. Describing the occasion, Ethel remarked in her diary on the contrast between the bridegroom's nervousness and the coolness of the bride. Louie wore a 'very simple white dress trimmed with chiffon & a white flower in her hair. She wasn't a bit nervous, very bright & talkative & laughing'. The couple drove off in a cab to their pretty cottage at Chatswood, Jack taking a few days off work at the Law Institute and on 20 January Louie had Ethel come over for a chat, assuring her that Jack was the 'nicest man in the world to be married to'. Ethel reflected that 'Perhaps being married isn't after all quite so-to-be-trembled-at a thing as I have been thinking.' She went off to look at a Queen Anne cottage that she fell wildly in love with but by the time she was ready to make an offer 'some wretched barbarian' had snapped it up.

Ethel and Herbert soon became convinced that they wanted to live at Mosman, especially after enjoying a simple tea and sitting watching the moon over Middle Harbour and the ocean from the heights of Balmoral. The ferry gave easy access to Circular Quay and to Herbert's chambers so on 31 March they took a year's lease on 'Yanalla', a cottage in Harbour Street. It was in the Queen Anne style on the heights of Mosman looking towards Balmoral Beach. Soon after, they settled on the place for their honeymoon retreat, 'The Chalet', a romantic house near Little Sirius Cove.

In the run up to the ceremony at St John's there were 'evenings' given by various family friends in Ethel's honour. One of Ethel's tasks was to prepare her children's pages to cover a five weeks' absence. With that done she surrendered to exhaustion for the final week and let life flow over and around her, lying on a nest of cushions under a tree two days before the ceremony and chatting to Lilian.

While a ship's awning was erected over the tennis court at 'Bukyangi' in readiness for the wedding breakfast, the study was being filled with presents, silver from the family and the

Pockleys and from Steele a handsome inscribed copy of Mrs Beeton's *Household Management*.

The events of 22 April were written up by Ethel in her diary a fortnight later:

My wedding day

I stayed in bed till 10, for last night I did not shut my eyes till 5 o'clock. Ella Pockley & Flo Barry came to help. It rained just a little now & again, not enough to wet anyone. All the morning the erection of arches & flags & the setting of tables went on. At 1/2 p 12 I went to dress, Rosie did my hair, Mother fastened my veil & put on my wreath. Had a fit of exceeding trembling at 1/2 p 1 but was calm at 2. The carriage came, Lil Rose Dolly Marion & I someway squeezed into it. Had no time for nervousness Rosie was so busy giving us our lines & we were all so anxious to keep ourselves uncrushed. The church crowded to overflowing, – beautifully decorated (at least the papers said so after, I did not see). Up the aisle on Mr Cope's arm, caught a vision of W. Curnow, H. Wolstenholme & Dr Barry, & said to myself mechanically their faces looked familiar. Then a glimpse of poor little Mother with tear wet eyes in the front pew. Then Herbert looking anxiously at me (I was so pale, he said). The beautiful service ... The plighting of troths, – we both spoke up bravely. Lily taking off my glove. Herbert taking my hand, putting on the strange little ring. Mr King's voice again, – then a burst of organ & Herbert lifting my veil for the first kiss. – And Mr Cope brushing roughly up, pushing him aside & taking the first before anyone could recover from the surprise. – it was cruel, wicked. Then Herbert, then Mother.

On then to 'The Chalet' to find the old housekeeper had everything ready and that Mrs Curlewis had put white flowers in all the rooms. 'And the loveliest moon in the evening. And the morning & the evening were the first day'.

chapter

Eight

The diary entries made by Ethel soon after the honeymoon at 'The Chalet' overlooking Little Sirius Cove suggest a time of unalloyed delight. The retrospective note written on 3 May 1896 on the eve of moving into temporary quarters at Rothesay, while she and Herbert waited for their house 'Yanalla' to be completed and made ready for their occupation on 13 May, gives some flashes of illumination as to the beginning of their life together. During those 'beautiful halcyon days',

We had perfect weather all the time, sunshiny cool days, & moonlight nights lovelier than ever moonlight nights were yet. Rowed on the harbour in the moonlight. Lazed all day on the balcony on a heap of cushions. I don't know how newly married people *can* go to crowded hotels. Here it is perfect, we have seen no one but Mrs Brookes all the time & yet have any amount of space & ground to wander about in, just ourselves for the dear little meals. No appearances to keep up, I wear my tea gown & pretty dressing gown half the time. Sometimes we go down to the beach. Once I paddled & H amused himself by trying his revolver that has lost its terrors for me, I have even fired it once myself.

With the end of the honeymoon Ethel began to have visits

from family and close friends. Mrs Cope was the first to call on the new bride, who felt that 'it seems months since I gave her the last kiss from the carriage'. Lilian was next on 6 May and Ethel went to the top of the steps to meet her, 'being too shy yet to venture as near to the public gaze as the wharf'. After an early lunch Lil departed and was succeeded by Rose and Rex, but 'the dear old lad', as Ethel put it, refused to accept the order of his going and challenged his half-sister to a game of chess, which he won with scholar's mate in four moves, Ethel reflecting 'where were my thoughts?' Just before Herbert was due back from his chambers Mrs Moors and her daughter came with a huge basket of roses and chrysanthemums, leaving Ethel to greet her husband and convey the tender suggestion that the evening was 'astretch before us'. A few days later came Louie Mack, with whom Ethel 'chattered like magpies all day' and took to see 'Yanalla' in the final throes of its preparation.

Ethel made her first public appearance as a married woman by taking an electric tram to the North Shore to buy furniture for Mrs Brookes, who continued to work for her as a general servant. 'Kept my veil down & was terribly nervous at the thought of meeting anyone,' she wrote. Herbert's parents came that night for dinner and next day Ethel cooked her first meal, a veal ragout, only to have Herbert decline to touch it because 'a carrot lurked within'. One can only wonder at the composure with which the diary entry was made. It seems likely that with the termination of their secret engagement and the beginning of Herbert's more secure and complete role as husband the balance of influence had moved significantly in his favour.

Rain came in torrents to complicate the Curlewises' move to 'Yanalla' in Harbour Street, Mosman. Next day Mrs Cope came to help unpack and Ethel rejoiced in her domestic tasks, which she felt 'quite puts literary things in the shade for a time'. And it was a 'dear little cottage, – plenty of sweetness & light & not particularly small; 5 fairly good rooms & a good kitchen'. Leaving her mother and Mrs Brookes to continue unpacking she went into town by Herbert's ferry to shop for carpets and ironmongery, returning also by the same boat, conscious of the notice being taken of them, Herbert in his tall hat and herself in a grey coming-away dress, looking 'very bride & bridegroomery'. Mosman Bay was a small community much aware of its new people, and for a long time Herbert and Ethel were generally referred to as 'the couple'.

At the end of their first week of housekeeping Herbert had his introduction to carpentry '& liked it exceedingly'. He made a servant's dressing table which Ethel decorated with a gay petticoat and planned to make shelves and cupboards for the whole house. That night they lit a luxurious fire in the bedroom and piled cushions onto a rug on which they relaxed while fortifying themselves with mulled wine.

Quite rapidly, it seems, Ethel had got over the feelings that had made her feel so repelled during the courtship by any approach to sexual familiarity.

The easy playfulness to which their relationship had developed after a year of marriage was shown on a wet Sunday towards the end of April 1897:

It rained too heavily for us to go to Gordon so we played games & sang songs & amused ourselves & were as ridiculous as two children. I think Alice must occasionally think we are bereft of our senses; she comes in to set the table & finds me being carried around the room or chased round or her master climbing in the window because I have locked him out of the room. And we've been married a year & should be growing sedate.

Another development that gave special value to the first months at Mosman was the quiet revolution that began in Ethel's relationship with Charles Cope. Sarah and Rex had come for a visit, 'then later – Mr Cope! Who was never going to darken my doors if I married!' Gradually her stepfather felt able to pop in and see Ethel in a casual way; she began to describe him in her diary as 'Charlie'. Presumably the formal 'Mr Cope' continued to be employed in speech for as late as February 1897 on his second unscheduled visit for dinner she made the point, 'I am not entirely forgiven yet'. Rex meanwhile began to perform for his brother-in-law the kinds of helpful offices that Herbert had conferred on Charles Cope for many years at 'Inglewood' and 'Bukyangi', assisting in a range of handyman activities. Neighbours heard the two men hammering and banging away on Sundays at tasks that ranged from making wood mats for the bathroom to constructing trellises that were designed to enhance the Curlewises' privacy.

One of the first callers who braved the trip to Mosman was Ethel's headmistress:

We carpentered all afternoon, at least H. did & I painted a table, and when I was particularly black handed who should Mrs Brookes come and say was in the drawing room but Mrs Garvin! I scrubbed at my hands, donned a clean housewifely apron over my paint and received her, – my first ordinary visitor.

That such a visit occurred says a good deal about the character of the relationship and the standing accorded by Ethel's old school to its first celebrity.

Long before Ethel and Herbert had committed themselves to purchasing land in Mosman and building their own house they were responding to the special charms of the area. Ethel learned that she was a Mosmanite when she visited the friends on inner-city Crown Street. Five years earlier she had been blissfully happy as a young woman living in the inner city but now she felt ... 'I couldn't *live* in such a neighbourhood, – so dusty & noisy & dirty; everyone seemed dingy & careworn & miserable. It was lovely to get back to fresh, sweet little Mosman again'.

Central to the formation of this attachment was a growing sense of neighbourhood, nurtured by the opportunity of uncluttered living in the midst of unspoilt bush with panoramas of the sparkling waters of Mosman, Balmoral and Sirius Cove. Contact with Circular Quay and the city was made largely by ferry, which sharpened the feeling of isolation and helped to define the community. At the same time the Curlewises' feeling for their home was strengthened by a network of local friendships, notably with the Cullens, the Arthurs and the Meillons, which began in 1896 and lasted a lifetime.

Herbert it was who made first contact, when he attended a meeting called in May by Dr Cullen, a distinguished lawyer. 'The Junior Bar is getting thick over here' Ethel observed. The true point of intimacy was established, however, by Ethel's returning Mrs Cullen's formal call in October and being shown all over their extensive grounds at 'Tregoyd' in Raglan Street three weeks later. 'They are lovely,' she wrote, 'inasmuch as they have left them almost as they found them, there is a lovely gully & waterfall, – a big piece devoted to flannel flowers, hedges of some wild flower, & all the native trees.' At her initial visit Mrs Cullen has promised Ethel a kitten; that gift was succeeded by a stream of plants and cuttings that were used by Ethel in her early gardens at Mosman and after 1901 in the terraces at 'Avenel' that ran down towards the harbour from Warringah Road. The gardening side of the friendship was largely between Ethel and Dr Cullen and later came to include their homes in the Blue Mountains; what the women shared increasingly was their experience of motherhood, though Ethel once took up the invitation to work in the quietude of her friend's garden when she was struggling with *Three Little Maids*.

Not only was this a satisfying and intimate friendship; it

also offered an entree to Mosman and Sydney society. The day after Mrs Cullen's first call Ethel had a visit from Mrs Geddes of whom she wrote, 'I like her very much, there's something very bright & breezy about her. She & Mrs Cullen are the "chief" people on the Bay I hear. They have certainly beautiful houses, not just imposing but picturesque.' In time Dr Cullen became chief justice and lieutenant-governor, confirming a trend for the young Curlewises to be on cordial terms with the Government House 'set', though Herbert found the formal functions tedious and Ethel herself felt less keen when her youthful passion for dancing diminished.

Chess and bridge were the games that most engaged the Curlewises and their friends. It was Dr Richard Arthur and his wife who became Ethel and Herbert's most regular opponents at chess, playing sometimes when they dropped in on each other for a game and at other times when there were tables of both bridge and chess. In late February Ethel played three games against Dr Arthur, opening each time with King's Gambit and taking an early advantage only to lose in the end games. Three weeks later they again visited the Arthurs but Ethel 'didn't care for it for I was stuck down with a lot of middle-aged women to play whist: I'd far rather have played chess with the men'.

From her diary for 1896, preoccupied as it is with the wedding and its aftermath, we'd have little indication of Ethel's literary ambitions. Yet there came from the indefatigable William Steele a barrage of letters, including a further request that she moderate her demands and give more consideration to the outlay incurred by his firm in launching her career. Just a week before Ethel's wedding, Steele had written from his Sydney hotel setting a date for the signing of an agreement relating to *The Little Larrikin* and asking her to leave the royalty at twelve and a half per cent as it had been for her previous two books, rather than insist on the fifteen per cent that had already been contracted for. In support he quoted recent letters from London, including one from James Bowden regretting that 'Miss Turner continues to be so exacting'. As he saw it her ambitions had been inflamed by the bids of rival firms whose interest had largely been sparked by the 'booming' promotion engaged in by Ward, Lock & Bowden.[1]

One of Bowden's initiatives from the previous year had been to urge Ethel to submit several stories to the firm's new *Windsor Magazine*, which had been launched in January 1895. The title was far from coincidental, as was made clear by the Foreword, 'making its obeisance to its Sovereign and to the public alike, mingling devotion to the gracious lady on the throne and to her three direct heirs, whose portraits are here presented, with loyalty to some of the best and widest interests of her subjects'. Beginning with 'The Saucepan Sketch', a lively domestic comedy, Ethel regularly published stories and poems in the *Windsor*, receiving prices of eight and ten guineas for the former and three for the latter, about double the local price. But Steele felt nervous about 'A Champion in Anklestraps', because it gave prominent and favourable notice to the Sydney *Bulletin*, a journal whose 'references to our magazine have always been insulting ... and insulting to the associations of the Royal Family which are cherished in 'The Windsor'.[2]

Steele's reservations about the *Bulletin* came as no surprise; what is fascinating is that Ethel, for all her royalism, stuck to her guns, declining Steele's offer to have Kernahan remove the offending elements from one of her most charming and vivacious stories. Even more surprising, except in the light of 'The Champion's' brilliance, is that Ward Lock agreed to publish, and sent a cheque for 21 pounds in August 1896 to cover it and another story, 'The School at

Jimbaree'. The 'Champion' is a girl of 6 whose widowed father was a cabinet minister, commonly the butt of *Bulletin* cartoonists who gave little thought to the sensitivities of little girls when they wished to debunk the father's policies on Land Reform. With the help of the postman, Dolly journeys by ferry to the *Bulletin* office to confront the artist and succeeds in having him draw 'my farvie' as he really is, virtually a front page retraction. And when the bearded cartoonist next calls on the father at home, he finds Dolly playing upside down games on the stairs with her little brother, though not too busy to encircle his neck with her arms and bestow a kiss.[3]

In October, Steele told Ethel of his disappointment at the departure from the firm of James Bowden, who had decided to go out on his own with Coulson Kernahan as his literary advisor. George Lock, who seemed likely to fill the gap in the firm, had written to Steele about Ethel's work. He much preferred *The Little Larrikin*, which had just been published and was soon to be on sale in Australia, to *Family at Misrule*, and considered that her books had been handicapped in the English market by the existing style of doing illustrations with line drawings instead of full page plates. Both Steele and Ethel preferred the latter, and this became the usual format from that time. Ethel was already involved as much as possible in the process of designing and illustrating the books. She had been sent the woodcuts made by Johnson for *The Little Larrikin* and especially approved the artist's rendition of Lol (i.e. the young hero), who bore a remarkable resemblance to Billy Curlewis, on whom he was based.[4]

An earlier letter had told Ethel of the arrival in England of a Danish edition of *Seven Little Australians*. Steele's fertile mind came up with the idea of having a copy bound in padded morocco, embellished with the Danish and Australian coats of arms and presented to the Princess of Wales:

it may be just the thing to set agog the interest in you which is so much longed for. Besides, if it leads to an acknowledgement which could be published, the result must be beneficial.[5]

Writing now began to come more easily. On 20 July Ethel made good progress with her gold rush story, 'The Camp at Wandinong' and Herbert came home early from his chambers and helped sort out the competitions for the weekly children's page she edited for the *Town and Country Journal*. Next day she wrote for hours, 'free fast & furiously ... Quite 3,500 words today,' and she added, 'Writing comes easier than ever now just the words I want rush to the end of my pen & I can't go quickly enough.'

Ethel had her long story, 'The Camp at Wandinong' ready to show to a publisher by the time Mr Steele returned from his New Zealand trip and came to dinner at 'Yanalla' in August 1896 but she was not yet sure if it would be offered to Ward Lock. Steele was getting 'splendid orders' for *The Little Larrikin* and the other books were all doing well. And he passed on Mr Bowden's opinion of Louie Mack's new book, 'that it displays a certain amount of cheap cleverness but nothing more', and warning against the acceptance of manuscripts without reference to London.

The confident spurt of writing had dried up by mid-September when Ethel reproached herself for remaining in a 'very dilettante mood' and only skirmishing with her pen. She was inclined to blame it on frequent visitors but the restlessness was in her own mind and the lack as yet of a work pattern that might be respected by family and friends. As a newly-established young matron she took the trouble to make obligatory social calls and have her own afternoons 'at home'.

Ethel's visit in October to Thea Cowan's studio suggested to her that literary and artistic people differed significantly in their self-perceptions. Miss Cowan had shown Ethel all over her things and had 'talked about herself & pictures as artists will. I believe literary people have too much sense of humour to do it, – at least they only talk "shop" to each other'. The first copy of *The Little Larrikin* arrived that afternoon and she quickly decided it was her best piece of work to date in spite of parts she would have given worlds to alter. Herbert also completed his first piece of light fiction intended for publication, 'Georgie Johnson, a Piratical Extravaganza', which Ethel successfully offered to Walter Jeffery as a serial for the *Town and Country*.

Lilian, still unmarried, though courting with Fred Thompson, came with him to stay with the Curlewises in June 1896, when they had the thrill of a visit from 'dear old Dr Barry' with his wife and daughter Flo. The sisters enjoyed some long walks together and at the end of the week, after a walk down Cowles Road, Ethel sighed, 'I don't think two sisters ever were as much to each other as we are'. Lilian, like Ethel, was a prankster, and the girls always enjoyed playing practical jokes, dressing their young male associates in 'drag' and passing them off on unsuspecting friends as elderly aunts. On 13 October, for example, while Herbert and Ethel were at dinner a ring came to the door and the maid appeared at table to say that Mrs Board was in the drawing room. (Lucy Board was the member of Henry Turner's family who had remained with her father after he married Ethel's mother and had accompanied the little party when they migrated to Australia. She had witnessed Sarah's marriage to Charles Cope at the end of 1880 and had herself married Thomas Board, but there was coolness between the families and visits from the Boards were not greeted with enthusiasm.) Ethel 'groaned in spirit & went heavily up the hall. And it was dear little Lil!' The visit, not untypically, was to seek the younger sister's help with one of the recurring financial problems faced by Lil and Fred, even before they were married.[6]

Ethel and Herbert sought to manage their own budget

with care, Ethel making jam and curtains while Herbert made kitchen furniture:

Night did accounts, we are spending too much, – when we put it down on paper we estimated our housekeeping at 150 pounds a year, we are spending at the rate of 250 to 300 pounds. H. suggests, – almost with a break in his voice – perhaps we had better not have quite so many puddings.

Yet some relief was in sight, for in the first week of November 1896 Cassell's and Ward Lock had placards competing with each other in seeking buyers for Lilian's book *The Lights of Sydney* and *The Little Larrikin*. Lilian's anxiety came to an end with an excellent notice in the *Telegraph* saying that her book had passages that were 'not unworthy of Charlotte Brontë'. A further boost to her finances and to her hopes of affording to marry Fred came in February 1897 with Cassell's offer of a hundred guineas for her new novel, *Felise*, which had been temporarily mislaid in the post.

For her own part Ethel had a warm, glowing, almost rapturous letter from Louie Mack about the Larrikin and generous congratulations from A. B. Paterson, with whom she was soon exchanging visits. He had made the interesting point, when his 'Man From Snowy River' was published in 1895 to critical and popular acclaim, that he had benefitted, as she had with *Seven Little Australians*, from the emergence of a new mood of acceptance for distinctively Australian material. As he put it, 'I think we have struck a lucky time when no one has done much for a long while & the feeling in favour of Australia is growing'.[7]

In relation to Louie, some problems were emerging that would eventually diminish her intimate friendship with Ethel. When Ethel went to the Creeds' little cottage at Chatswood for lunch in November she was sad to see how shabby it had become in less than a year. There was no money to spare for renewing the few things that had been bought at the start and Ethel told herself she would set something aside from the sale of her next story to give Louie some help. More significant was the discussion they had a week later when Louie rushed over to Mosman to inform Ethel she had just been accused of basing the character of Jean in *The World is Round* on her old friend and of holding her up to ridicule because she was said to be jealous of Ethel's greater popularity. At first Ethel felt 'the thought was too unworthy to be entertained' but at length her suspicions were reawakened by Louie's letter of self-justification explaining that she 'could not be guilty because she did not envy Ethel, implying in a naively superior way that hers was the life of the true artist while Ethel's was merely that of the successful authoress'. More and more Ethel and Herbert, especially the latter, came to feel they could not trust Louie.[8]

By April 1897, after a year of married life, Ethel found in the course of a morning with Louie how much they now differed in their values:

Talked royalties & publishers & housekeeping. Louie says she hates the latter, that it cramps & cripples her etc. I'm afraid she is growing inclined to think everything an author does but write is infra dig to the author. The housekeeping both of us have won't hurt us; with our dear, new little homes & a good servant each we haven't much to grumble at. I wouldn't give up the reins of my little house for anything.

A remarkable feature of Ethel's marriage, and one perhaps missing from Louie's, was the readiness of both husband and wife to communicate and take stock. Ethel's sister Rose came to stay for the second weekend in March and on Sunday night, when the sisters returned from a little walk, the husband and wife had a brief quarrel. 'He says he has an aggrieved feeling all the time, for four Saturdays & Sundays he has not had me all to himself & he has been longing for it. I must manage better, Sundays at all events I must try to keep free, & more evenings than I do at present'. Next day Rose went home early and at night Ethel 'put away all appearance of work & we had a lovers evening.'.

Equally impressive was the degree to which husband and wife supported each other's professional ventures; Herbert contributed significantly to Ethel's work not only by criticising her manuscripts but also by slogging through the mountains of mail involved in the competitions she ran for the Children's Corner as 'Dame Durden'. For her part Ethel kept an eye on the appearance of Herbert's chambers and when he moved to a much bigger, nicer room at 93 Elizabeth Street she scoured the city to find a 'chaste, legal, strong floor covering' for the very modest price of one pound. At the same time she got some serge for a curtain to his bookshelves and bought a picture for the wall. They spent the following Saturday putting everything in order and caught the late afternoon ferry home feeling 'well pleased with ourselves'.

Another activity enjoyed by Ethel and Herbert was swimming, whether in baths, bays or in later years increasingly in the surf. During Herbert's January vacation they made up a picnic basket and tramped to Pearl Bay where they found themselves the sole occupants of the baths and so able to have their first swim together in those days of segregated bathing:

H. swims splendidly, & he says I swim very well though I get breathless after a time. We jumped off the spring board several times & I also dived. It was simply glorious. Then we had lunch in a little summerhouse, & afterwards I read for a time ... & H smoked. And then he read to me & I knitted.

New baths were opened at Balmoral in January 1897 and Ethel made up a party to take Dolly Curlewis and a little friend for a swim and to enjoy lunch together, but the pool was so crowded that she yearned for the peace of Pearl Bay.

In April 1897 the Curlewises went away for their first holiday together, choosing a guest house at Kurrajong in the Lower Blue Mountains. From Richmond station they took the coach and enjoyed the dust and the scenery and rather disappointed their fellow guests by assuring them after tea that they were not the least bit musical, fleeing to 'the safety of the verandah while a schoolgirl performed conscientiously the whole evening & the others all sat stiffly round the room'.

During their first holiday outing they were taken by friends to see the local showplace, a garden of 600 acres called Northfield, created over the previous forty years by a fascinating man now in his eighties. He was Mr Comeri and inevitably he and Ethel became the best of friends for he revealed that he had read everything she and Lilian had written. She also spent a good deal of time with Miss Bass, a crippled girl who made Ethel feel almost ashamed of her advantages of health and happiness. Soon the girl learned that her new friend was a famous writer and when Ethel regretted the discovery made the point that it gave great pleasure to her. As she explained, when she had been struck down by illness it was *Seven Little Australians* that had cheered her up when nothing else could.

For a Sunday outing Herbert and Ethel joined a small party of choice spirits, went to the Sylvan Shades, and found a comfortable nook where they spent the morning talking and looking for wallabies. Ethel took special pleasure in being able 'to make a remark a little above the commonplace & know you will be understood'.

Their first day back at 'Yanalla' was celebrated by Ethel with reflections on the past twelve months of married life:

Just a year. I wonder if any other couple had so ideally perfect a first year. There has not been a shadow of a cloud on our sunshine ... We have both been splendidly well [*Ethel was forgetting here the awful steel instruments that Dr Brady had been poking up her eustachean tube in a peculiarly destructive effort to improve her hearing*] & full of spirits all the time ... We have been such friends as well as lovers & husband & wife, – done everything together & gone everywhere together. Not a single Saturday or Sunday or night apart. I wonder what I shall have to write this day next year, it seems hardly possible we could be allowed another year of such happiness. *And yet there might be even greater happiness, – I am thinking so now. And H. will not mind now we have had one year alone.*

As Ethel alludes shyly to the fact of her pregnancy her handwriting becomes as tiny as a whisper.

She was less retiring about her literary future. On the following day Ethel wrote to A. P. Watt, the literary agent in England, and put all her affairs in his hands for six months at least. Somewhat nervously she wrote to tell William Steele of the arrangement and answered the letters of advice she'd had from Ada Cambridge and Rolf Boldrewood. Her reading was going at a good rate; in May she frequently neglected more formidable chores in order to read *Vanity Fair* and *Henry Esmond*. On completing the latter she felt the pang of disappointment suffered by every true reader when a rare experience has come to an end. She and Herbert 'went to the extravagance' of paying two guineas subscription to the Angus & Robertson library for a year but by 4 June they had both raced through the three books with which they had started and had nothing left for the weekend.

A. B. Paterson had written early in June asking Ethel to write a story for a collection in the *Antipodean;* her first response had been to decline the opportunity but a week later he pressed her to reconsider because:

they want to show what Australian writers *can* do & ... Brunton Stephens had said in his letter 'It is important to secure Ethel Turner' etc. So I shall be 'patriotic' & write something though I can't afford to when I get so much bigger prices in England.

She completed 'Golden Syrup', her short story for the *Antipodean*, on 17 June, feeling confident that it was her best yet.

An illustration of the superior buying power of English magazines came soon with a letter from James Bowden's Religious Tract Society offering 46 pounds for the serial rights of 'The Doll's Dressmaker', a squeaky clean story of 11 000 words Ethel had sent at their request. While accepting the money, Ethel felt ashamed of herself, writing, 'It is absolute fustian & they ought to have refused it. I'll never put pen to such stuff again though, – & never, never drag a moral in when I don't want to'.

Socially this was still a busy time for Ethel. An English writer named Dolman arrived with a letter of introduction from Coulson Kernahan and was invited to dine with the Curlewises in company with 'Banjo' Paterson, starting off rather 'dull & quiet' but improving greatly on acquaintance. Next day, a Sunday, Herbert and Dolman joined Ethel at 'Bukyangi' so he could meet Lilian; it was not till the Tuesday they returned to 'Yanalla', laden with violets and jonquils. The flowers were the more appreciated because Ethel and Herbert had eleven friends coming on the Wednesday night including their neighbours the Arthurs and the Meillons, making two tables of whist in the drawing room and three sets of chess in the dining room. They were busy again on Thursday night, going to the Lyceum Theatre to see an amateur performance of *Caste* in which their friend Mr Pridham had a major part. 'Still though we were in front row of d.c. I could only hear about half, – oh this wretched wretched deafness.' This seems to have been the first such experience and it may be significant that when Herbert took Mr Dolman to the theatre a week later Ethel stayed at home, her first occasion alone since her marriage, working at a dress for the baby and dreaming 'sweet dreams, over the tiny garment'.

Literature's claims were revived by Ethel's reading Shorter's *Charlotte Brontë and her Circle*. She commented in her diary:

The life of those three sisters has a strange & intense fascination for me. How in earnest they were, – they worked with their very heartblood. What a trifler I seem beside them, nearly everything is made smooth for me, I've health & happiness & enough money to keep me from the necessity of pot boiling, & I waste my time & work half-heartedly & grudge trouble very often. – I'm not fit to be trusted with a pen.

It is interesting that Ethel should compare her life favourably with that of the Brontë sisters when one considers her own childhood, the loss of two fathers and the anxieties of poverty and emigration. The immediate consequence of this reflection was for Ethel to reread her manuscript of *Three Little Maids*, facing it sternly and deciding to scrap what had been written so far and put the idea away until she felt a stronger inspiration. And she took the further precaution of writing to A. G. Stephens, who had recently set up as a literary agent, asking him to advise her on whether it was worth going on with.[9]

Stephens's reply has not survived, although Ethel wrote again thanking him for his 'long and careful notes', agreeing with his strictures but explaining how she had conceived her task in writing an autobiographical novel. These remarks deserve to be quoted extensively because they illuminate her special qualities as a writer for children and her power as a correspondent.

My idea was to make a book of the quiet, somewhat uneventful life of three small girls.

Such life naturally is a quiet, trickling stream. To bring in big incidents & strange happenings might be better art but not half so true to nature. But do you know I am beginning seriously to find my imagination does me better service than my observation ... Those three little girls are absolutely true to nature, whatever else their faults: & so far not one single incident of their lives has been untrue. [*She was writing of the first draft, which was much altered in the light of Stephens's comments.*] Yet I felt as I wrote it was a tame record, & I was tempted several times to let imagination in to run riot. But as an experiment I did not – & behold.

The Seven Australians, & Misrule are really the most fanciful things I have done. I took a peg or two to hang their characters on & I got to know them so well as I wrote I knew just what each must do under given circumstances. But the rest is an airy fabric & you praise it as the real, substantial article. Then I sit down & weave a genuine material, with each thread tested & strong, & lo, you carp at it & call it gossamer. – It is bewilderment, isn't it?[10]

The experience made Ethel determined to 'make friends with imagination again'. She then went on to reject Stephens's misgivings about her picture of child behaviour, claiming to 'know children pretty well' and insisting that in the intimacy of home life 'there is hardly anything I find that you can put it past a child to say – or do'. Stephens, she thought, in his capacity as a school examiner would see nothing at all of this side of children's lives. She then played her trump card, the half-brother Rex who was ten years her junior:

At school doubtless the masters regard him as a shy, awkward, somewhat dull boy ... But at home he might be any character I have ever written about, & I have never yet been able to do his sayings & doings justice. It was he at 4 who did the Larrikin's trick of washing some live ducks & hanging them to dry on the line. At 3 ½ he climbed, in company with a girl of 3, right up two ladders, walked round on the scaffolding of the half-built church, pulling the little girl behind him.

Ethel agreed that the Larrikin might have been better placed at seven or eight:

but after all there are countless street arabs of five & six selling matches, papers, jumping on trams, – hardened & wily as boys of 10 & 11. And circumstances had made Lol very little different from these street boys.

The same with the little maids. Take any three delicately reared little girls, touched with imagination, shut them up in a rather lonely home with only occasional outside playfellows, & you would have the same result.

She insisted that near her were three girls who were 'Lal & Dolly & Weenie over again' playing wonderful games and talking in the strangest way among themselves. 'They make me know I am not exaggerating'. So she would put the story aside to see if it would 'mature', reduce the English story to four or five chapters '& let the sun & Australia make the rest bright'.

Ethel by this time had begun her ninth year in charge of a children's page, starting with the *Parthenon* in 1889. When she ended her term as Chief Sunbeamer with the Sydney *Sun* in 1931 she'd had the best part of forty years experience in this line of work, on four different newspapers. Apart from providing Ethel with a reliable income, a source of that financial independence which meant so much to her as a woman of the 'new age', this work taught Ethel much about the craft of writing for children.

On 6 April we get a rare view of 'Dame Durden' at home and a surprisingly candid opinion of the literary standard of the Children's Page when 'the little girl Hogue' came to see her:

I don't know if she thought she was coming to see an ogre but she was so white & trembling & nervous for a long time she hardly knew what she was saying. Later, she seemed to think I was not so dreadful a person & told me all about her writing hopes. I don't often encourage 'Corner' children, – their work is very poor as a whole – but I thought this one needed it & deserved it so I did.

Ethel's writing commitments did not leave her unlimited time for household management. Finding and keeping reliable servants was a recurring problem, and particularly trying during her pregnancy. By the final week of August Ethel was struggling to come to terms with Esther, the third girl of the month and wrote, 'At night we sat up till 11 waiting for Esther to come in. And finally discovered she had quietly packed up her clothes & marched away without a word.'

Joseph Carruthers, later to become Premier of New South Wales, who had written in February 1896 to praise Ethel for her 'great service to Australia' in her writings with their purity of feeling and thought, was due to come with his son to dine the following day. So Ethel went to Esther's home and demanded she should return for the day at least. 'She had found the washing too heavy & "didn't like the place"' was the verdict, but she came back which was everything, though afterwards Ethel had to manage by herself till a new servant arrived. Meanwhile she entertained Mrs Cullen and two other young matrons who had come for afternoon tea with their three babies and at the end of the day cooked dinner for Herbert, by which time she was 'fairly wrecked'. So

Herbert put his pregnant wife to bed, turned the gas down and bade her go to sleep while he washed up the breakfast, lunch and dinner dishes and tidied the kitchen. Which prompted Ethel's heart-felt comment:

Morning very busy with housework, – despite the trouble servants are I wouldn't be without for worlds permanently, – it is such a shocking waste of time doing the thousand & one details of work in a house.

Early in September they went to a Conversazione at Government House 'which I thought very nice & H, very deadly. But then I was being flattered'. Carruthers introduced her to lots of people including Sir Fowell Buxton, governor of South Australia, who told her he had read her books and liked them very much.

Flattering experiences of this kind tended to spur Ethel to seek further achievements; books were, after all, the source of her fame and income. After a month of desultory activity Ethel paced about the house 'bitten with a longing to write a magnificent book, & crumbling to nothingness the minute I touched a pen'. At night more pacing and an attempt to write 'something good as a sequel to Larrikin' but confidence increased only slowly for the next day or so.

The big occasion involving the Curlewises in September was an excursion given by Carruthers, then a cabinet minister, to the delegates who were assembled in Sydney to discuss the federal constitution. Their destination was Kiama, a town in the Illawarra district where Carruthers had grown up in a Scottish farming family before going on to school and legal studies in Sydney. Herbert and Ethel joined the special carriage laid on for the delegates and were introduced by Carruthers to many of them, whom Ethel described in her candid inimitable fashion:

Politics crept in everywhere of course & I picked up more crumbs of knowledge from the men themselves than I have ever collected from the papers. I liked Mr Deakin greatly, – such an impressive personality he has, a force & vigour not often met. Mr Symons, too, an Adelaide delegate & leader of the Bar; he seemed a forceful man. Sir Philip Fysh seemed a harmless garrulous old donkey but kindly natured, his wife a queer, vulgar, genuine creature. Mr Simon Fraser told me all about the referendum & his intense desire not to have it; such a simple, good, clear-headed old fellow. Everyone was very nice to me & several said they had read my books & made kind remarks about them.

Feeling worn out by the day Ethel stayed overnight with Herbert at the Royal Hotel in Kiama instead of returning with the official party. The coastal scenery she pronounced the most interesting in the colony, being struck by the dramatic contrasts afforded by the proximity of mountains to the sea, which gave travellers the thrill of emerging from dark tunnels and bursting into the sunlight where they caught glimpses of white crested waves on the one hand and hills on the other.

Lilian came to stay at 'Yanalla' for a few days, when the sisters talked about books and marriage, agreeing on the following April as the likely date for Lil's marriage to Fred Thompson.

Then, stimulated by a talk we had about the funny things we used to do & think when we were little I got a brand new exercise book & started a brand new version of 'Three Little Maids', – I feel sure I *can* do something with the subject but the last attempt of 12 chapters is certainly worthless & wishy-washy. Only wrote 10 lines but it has started me.

The post brought an early copy of *Miss Bobbie;* it looked nicer than the other books but Ethel felt that the matter was 'miserable', a judgement with which many of us will concur, though the book's popularity was immediate. However, she soon got into a good mood for writing and turned out 3 300 words of *Three Little Maids* during a Saturday on her own.

In October, with four months of her pregnancy to go, Ethel began to wear a maternity cape '& felt horribly self-conscious & shrinking', determined to cease going to town. At Anthony Horderns she bought an ice chest, which she expected to be a great boon. The approach of her own confinement made the friendship of Lil Cullen the more attractive and Ethel spent a day in the garden at 'Tregoyd' hoping to find there the peace and inspiration she needed:

She found an ideal summer house place for me, near a tiny creek where the birds come to bathe. Couldn't settle down at first for the distraction of the flowers & birds & bees – & mosquitos. But finally gave up pacing the fascinating paths & wrote half a chapter of 3 Little Maids & started Ch III.

After lunch in spite of good intentions the two women played with the Cullen children and gossiped.

Louie Mack's *Teens* arrived from the publishers, 'beautifully got up, sage green & gold' and Ethel lay on the sofa and read it all one evening. She pronounced it a disappointment, lacking the brightness and cleverness of *The World is Round* and seeming 'tame & insipid' with very little happening. Two days later she was surprised to see favourable reviews in all the papers.

As summer approached the hot winds left Ethel crawling limply about the house. But on 28 November it was a cool 65 degrees and Herbert 'clipped & rolled away at his grass till it looked a thing of beauty, & then, as usual, looked over the next fence to reward himself & gloated over the Knight's dandelions & general want of order'. How thoroughly human, yet so inconsistent, for the Curlewises took the greatest pains to protect their own privacy by building trellises and growing tall shrubs. A week before Christmas there was a 'truly drefful day', so hot the jellies would not set for a children's party. Nevertheless Ethel and her friends got dolls and toys ready for the City Mission and by night time it was Herbert who had to take over the house.

At the end of 1897 Ethel took her usual stock of the past year. She and Herbert had a total of 547 pounds in three different savings banks, the greater part in Ethel's name. Her literary work was not as formidable as before: *Three Little Maids* had been written and rewritten up to chapter 14; 'The Doll's Dressmaker' had been written as a short serial for *Sunday Hours* and four short stories completed of 4 to 5 000 words, 'A New Lenore' sent to Watt, 'Golden Syrup' to the *Antipodean*, and 'Letters to a Mother' and 'Second Nature' to the *Windsor Magazine*. And she was by now in her eighth month of pregnancy.

Her own thoughts about the approaching confinement were not eased by an awareness of the difficulties experienced by her friend and neighbour, Mrs Pridham. She had 'one of those old nurses who muddle everything', got up too early and was now feverish and depressed, convinced she would not get better and anxious about the three-week-old baby, which had been given gruel when only two days old.

In January Herbert occupied himself making a stand for the baby's cradle and Ethel with writing out recipes with which his favourite dishes could be made 'when I am ill'. The nurse whom Dr Arthur had chosen to look after his patient returned from her honeymoon and impressed Ethel with her capability. Letters from Lilian and Mrs Cope filled Ethel with wrath for the Thompsons had insisted that Fred could not marry during Lent which meant bringing the wedding forward to 22 February, with or without Ethel present, or deferring it till 11 April.

At the end of the first week in February, Ethel had a little mishap when a leg broke on her verandah chair and she dropped to the ground. Yet she was able to join Herbert in their regular walk in the cool of the evening when they called on Richard and Jessie Arthur. While Herbert played chess with the doctor and his brother Ethel and Jessie walked in the garden, taking advantage of the 'loveliest moonlight night'. Next day Ethel superintended the making of a rockery in the bush house and Herbert worked on the lattice; in the evening she finished writing 'The Museum at Koonaworra' and started on her walk but suddenly felt ill and barely able to make it home.

It was not till Sunday that labour began. The nurse and doctor were sent for, the Copes were telephoned and came rushing from Gordon and Herbert walked Ethel up and down the drawing room 'cheering me up between each pain'. At night when things began in earnest Herbert took to the street 'and walked up and down half mad the whole night'. As she wrote later, showing in her words a remarkable concern for the strain suffered by her husband:

My little girl was born at 20 mins past 7. I was seventeen hours ill; the last eight being exquisite agony. Pain will always be a matter of comparison now; I believe I should be able to smile over a trifling matter like having a limb sawn slowly off. They used a 2 oz bottle of chloroform on me but it had scarcely any effect; I was never quite unconscious a moment, & knew all the time what they were doing. They owned that I had a very bad time, being so small but the moment I heard that strange little urgent cry! 'Is that my little baby' I said & fell to crying myself. Later Laddie came in – just one moment to kiss me & I cried again at his face. And yet he had put his head under the shower-bath & dipped his face in water & drunk half a tumbler of brandy to try & get it under his control again so that he might not hurt me. My poor old Laddie.

chapter
Nine

*J*ean's birth on 7 February 1898 began a major
new phase in Ethel's life. For the first time since
she had started keeping a diary in 1889 the
central fact of her existence was no longer the determination
to make good as a writer but rather to succeed as a mother
and homemaker. For some years, and this continued long
after the birth of son Adrian in January 1901, the demands
of writing took second place to domestic needs, though eventually her professional work returned to its old vigour, not
least because it was seen as making a vital contribution to
the family's prosperity.

Not a word was written in the diary for five days after
Jean's birth, then Ethel recorded first impressions of a new
state of things by writing:

Not quite so well, – low spirited. Rosie came to see Babe for the
first time. H's father & Mother came late in evening & I suppose
I must have been tired & overwrought for I alarmed them by
bursting into tears before they had fairly spoken to me.

A week later, after feeling low-spirited all day Ethel suddenly
dissolved in tears at tea time, when her temperature was
found to be 103 degrees Fahrenheit. Dr Arthur was puzzled
as to the cause of the fever and called in a specialist, Dr

Foreman, who diagnosed abscess of the breast. Fever and headaches continued for two more days when another specialist was called in and he pronounced the cause to be septic absorption. It was decided, with Dr Arthur dissenting, that an operation would be performed if no change occurred by the following morning. Sure enough she then turned the corner and there was no need for Dr Worral and his 'horrid black bag'. As she wrote on 23 February, 'Almost well again. 'Twas influenza for "a morality".'

The illness kept Ethel away from the ceremony that took place on 22 February at the little Anglican church at Gordon:

Darling Lil's wedding day & I away! When it was two o'clock & I was thinking & thinking of the darling I couldn't help having a cry to think I was not there. I shall never forgive the Thompsons for their absurd 'No-wedding-in Lent' insistence. Little mother came flying to me the second the wedding guests began to go, – she and Mr C. And they couldn't let me see her, I was in such a nervous, strung up state & crying & crying till Mother said I nearly broke her heart. Little Lil almost put off her honeymoon trip only H promised to keep wiring my condition.

When another few days had passed Ethel was well enough to be carried onto the drawing room sofa to enjoy views of the lawn, the scarlet cannas and gum trees which 'looked things of exquisite beauty'. Jessie Arthur and her mother came for a visit to admire the baby and administer comfort to the young mother, who was disappointed at being unable to maintain a sufficient milk supply, telling her of all the fine babies they knew who had been partially or wholly hand fed. By the end of April Ethel had given up breast feeding.

On 4 March Ethel was able to take stock of the consequences of her time of indisposition. Her home, she lamented, was 'half ruined, quantities of china & glass broken, grease dropped on carpets & matting, mildew & ironmould on linen, – everything possible spoiled – the result of an incapable servant at such a time'. Next day with the aid of her nurse she set off with the baby to stay at 'Bukyangi' to try the benefits of a mother's tender care and the still rural peace of Gordon. Though she felt tottery in the walk up to the tram 'the little journey was quite intoxicatingly lovely to me, the harbour & the gum trees & the blue sky after bedroom walls'. A cab from the station took her to 'the lovingest of welcomes home', the nurse departed at 5 p.m. and that night Ethel and Herbert were left:

absolutely alone for the first time – at least with no one else in the room – exposed to all the terrors of that 20 inch infant of ours. I was afraid to go to sleep, it seemed so easy for her to smother herself in her pillow, or choke silently. And H was up every little time to 'see she was alright'. She had slept harmlessly however most of the night.

At 'Bukyangi' Ethel and the baby basked for hours in the sun while Herbert made the long journey into the city. When Mrs Cope went off for the day to help Lil and Fred get straight in their new home at Chatswood on returning from the honeymoon, a Mrs Taylor was called in, since 'I was too much of a coward to be left alone with such an alarming personage as my infant'. Ethel got up late and spent hours in the summerhouse writing letters while Jean lay in the cradle soaking up the fresh air and sunshine. One day Ethel shocked the Reverend King, when he visited her at 'Bukyangi' and asked if the baby was to be christened at Gordon, by telling him she was not to be christened at all. Clearly Ethel's thoughts about religion had changed since the days at St Matthias's in Paddington, though it was Herbert who answered for both parents when the rector asked them to reconsider.

A fortnight of being spoiled prepared Ethel for a return to 'Yanalla', and she began a trial of wills with Jean; it started with a display of tears when the baby was withdrawn from the bath. The screams continued till the mother was almost in tears herself, at which point Jean smiled complacently and dropped off into a lovely sleep 'as if that were her sole object'. Victory went to Jean again on 12 May when she refused to go down to sleep on the occasion of a visit from Dr Arthur. At length Ethel laid her on the table amongst soft cushions '& she lay & blinked victoriously at the light while we played chess'.

Friday 13 May marked the effective end of the war between parents and babe. Details of that battle deserve to be quoted in full:

Night we both read. A long fierce struggle with the little babe; she resisted most vigorously any attempt to put her in the cradle & shrieked wildly. Once or twice I gave in & lifted her thinking she might be in pain. And she immediately looked round in her interested fashion at everything & bobbed her little head & laughed. Then down she went again & again the evening air was pierced with her yells. I had to go away & leave her to H finally for the yells began to give way to sobs of sorrow & woful little hiccoughs of vanquishment. Even H's stony heart was touched. Finally she fell off to sleep with her dear little hand spread on the pillow & a tear on her cheek & her lip dropped. Heigho I hope the battle will not last very long, but the victory must be to us, I couldn't bear the little girl to be one of the spoilt, tyrannous children one is always meeting.

During this period of domestic preoccupation Ethel took particular care of her relationship with Herbert, which was conserved in many ways, above all in their sharing enjoyable pastimes both of an active and reflective character. In January 1899, for example, they joined with thousands of Australians in being swept up by the craze for bicycling. It was something they did together, especially when Ethel was being taught to ride by her already expert husband, though later they went for long solo rides and joined in expeditions with the Arthurs.

Women had been encouraged since 1890 by Louisa Lawson's feminist newspaper, the *Dawn*, to take regular exercise out-of-doors and ladies' cycling clubs had soon been formed. Such advice had a ready appeal for Ethel, who delighted in physical achievement. She used *Seven Little Australians* to express her ideas about the need for young women to break free from unhealthy restraints and develop their bodies. The 'rebellious, tomboyish Judy' embodied such impulses during the whole of her short life. Her older sister Meg, who has a somewhat purposeless existence and uses corsets to crush 'her beautiful body into narrower space', pays for her foolishness by falling down in a faint in front of her father and his guests.

Bridge and chess were games the Curlewises enjoyed regularly, not only at organised occasions but frequently on the spur of the moment as the climax to a nocturnal ramble in leafy Mosman. Again, the Arthurs were a constant element in this part of their lives.

Richard Arthur (1865-1932) had graduated in arts and medicine at the universities of St Andrew's and Edinburgh before coming to Australia where in 1890 he married Jessie Sinclair, the daughter of a Presbyterian minister. Returning briefly to Britain, Arthur worked as a medical missionary and wrote a thesis on the therapeutic use of hypnotism for his Edinburgh doctorate. Settled soon after in Mosman, he specialised in problems of the eye, ear-nose-and-throat and dentistry till he moved in 1900 to Macquarie Street. Hypnotism was a continuing interest and he used it in a vain attempt to cure Ethel's deafness. He took strong stands on public issues, opposing Australia's involvement in the South African war and warning politicians and people of the dangers posed by the rise of Japan. In 1904, the year that saw the beginning of the Russo-Japanese War, he was elected to the Legislative Assembly with temperance and Protestant support. One of his passionate concerns, many of which Ethel shared, was to provide good cheap homes for servicemen returning from the war. Immigration and closer settlement occupied much of his attention and, like the issue of temperance, found expression in Ethel's novels during and after the war. *St Tom and the Dragon*, published in 1917, was the story of a young medico who gave his life to the temperance cause. So we can imagine that the Curlewises and Arthurs had much to talk about when they played chess or sat on their balconies and looked out on the soft beauty of the harbour on balmy summer nights.

Ethel felt by mid-April that her strength and mental vigor had returned, for she had the thrill of defeating Dr Arthur at chess in two out of three games. She was sure that, given time, she could write 'a really good book'. Royalties had been encouragingly strong and had amounted to 220 pounds for the past half year, largely because of the success of *Miss Bobbie*, which had done the best of all her books thus far, selling over 9 000 copies in three months.

Miss Bobbie was the expanded version of a story Ethel had written for the *Parthenon* in 1889 employing the theme of the blended family which she used in her books with endless variations, reflecting her own experience of the intrusion of death and transplantation in human affairs. The heroine was an eleven-year-old redhead who was left in the care of a widower and his five boys while her squatter father travelled abroad with his new bride. Control of the household is in the hands of a gaunt but loyal servant who could almost have been an Englishwoman. The gentle and ineffective Dr Wallace is typical of Ethel's fictional fathers in his distance from the children.

Interest is provided by Bobbie's enthusiastic attempts to

win acceptance from the boys but the book is flawed by the unreality of the final adventure when she saves Issie from the bush fire, and by the absurdity of some comic situations. The moment when Suds is gulled into thinking he has pulled the girl's red hair out by the roots provides good theatre, but the afternoon tea party fails at every level. Certainly for a modern reader its assumptions and language are dated to the point of being embarrassing. When Bobbie invites her rich friend Isobel to afternoon tea she confesses to the boys her discomforture at having only one servant so Ted offers to help by blacking his face and dressing as a manservant named Sambo: 'I'd make a good nigger,' he said, 'she'd be quite impressed.'

While the cables from overseas told of the beginning of hostilities between the United States and Spain which terminated in the extension of American power in the Pacific, Ethel and Herbert celebrated the second anniversary of their marriage. He had taken a half holiday and they made a little pilgrimage to 'Rothesay', the house in which they had spent their first weeks of married life, using a new Kodak to record some photographs. In the evening they played chess and she reflected:

Well, whatever the future brings we have had two of the most perfect years possible in this world. I think every month we grow more deeply happy & grow more dear & necessary to each other. That is because we are playmates & chums as well as lovers, as well as husband & wife, as well as mother & father.

In spite of her earlier feeling of mental vigour Ethel found great difficulty in making a new start on *Three Little Maids*, the autobiographical novel that tells us so much of the young family's formative years in England. On 26 April she could only write a thousand words against a background of constant interruptions; a whole chapter was torn up in disgust on 6 May. Almost a month passed before work resumed on the manuscript on 2 June when Ethel sent Jean down to the Spit for a walk with Rose and again the next day, 'The great day to decide Federation!', when Herbert went into town at night to watch the progressive results being posted up in Martin Place. Freed from his distracting presence she wrote 'for a couple of hours at Maids'. Concerned to maintain the level of her income, she wrote in July to Watt, the English literary agent whom she had appointed the previous year, to Steele's disappointment, enclosing three stories. He was told 'only to offer them to a children's paper, they are such poor stuff I won't risk my name with them. But I wanted the money'.

An over-riding sense of romance, if not fantasy, lay behind the move in August 1898 from 'Yanalla' to 'The Neuk', a two-storeyed brick house in Moruben Road, Mosman. Herbert and Ethel had been restless for some months, seriously considering the purchase of land in Military Road and also inquiring at real estate offices. A decision was made in favour of 'The Neuk' provided that the rent was reasonable and on the following day it was settled, as the agent agreed with Ethel to drop the price from 72 pounds to 66 pounds for a year's lease.

An early photograph of 'The Neuk' with Jean in the foreground, a toddler wearing a huge hat decorated with flowers, shows an almost new house in Federation style with outrageous bargeboards and roof decorations. It was chosen in spite of many inconveniences and after Ethel measured the floors she wrote:

It is the dearest, loveliest little place, & oh so mad ... But the view & quaintness compensate for everything. The draw. room & din. room too are very pleasant rooms, – with the end of each given up to windows looking out on the view of dancing blue water & hills & beaches & the red, winding hill.

On the last Saturday in July, 1898, Herbert and Ethel left Jean in Rose's care and visited Joseph Carruthers' home at Kogarah, where there was a grand party to celebrate his overwhelming majority in the recent colonial elections that put George Reid and his Freetraders in power. The garden, with its fine tennis court separated from the George's River by a row of clipped black pines attracted Ethel's special attention. Flowers were in such profusion it was hard to believe that winter was at its height. She liked the new Mrs Carruthers very much but felt sorry for the divorced first wife 'shut out as she is by her own doing from her kingdom', and enjoyed 'the picture of the hard-worked politician resting in his beautiful home'.

September was a month of literary promise. Ethel learned that Watt, her agent, had sold 'A New Lenore' to *The Gentle-woman* for 25 pounds, double the best price so far for a short story. Another one, 'Not always to the strong', was published in the *Queen* on 24 June and 'What the postman brought' in the *Windsor Magazine* for June. Yet another of her titles appeared in a foreign translation with a Dutch edition of *The Little Larrikin;* no money was involved but much satisfaction.

In mid-October the Curlewises spent a Saturday together gardening in the sunshine at 'The Neuk' implementing suggestions offered by Dr Cullen. His magnificent garden with tall exotic palms and native bush cascaded down Raglan Street towards Balmoral Beach, giving a peaceful setting for 'Tregoyd', a large home in Federation style which still looks towards the harbour. Herbert and Ethel challenged each other that night to write a 'Child Song'. He wrote 'As Baby sees' and she 'A Trembling Star', a charming little poem that was published first by A. G. Stephens in his effusive article about Ethel in *The Bookfellow* for March 1899.

The most important development was the completion of

Three Little Maids which gave 'exquisite relief' after so many false starts and the repeated temptation to consign it to the fire – 'perhaps that would have been its best place' she still suspected. She began immediately to have the manuscript copied by two professional typists, Mr McBlain and Miss Anderson, so bringing to an end the tedious old task of copying it out herself in a fair hand.

December found her suffering again the attention of the ear specialist, Dr Oram, 'and got hurt rather badly; he pushed the instrument further than ever yet, for I told him I was deafer than ever'. Distressed, she called on Herbert at his chambers and he bought a particularly nice lunch and found a little white teapot to bring a smile back to her face. A more pleasant task, which became almost an annual event, was her attendance at the Sydney Girls' High Speech Day. She gave a prize herself, a padded morocco-bound book, for a short story that was marked by its author's lively sense of humour, and heard some flattering words from Hogue, the cabinet minister who presented it to the winner.

Christmas was spent as usual at 'Bukyangi' though present giving was done quietly because Lil and Fred were in no position to take part. Produce from the garden, orchard and pastures of Charles Cope made the fare abundant. A few days earlier Ethel had packed a Toy Box with 200 gifts for distribution to the City Mission; an often repeated gesture of interest in those less fortunate than she. January, 1899, marked the beginning of the Curlewises' enthusiasm for bicycling. Herbert had been one of the founders of the bicycling club at Newington, which revelled in long and demanding expeditions. Ethel's first real exposure to the machine was by courtesy of a friend who brought her cycle over to 'The Neuk' for Ethel to try out on the quiet road outside. In that first attempt Herbert held the saddle all the time but like Mr Toad with the motor car she was an instant convert.

On the following Friday Ethel met Herbert in town and

went to Bennett and Woods to hire a Rover bicycle. After spending five minutes over dinner they went to a flat stretch of Spit Road to try it out. They had to desist at 8 o'clock since they were promised for chess to the Arthurs but talked 'bikes' most of the evening. At 6 a.m. they were again practising on a level piece of turf where Ethel had fifty bruising falls before breakfast. In the afternoon they were at it again and by 7 p.m. Herbert pronounced his wife sufficiently advanced to cycle on the road where she 'rode up & down in style'. From this point there was no halting her progress: they practised mounting, turning, riding 'no hands' and every possible refinement until it became possible for them to use their bicycles, in the absence of horses, carriages or motor cars, as a means of transport.

January was also memorable for the beginning of Ethel's personal association with Henry Lawson. On the 25th there was a letter from the poet saying he was 'both surprised & delighted at my kind invitation, & that it came just as he was suffering from a reaction after his bitter outburst in the Bulletin'. He had written to the *Bulletin* in terms that appealed irresistibly to Ethel, of having started as:

a shy, ignorant lad from the Bush, under every disadvantage arising from poverty and lack of education, and with the extra disadvantage of partial deafness thrown in. I started with implicit faith in human nature, and a heart full of love for Australia, and hatred for wrong and injustice.

Despite popular and critical recognition he could not earn enough to keep his wife and family and proposed therefore to seek a better living in London.[1]

Ethel asked him to visit her. Assuming the invitation included his wife and baby they came together for afternoon tea, and Ethel wrote in her diary:

Mrs Lawson told me – we grew friendly quickly over our babies – all the troubles they have had, & quite broke down, poor thing, when she told me the Doctor said her husband is in a consumption & must *not* go to England. And so poor they are, – he is depending entirely on his pen & has to keep it going ceaselessly to pay boarding house dues. I like him muchly, & he said the afternoon had done him worlds of good, taken him out of himself.

Earlier in the month Ethel had sent her child verses, 'Trembling Star' and 'Leila Watering' to the *Bulletin* and began two short stories which she had promised to the *Windsor Magazine*. The first appeared at the end of 1900 as 'A Vagabond Day', which tells the story of two boys who spent their sixpences intended for haircuts on lollies, cakes and tobacco, very much in the tradition of the naughty Australian child that Ethel had established with her early novels. They attempted to deflect retribution by cutting each other's hair with blunt children's scissors, using a basin to establish the line. 'Early Morning at Browns' came out in the June 1901 issue; it is a well-constructed tale of the very beginning of a family's day with the baby waking to the sounds of birds welcoming the new morning and gradually imposing its will on parents and siblings until the father kisses them all, slams the gate and sprints down the hill to catch his train.

February saw a continuation of Ethel's revived zest for writing with a start being made on a new book, 'my great novel with a purpose', which was soon given the provisional title of *The Common Problem* and published in 1901 by James Bowden for The Religious Tract Society as *The Wonder Child*. This event carried the supreme irony, that by gravely disappointing Ethel's expectations of enhancing her receipts by moving away from Ward Lock, he was himself bringing to fruition a prediction he had made in December 1895 while he was still top man at that firm.

What I should try and bring home as forcibly as possibly to Miss Turner's mind [*Bowden had then written*] is that no one could spend as much money as we have done in producing and advertising 'Seven Little Australians' and pay a 15% royalty [*on a cheap edition*] without losing money. For many reasons, it would not be a bad thing if Miss Turner had an experience of another house, as we feel sure she would come back to us.[2]

Literary associations remained uppermost, with A. G. Stephens coming to dinner at 'The Neuk' on the last day of the month. He desired information for an article on Ethel's work intended for his magazine *The Bookfellow* and she wrote cautiously 'I think I like him – fairly – . He certainly has an excellent opinion of Mr Stephens'.

The article 'An Australian Authoress' published in *The Bookfellow* of 25 March 1899 makes it clear that Stephens also had an excellent opinion of Ethel Turner. He wrote of:

the quiet persistence of the small figure at the desk in the Red Road Country, writing and destroying, destroying and writing again, perfecting style and art, and winning at last a well-deserved success, holds a lesson for many an ambitious author who refuses to learn that the second-best of genius, the best of talent, is the capacity for taking pains.

Stephens went on to detail the sales of Ethel's books, which made the impressive total of 115 000 copies in five years, starting with *Seven Little Australians* going through seven editions and 30 000 copies and five of the six other titles selling 10 000 or more. The best-selling books, he pointed out, were those that did not pretend to 'the high plane of intellectual or imaginative achievement' but they were among the 'few charming stories written for and about children'. Agreeing with most of the critics, he thought that:

though her charm never leaves her, it is only her childish characters who are fully realised – made lifelike, genuine, convincing. Ethel Turner's 'grown-ups' are still childish characters – have some quaint air of delightful boys and girls masquerading in their elders' clothes. She has the key of the children's paradise only. That is enough; but there is one person in the world who demands more, and her name is Ethel Turner. 'I am so tired of writing children's books,' she says. 'I do wish to write a big book.' So she is trying.

As she still hoped to write for the theatre, in March Ethel began a collaboration with a Mrs Kearney, an unpublished would-be dramatist. After their first long discussion Ethel remarked, 'She certainly has dramatic notions, though also somewhat hackneyed ones'. They spent a day together on their play drafting the first act and worked on it again in July when Mrs Kearney stayed at 'The Neuk' for several days during which the work was brought to a conclusion. When her visitor left 'a sense of relief came over us all':

Thank goodness, Lil and I are only literary as far as our pens are concerned. I couldn't live with anyone like Mrs K. She is untidy – horribly so – not over clean, & always in a confusion of some sort.

The manuscript was taken in to Mr Brough, manager at the Theatre Royal, who sent Ethel a note of icy rejection on 1 August, finding himself unable to say anything good about the play. She accepted the opinion philosophically but felt concern for Mrs Kearney, who had set her heart on success.

Some weeks earlier Ethel had the disappointing experience of going to the theatre with Herbert and hearing not a word, despite their taking the front row of reserved stalls. One possible recourse was to use an ear trumpet when the lights were low, but it was 'a great strain'. Yet another, which she tried at a performance of 'The Amazons' in September

1901, was to sit close to the front and have Herbert whisper the essential parts to her; she got on very well and had a pleasant evening. The Arthurs had gone with them and it was typical of the doctor's solicitude for his friend that he turned up two nights later with the present of an 'unobtrusive ear arrangement – just a tube & mouthpiece & I can sit at theatre or anywhere & hear without being seen to put anything up. Nothing so horrid as an ear trumpet'. What continued to puzzle her was that she could still hear ordinary conversation at table without difficulty.

A more promising literary collaboration was embarked on as a result of Ethel's meeting in town with Mr McMillan and the famous artist – illustrator D. H. Souter. At her suggestion they were to join forces in producing an annual for children to be known as *Gum Leaves,* with poems and stories and rich illustrations. Several meetings were held during the year and the manuscript was ready in December for the printer, Mr Brooks, who suggested to Ethel that he should pay 45 pounds to each of the three contributors early in 1900 on account of royalties. The volume that resulted was 'an elegant piece of typographic design [with a] feeling of art nouveau ... an ageless beautiful book'.[3]

Souter went on to illustrate four more of Ethel's books, all published by Ward Lock: *Happy Hearts* (1908), *An Ogre Up-to-date* (1911), *The Raft in the Bush* (1910), and *The Sunshine Family* (1923), a joint effort by Jean and Ethel. Though an illustrator rather than an 'exhibition artist' Souter appealed to Ethel with his elegance and professionalism.

Despite a degree of coolness between them, Ethel still saw Louie Mack from time to time, though she was aware of the gradual erosion of Louie's marriage to Jack Creed. Ethel had expressed concern about the curious alteration in their behaviour to each other after the Creeds came to 'The Neuk' for Sunday tea in January 1899. A more dramatic development occurred a year later when Herbert, as a loyal friend, brought 'the Admiral' home drunk in a cab from the Law Institute and got Ethel out of the way while he put Jack to bed in the spare room:

It would have been no use taking him home to Louie, she would have been out & has no influence at all with him now ... It is a dreadful thing that that marriage should have turned out like this, – just 4 years ... I'm sure Louie does not do her best, – more than anything a home would reform him & she will not give him one.

The next manifestation of the decline was just before Christmas 1900 when Herbert accepted an invitation to tea with the Creeds at their Pymble boarding house, Louie having by now abandoned the idea of a conventional middle-class cottage. Jack was 'too unwell' to appear but Louie said nothing against her absent partner, impressing the Curlewises with her loyalty, which contrasted with Creed's verbal abuse of his wife. Louie by now was ready to escape the scarifying cruelty that she and Jack commonly inflicted on each other and in 1901, after three years of writing the woman's letter for the *Bulletin*, decided to seek her fortune alone overseas. On 11 April a hastily convened meeting was held at Sid Long's studio to arrange for a purse of sovereigns to be presented to Louie, who was planning to leave Melbourne for London on the *Omrah* at the end of the week. Ethel found it impossible to forget that in going off for an indefinite time Louie was leaving a bankrupted and unemployed Jack Creed to drink himself to death.

Henry Lawson, another of Ethel's friends who'd suffered a drinking problem, had already left for London a year earlier, convinced that his expectations as a writer, even as a great writer, would condemn his family to poverty while ever he remained in Australia. So urgent was his need to escape that he had applied to Lord Beauchamp, the new governor, and David Scott Mitchell, a wealthy collector of Australiana, to assist with his expenses.

With her passion for helping lame dogs, Ethel was determined to see what she could do when she'd discovered in March, 1900, that Henry, Bertha and the two rather sickly children were to sail in a month's time. As we learn in a surviving letter of Henry's, Ethel had chosen to make an eminently practical contribution to her friend's outfit for the journey:

Thank you very much for your thoughtfulness in sending linen. Shirts especially acceptable to me. Some time ago a brother of mine was going to North Queensland and I, rushing to see him off, packed up every old shirt &c I had in the house and gave them to him, which left me awfully short for the voyage.[4]

Another of her literary friends, A.B. Paterson, was also leaving the country at about this time, going to the Transvaal to cover the Boer War for the *Sydney Morning Herald*. Ethel's first diary reference simply reports the fact of the contingent's departure but ten days later, on 13 November 1899, she wrote for her Children's Page in the *Town and Country Journal* a story entitled 'War! War! War!' in which 'the Court Jester makes the whole court volunteer'. It would seem from this that Ethel was fairly critical of British policy in southern Africa; her friend Richard Arthur was a well-known early opponent of the war.

But on 20 February 1900 the Curlewises and Arthurs attended a local Patriotic Concert which was interrupted by the news that a detachment of Victorian troops had been 'entrapped & slaughtered to a man'. Under this influence Ethel got to work on her novel, *Wonderchild*, and enthusiastically wrote a new chapter set in the Transvaal in which the hero was a prisoner in a Boer farm house.

The diary entry for 28 February 1900 appears to reveal the

completion of Ethel's conversion to the mainstream view of approving the war. On the public holiday in Sydney when people watched the departure of the Bushmen's Contingent, she and Herbert went to see the procession of 'all those fine Bushmen & their splendid horses' from Dr Pockley's rooms in Macquarie Street; 'the enthusiasm was immense, – contagious, it brought a lump to my throat'. Influencing her feelings was the raw power of sturdy men marching to martial music and her share in the collective emotions of a jingoistic crowd; there was the further fact of many friends going to join the conflict including Jack Antill, Harry Pockley and Charles Cope's brother William.

For some time the Curlewises had been seeking a larger house and on the first day of Spring 1900 Ethel's eye was taken by a block of land in Warringah Road, Mosman, with a commanding view of Middle Harbour. The owner, Mr Rohde, happened to be on the spot and next day she took Herbert to see it as she liked it best of all seen so far. 'Even H likes it muchly,' she wrote, 'such a glorious view'. So she drew plans all the afternoon while Herbert worked on his new bench. On the following Monday, after taking an architect's advice on practicalities, Herbert made a written offer of 130 pounds, but they were happy to close the deal on 4 September at the owner's price of 150 pounds.

Ern Thompson, a brother-in-law of Lilian's, was promptly appointed architect; final plans were completed by 1 April 1901. Ethel found it difficult, living so close, to resist the temptation to bicycle over and maintain a constant surveillance of progress. The brickwork was well advanced by July and in September a start was made with shingling the roof. At the same time work began on laying out the extensive grounds, which fell away to the harbour in several levels that offered marvellous opportunities to a gardener. Ethel went with Ern Thompson to choose mantelpieces, hearths, bathroom furniture and gas fittings, returning home after so much excitement with a frantic headache.

What made the building of a new and larger house practicable was the improvement in Ethel's income from writing, which jumped from 345 pounds in 1900 to 631 pounds in 1901, after which her Pen Money Book shows it to have averaged more than 500 pounds for ten years. With such resources it was easy to service the interest of 35 pounds per annum on the mortgage raised for the construction of 'Avenel'.[5]

The building of 'Avenel' had been made desirable by an expansion of the Curlewis family on 13 January 1901 when Adrian was delivered to a heavily sedated mother after a relatively straightforward and brief labour. Ethel had shown the classic signs the day before, directing major changes to the disposition of the furniture. The only real drama came with the onset of contractions, when Herbert rushed off to get Dr Arthur only to find he was away in Bowral. On Herbert sped to Dr Doak and found that he too was absent on holidays. Even the midwife could not be contacted but a third doctor, Van Someren, was discovered and he produced a good nurse. Loyal though Ethel was to her friend Dr Arthur, who had not expected action for another week or so, she was glad to have had a doctor who was more generous in the use of chloroform.

On 6 November they said goodbye to the 'little grey house' which they now found cramped and inconvenient. Ethel immediately attacked the confusion, assisted by Jean's absence with the Copes at Gordon and had little time for her diary till 13th, when she wrote:

The drawing room is almost itself, – looks very nice with its pale green walls & ivory paint, the soft moss green carpet with careless flowers on it here & there & the big wide bay looking out over the dancing blue harbour.

And so by the end of 1901 the 'Three Little Maids' were all settled, Rose, after a protracted courtship, having married Harold Pockley at St John's, Gordon, on 18 June. There were five bridesmaids including two Pockleys and Ethel's darling Jean, who wore a tiny white silk frock with a 'wreath of violets on her curly gold mop'.

*T*he move to 'Avenel' in November 1901 repre-
sented for Ethel an arrival in a safe haven. The
Curlewises were to enjoy the combination of
acres of unspoilt bush overlooking Chinaman's Beach with
ready access to the city by ferry, an almost complete freedom
from immediate neighbours and the opportunity of gradually
developing a terraced garden site that began within easy
walking distance of the Mosman shops and ran down towards
the water.

At ground level the house was brick but rose to an upper
floor and a roof of dark painted shingles. On the southern
side of the house facing a broad lawn a small half-hexagonal
room jutted out. Situated on the ground floor with access
from the dining room, this was later extended to keep pace
with the growth of Ethel's library. It was here, in 1927, that
Harold Cazneaux took the well-known photograph of the
author which shows her leaning out from the open window,
below which can be seen a long box of geraniums in the best
Parisian tradition. On both floors there were large verandahs
facing east towards the sparkling waters of Chinaman's
Beach. When the family entertained, especially during the
adult years of Jean and Adrian, the open verandah on the
ground floor was set up for dancing with coloured lights and
magic lanterns.

Ethel's diary for 1902 began on 9 January with a visit from a writer and his sister who 'said something cutting and unkind of everyone we spoke of'. Ethel expressed doubts, not for the first time, about whether she liked literary people at all. Next day she went with Jean and Adrian to the beach at the Spit, where they met some of Ethel's old school friends and had a lovely swim. After remarking how infrequent such adventures had become she reflected on the complexity and busyness of her life.

I don't think 48 hours to the day would see all my work finished – there are too many 'departments' in life to be head of – probably it is I am a bad manager. But there is the roll-top desk department, & the garden (a big matter at present) & the nursery, which mustn't be neglected, & Society – which is neglected – I've a 100 calls at least owing I believe – & the Clothes department & the House Linen & the Pantries, & the orders & the servants ... & H does get his buttons off dreadfully. And then there is Shopping. And the calls of one's family, – & the rights of one's husband to have me at leisure in an evening, & letters, & accounts, & & & & &

I suppose it is the removal & the summer & disturbed nights with the boy – when I get alright again I'll steer my boat better.

In late March Ethel took the children, with their nanny in attendance, to stay for a fortnight at Hazelbrook in the Blue Mountains. Herbert saw them off on the 4 p.m. train. At Miss Rahm's boarding house they settled into a regime of short walks, weather permitting, and almost every day Ethel was able to do some writing. She worked on the Dame Durden competition page for the *Town and Country Journal* and wrote two school songs that had been requested by Angus & Robertson, 'Cooee' and 'A Song for Rain'.[1] The manuscript of the first verse concluded with these lines:

Just be kind, great Sun, today,
Hide your burning face away
Let the clouds roll up & darken till the
Sky is all deep grey
Just be kind, great Sun, again
Let your glory quickly wave
And bid your Queen rule over us,
The Rain, sweet Rain.

After a separation of nine days, Herbert joined his family for the weekend, when he and Ethel walked to the Terrace Falls and to nearby Lawson. It was a pattern that was to be repeated many times, especially when the Curlewises had their own cottage at Leura.

When Ethel and the children were back within their 'own dear walls' they went to see Rosie, whose first baby, 'such a dear, pretty, big boy' was baptised Robert Campbell Pockley at the Anglican church in Gordon where all of the three little maids had been wed. Soon after, Rose and her child travelled by coastal steamer to Coraki to join Harold at his farm in the Richmond River district.

While at Hazelbrook Ethel had begun work on a play, 'The New Tutor', for the hope of succeeding as a writer for the professional theatre had not been extinguished by the failure of *The Wig* in 1895. The collection of her papers at the Mitchell Library includes a volume of incoming correspondence from the principals of theatre companies dated from 1900 to 1921. It begins with Charles Arnold of the English Comedy Company and goes on to reveal such famous names as Edward Terry, Frank Thornton and J. C. Williamson, most of whom showed a genuine regard for her standing as a writer and a desire to guide her to success as a playwright. During this time Ethel wrote as many as ten plays – their titles are often not identified – but not one of them was performed.[2]

Within two days of returning from the mountains Ethel was visited by Mr Marriner, agent in Australia for The Religious Tract Society, which had published *The Wonder-Child*. The fruits of that visit became evident at the end of May when she started writing a new story for the society provisionally entitled 'Under God's Sky'. It was a productive period, for on 17 June she posted to the *Idler* in England a story entitled 'The Marriage Morn', which was published nearly three years later in *McClure's Magazine*, New York.[3]

Illustrated with sensitive, tinted drawings by F. Y. Cory, 'The Marriage Morn' is one of Ethel's happiest stories, redolent with the glow she still felt in thinking about her own wedding day. Ellice Layton is woken from a deep sleep by her young sister who has her own expectations about the approaching ceremony:

'How *can* you go on sleeping and sleeping? ... why, it's the very day!'

Then Ellice sat up in bed ... 'What day?' she said faintly.

The child gazed at her speechlessly. 'You can't have forgotten,' she cried; 'why, it's the day I'm going to be bridesmaid!'

The story is strongly autobiographical, for the Laytons are modestly circumstanced and struggle to maintain two maidservants. Ellice had been tempted the night before to slip away in the morning, telling her parents in between sobs that, 'She couldn't dress up in all those strange white clothes and be stared at by crowds of people ... She would rather just stay herself, and not plunge blindly into any strange waters'.

The father, a big, gruff man, reminds us of Charlie Cope:

fretting and fuming in the passage. He kissed her with sudden violence when she ran out to him, then blew his nose stormily ...
'What's the use of bringing a daughter up to the age of twenty-

two and then having her desert her home? But you girls have no gratitude. Off you go at the first chance, and never care a button about those left behind.'

There is as well an anxious mother who has similar skills in household management to Sarah Cope and a sibling, in this case the younger sister, 'poor fractious, delicate atom, whose little body had been brought up with such difficulty that her nature had been entirely spoiled'. Lilian, without a doubt. At the ceremony itself the bridegroom showed no sign of nerves, but the gruff old father was in tears and shaking like a leaf, though he did not follow Cope's lead by seizing the first kiss.

During these months Ethel and Herbert saw a good deal of both of their families. Charles Cope made several visits to 'Avenel', usually on his own, often staying overnight and spending long hours helping with the task of erecting trellises around the house and garden. It was a timely return for the labour Herbert had performed at 'Inglewood' and 'Bukyangi' almost ten years earlier. At the beginning of June, in spite of threatening weather, the whole family went to Burwood to spend a day with Lilian and Fred, Ethel sewing with her sister and Herbert helping Fred painting, for the Thompsons were still 'very upside down' in their new home. Later in the month Dolly Curlewis had a few days at 'Avenel' helping Ethel when she was busy writing 'The Marriage Morn'; this was followed by a visit from Marmee, as Herbert's mother was called (after the character in *Little Women*), when she came from Stanmore to 'play with the children' while Ethel sped off to see her own mother, who had injured her leg tripping on some damaged carpet in a railway carriage.

Affectionate and useful co-operation within the extended family was continued when Sarah Cope came in August to lend her formidable skills in making bed drapery for the spare room at 'Avenel' and next day Ethel took Jean to see the Glass Works and Bakewell Pottery that Mr Curlewis managed. After lunch Jean announced her desire to stay at 'Hermsley' for several days, which seemed a good idea as it gave Ethel the chance of writing chapter four of 'Under God's Sky'. But late the following afternoon Marmee rang ... it seems both families had the telephone ... to say they were returning Jean as she was homesick. 'I wanted my own little Mummy,' she said, when she got back within the circle of Ethel's arms.

These idyllic images of family life contrast sharply with the constant upsets described by Ethel's diary during the 1890s. The peace that descended upon 'Bukyangi' after the last of the three stepdaughters married suggests that the mixed composition of the Cope family had been the genesis of the problem.

In spring Ethel went again to the mountains in the hope of breaking from domestic routine and stayed for two weeks with Jean, Adrian and a nurse at Wentworth Falls. Within six days she had completed the second and third acts of her play 'The New Tutor' and had to buy another exercise book at the local store. Herbert came up for the second weekend during which Ethel took Jean to church for the first time; she caused some embarrassment to her mother by asking in a loud voice as soon as they entered, 'Mumsie, did you remember to bring the money?'

Soon after their return to Sydney Jean embarked on the great adventure of having daily lessons. Ethel had engaged Miss Evans, a kindergarten governess, to come to 'Avenel' to teach her own and four other children each morning. Jean was 'intensely excited & had a little stack of books & "properties" prepared long before breakfast'. The actual classes are not mentioned in the diary until the following June, when the teacher did not come and Ethel took her place, quite enjoying 'giving the chickens their drill & songs & clay modelling'.

Miss Evans, however, is discussed at length in the 'Baby

Book' Ethel kept for about twelve years to record Jean's progress. From this document we learn that Ethel Jean Sophia was 'the most wonderful baby ever seen', that she was 'short coated' at seven weeks of age, by which time she slept contentedly all night except when she wakened for her food. At 18 months she was very fond of the beach and ran bravely into the waves without being held, liked having stories told or books shown more than anything and was soon:

very great chums with her father, & always has half an hour with him in the rocking chair after the bath, – 'Ing' she commands & he sings 'Here upon my vessel's deck' & songs from Comic Operas.

After seeing the governess at work for two months Ethel wrote confidently:

Miss Evans seems the very right person in the right place, she is gentle with the children & yet firm, has a thorough knowledge of her work & interests them all the time.[4]

Ethel had no desire for her daughter to be exposed early to formal lessons. A year earlier Jean had gone to kindergarten, for companionship and to learn to use her fingers and occupy her time, but not until ten o'clock each day when the lessons in reading and writing were over.

At her fourth birthday Jean was 'tall for her age & as pretty as ever, clear hazel eyes, clear skin with good colour, golden hair – darkening a little – a fluffy, curly mass all round her head'. And her mother added with evident satisfaction, 'Barely knows her alphabet which she has picked up someway' and though she could add and subtract in her head she could not write numbers at all.

Not surprisingly, Ethel tells some charming little stories of

Jean's sayings and adventures. At two and a half she told her parents:

'Well an' so was once a little girl an' had lovely golden hair tight down her back, – all *this* long, an' her Mama said not go up steps an' get lost for anysing. An' her Mama went to town, an' little girl *went* up steps an' she walked an' she walked sroo the bush an sud'nly zere came a drefful monstous noise an' (finger up, voice fallen to a sepulchral whisper) an' what you does fink it was? It was ze Plague'.

– she has heard Nurse & Nellie talking of the Plague & imagines it I suppose like some Ogre.

After being taken at three to see Nellie Stewart and company in 'Cimbrella' she dressed herself every day in ribbons and bath towels and came to Ethel continually with one of her shoes on a cushion, insisting on her trying it on, making the rest of the household perform their parts.

The first of the theatre entrepreneurs to see 'The New Tutor' was J. C. Williamson, who wrote an encouraging letter in February 1903 saying he thought well of its dialogue and literary qualities but considered the plot insufficiently strong and 'rather too ingenuous for present day audiences'. He thought she could achieve success with a good plot and advised her to map out the details and write a full scenario before going on to the play proper.[5]

Impatient for progress, Ethel sent 'The New Tutor' to Charles Arnold, who had advised her at length two years earlier. Now back in England, he wrote from Beckenham in similar terms to Williamson. It emerged that one of Ethel's problems was a lack of familiarity with the mechanics of the theatre. As in 1900, Arnold considered that the play was 'not actable', largely because of the 'fatal' error of long and frequent asides, which created the most awkward situations for the other actors on the stage. As he said, 'It is bad "construction" to keep them silent so long – they must be off the stage.' Williamson's solution to this mechanical problem, passed on in relation to a new manuscript, 'Keeping up Appearances', was for Ethel to get an amateur society to perform one of her pieces to 'assist your idea of construction and stage business'.[6]

One of the larger changes in Ethel's life and outlook had occurred when women in New South Wales received the right to vote in state elections as an indirect result of the Commonwealth Franchise Act of 1902. On 1 February 1903 Dr Arthur visited 'Avenel' in company with Mr Campbell, a candidate for the Warringah electorate who 'gravely said he came to solicit my vote. How important we feel with our new dignity'. So, in contrast with her earlier view that the business of politics was somehow unfeminine, Ethel now began attending political meetings in Mosman homes in the Liberal interest and even going on committees, for her involvements were never half-hearted.

For the first time Ethel as a writer went beyond the role of an entertainer to express views on issues of broad significance, though not of a party political character. It had been a year of severe drought in eastern Australia and something, perhaps the fact that her sister Rose Pockley was now on the land, brought home to Ethel a consciousness of the hardships endured so frequently by Australian farmers. On 28 November she had published in the Sydney *Daily Telegraph* a long 'Appeal for Bush Sufferers' intending to draw attention to the frightful distress in the bush and suggesting a 'Bush Box' scheme that might offer practical relief.

This concern was carried further in Ethel's letter to the editor of 7 February 1902 expressing astonishment at the apathy shown by the public in responding to appeals by the Drought Relief Committee and contrasting the 17,000 pounds collected by the Melbourne fund with the puny 700 pounds collected so far by Sydney. Part of the trouble, she thought, came from the tendency of the bush to accept evils and suffer long and hard before calling for help. The free distribution of seed wheat by the Government would be of long term value but more immediate charitable efforts were essential.

The *Daily Telegraph* responded to the suggestions made by Ethel and another correspondent by beginning its own Drought Relief Fund on 11 February, though publishing on the same day a letter from William Holman, one of the leading spirits in the State Labor Party, pouring scorn on her suggestions. Holman felt the 'appreciative recollection of several charming works of Ethel Turner' would temper the indignation felt by distressed selectors at reading her 'condescending patronage' but he denied that they were 'mendicant Ishmaels of the Bush ... The settlers of Australia,' he added, 'so far from being the objects of cheap benefactions of this kind, are as proud and independent a race as the men of the American backwoods.'

Most of the following letters sided with Ethel rather than Holman and, with the help of friends such as Jessie Arthur and Mrs Storm who collected from door to door, a good start was made for the *Telegraph* fund. Ethel herself gave ten guineas and on 14 March, 'Spent a strange & horrible day, only made endurable by the thought of the suffering Bush, – viz, took post on the Mosman wharf as one of the collectors for "Drought Saturday" for eleven hours'. Four days later she and Jessie Arthur attended the concert given by Nellie Melba in aid of the drought fund. As another gesture the family took tea into the bush and Ethel finished off a story entitled 'Giving Up', which she described as a Drought Sketch, but there was still work to be done packing Drought Relief clothes with Jessie Arthur.

From this kind of involvement in community affairs it was not difficult for Ethel to take the further step towards party politics. Richard Arthur, her friend and doctor, was about to stand for the seat of Middle Harbour as a Liberal and Reform candidate for the Legislative Assembly, joining the association founded in 1902 by Ethel's old friend Joseph Carruthers, soon to become victorious at the July 1904 elections by forming an alliance of 'Liberalism, temperance and Protestantism'. Early in June 1903 the Curlewises went to hear Carruthers speak on political reform. Though Ethel had formerly appeared unconcerned about the issue of female suffrage we now find her making the supreme sacrifice by speaking for the Political League to an audience of fifty women. Sir James Graham introduced her and she asked permission to read her speech as 'every idea would have vanished if I tried to speak "without the book".' In September she attended a Women's Political Social at Mrs Cullen's home 'Tregoyd', which she later thought had succeeded in its purpose in widening the net of political influence to include more women.

In June Ethel had felt a new book starting to take shape in her head; by late July it was given the provisional title, *The Child that was Lost*, and to her great pleasure she succeeded in writing a whole chapter, 'an event I felt was never coming off again'. Her pleasure and satisfaction in balancing various commitments is evident in the diary entry of 22 July, 1903. 'Played with the chickies, sewed with H in the tool room, & wrote again at night.' A silly accident, however, soon upset the balance: Herbert was playing with Adrian – who is still described usually as 'Little Boy' just as Jean for years was 'Little Girl' – and when swinging him by the arms as so many fathers do, dislocated his left shoulder. Two doctors came to look after him and Ethel held his hand while the chloroform took effect. After the X-rays had revealed no fracture Adrian was taken to town to be feasted on sponge cake, indulged with all the toys he desired and given a pet canary.

Two months later, Ethel and the children set out early for the Blue Mountains, picking up Lil and her son at Strathfield, intending to look at land on which to build a holiday cottage. At the end of the week, Herbert came to Leura with Rex Cope to inspect the land the women had been looking at. All agreed that the best blocks were in Balmoral Road, forming part of a large holding owned by the writer John Le Gay Brereton. A decision was made on a corner block for which they paid 60 pounds, securing a hundred feet of frontage. It had been a happy holiday with the children enjoying each other's company and the two sisters having close contact of the kind they'd been denied since they were married. In November Ethel went to Leura again with Rex Cope to take the levels for the foundations and arrange a contractor.

Into the new year, not a week passed without some shopping being done for the furnishing of the new mountain cottage and even the nurse was pressed into service making up linen for the cottage from forty yards of sheeting.

For Jean's birthday treat in February the Curlewises and Thompsons all went to Manly, advertised on the old ferries as being 'forty minutes from Sydney and a thousand miles from care'. Rides for all on the donkey and for Jean a hard gallop on a white pony. In the big pool they tried the much vaunted water chute, which took a bit of nerve to put one's trust in but delivered a splendid thrill. Even Herbert had three goes though the nurse was too timid. Jean declared it was the loveliest birthday yet. Next day a quick trip to check on progress at the Leura cottage, which Ethel found more appealing than expected. Tea at Knight's Boarding House and back to town for Herbert to meet her.

A year earlier there had been a rash of robberies in Mosman including a desperate struggle between a householder in Raglan Street and an intruder. Perhaps this had lain heavily on Ethel's mind, for in February 1904 Ethel had a 'burglar fright' in the night and Herbert went downstairs with a revolver but found nothing. Always ready to make use of such a stimulus, Ethel sat up in bed till late writing a story, 'In the Silence of the Sleep Time'.[7]

This story, which was soon published in the *Windsor Magazine* and again in another Ward Lock collection entitled *The White Roof Tree*, was indeed a thriller. Jim Charlton, a wealthy young householder, had gone downstairs in the dead of night and shot a burglar, who was now lying on the white bearskin hallway rug, staining it with his blood. While doctor and police are on their way the intruder is revealed as Wilkins, who had been given temporary work in the householder's garden to tide him over a lean time. Passing through his mind as he lay on the floor was his hatred for the upper class and awareness of the contrast between his own hulking shape and the figure of the man who had shot him, 'well proportioned, athletic, graceful in its light flannels'.

A distraction gives the intruder a chance of using his own revolver, which he aims at the breast of the woman, clad in a pale blue trailing gown, thinking to give his enemies a taste of how it felt to 'lie and welter in one's own blood'.

What saves the day is the appearance of the little girl, whom the burglar recalls with sudden tenderness as having tried to enlist him in her play, acting as the prince to her Cinderella. So he abandons thoughts of revenge and to reward him, Charlton takes his family upstairs and carelessly leaves the front door open, through which the intruder can make his escape.

Giving penetration to the story is its use as a vehicle for Ethel's social conscience, expressed as a concern about the long-term effects of a child's formative years. She tries to imagine what pointed the burglar towards crime and considers how the little girl had touched his heart, clearly thinking of Jean's relationship with old John, the gardener at 'Bukyangi'. As in *The Little Larrikin* Ethel voices dissatisfaction with the existing system of rewards and punishments and the crippling disadvantages of society's victims. 'What chance had he ever had,' was the thought that ran through the intruder's mind as he lay on the floor.

During the first week in March cases and furniture were despatched to Leura and on the Saturday Ethel and her mother took an early train with the children and a nurse and began unpacking. Workmen were still busy, held up especially with the outside painting by wet weather. Mrs Cope left after several days of hard labour and was replaced in the spare room by Lil who looked much in need of a break. The household was expanded next day by the arrival of Herbert, missing his wife and taken aback by the realization that she felt their time apart had passed with breathless speed. The little three-bedroom cottage became very cramped with the arrival of Mrs Cope's servant, Alice, who came unexpectedly to take the mountain air with her little boy because she was run down. Small wonder that Ethel wrote 'the holiday rest is very like real hard work'. And of course the tanks were emptied by the crowd, for they forgot to be careful with water.

With the departure of Alice and her son Jack, 'a dreadful child' who made a deafening noise all the time, life began to return to normal but 'before there was time to draw breath' Rosie arrived with her young nurse and two babies thus re-uniting the three sisters in a rain-beseiged cottage which Ethel now wished she had never built. She was longing for the quiet & comfort of home and was relieved to re-enter 'dear old Avenel' just before noon on 2 April.

Able now to resume her normally productive life, Ethel arranged for *The Gift Impossible* to be professionally typed and sent off to Ward Lock; it was the subject of an earnest discussion over dinner with William Steele in June, for Ethel tried to insist on its being presented, at least to the English public, in a form that broke away from the 'peas in a pod' format which troubled her about the Australian editions of her books. Steele cabled the firm in England putting Ethel's view and at the end of the week Herbert helped her compose a letter to Steele absolutely refusing to give way. She learned in September that the firm was immovable on that point and had also changed Ethel's *The Gift Impossible* to *Mother's Little Girl*, which she described angrily as a 'vulgar, namby pamby title'.

Vexed as Ethel was by this dispute with Ward Lock, *Mother's Little Girl* sold almost as well as her other titles, except for *Seven Little Australians, The Little Larrikin* and *Miss Bobbie*. In the nine years to January 1914 it had made over 347 pounds for its author in royalties and serial rights and the first edition of 13 000 had sold in eighteen months.[8] Its theme was the familiar one of transplantation; in this case a poor and sickly young mother with a big family is induced by a childless elder sister married to a Queensland grazier to give her last baby up for adoption, just as Ethel herself had been sought from Sarah Turner by a rich English uncle.[9]

Another issue Ethel took up at this time with Ward Lock was her desire to abandon an exclusive identification as a children's writer and join the main players in the literary game. G. E. Lock wrote to her in September 1904 noting her remarks about 'wishing to appear not as a writer *for* children but *about* children' and warning that the consequence would be a hundredfold drop in sales. This letter from the London office is one of several in which the head of the firm felt obliged to use plain speaking to clear up misconceptions, while assuring Ethel of his continuing desire to publish her work.[10]

On the matter of royalty levels Lock insisted that the firm was giving her better terms than afforded to any other writer including such people as Anthony Hope, Phillips Oppenheim and A. W. Mason. They had made a mistake from the beginning in publishing her books in a costly form though at the low price of 2 shillings 6 pence, a formula from which it was difficult to depart now it was well established. Though selling in large volume her books had the tendency in the Ward Lock list to 'drag other books ... down to the same unprofitable level'. Their further mistake was to spend much money and time advertising her books in the English market, 'not having sufficiently grasped in the first place the fact that it was their Australian character that conduced so much to their success in Australia'. Ethel persevered with Ward Lock for several years before trying other firms in the hope of gaining access to the English and American markets and seeking an adult audience, at length attempting to write thrillers under a pen name.

Chronic financial problems within the family of Herbert's maternal uncle Lucius O'Brien, who had never really recovered from the depression of the 1890s, are mentioned in Ethel's diary in May 1904. The O'Briens were now living in Mosman in reduced circumstances, obliged to supplement their income by using the home as a boarding house. Ethel sees a characteristic solution:

Worried over the O'Briens troubles & Lil's troubles & H's brothers troubles till I could only see one solution – I must write a play that will bring at least 10,000 pounds. Book writing only produces a quiet, unsensational income. Sketched out a plot that I have had 'simmering' for some time.[11]

Ethel worked on the outline of her projected 'Drama' during the next ten days and sent a sketch of it to J. C. Williamson at the end of May. Three days later he sent a note saying there was 'good stuff' in the play and that it would be all right with a few alterations. He would see her, he said, when he returned from a projected visit to Melbourne but nothing came of the venture until January 1905, when she picked up her long neglected outline and began writing again. Soon after there were encouraging letters from Williamson but it seemed she was still having the same problems as before.

The play [*he wrote*] is well written, full of merit: at the same time, faulty in construction, particularly as regards the arrangement of scenes. The changes could hardly be practicable in its present form.[12]

At the end of her 1904 diary Ethel put together a formidable list of her writing for the year. It had produced a total income of 480 pounds including 293 pounds in royalties from Ward Lock, 78 pounds for the 52 children's pages for *Town and Country*, and 80 pounds in serial rights for England, New Zealand and Australia. A good start had been made on two novels, four short stories had been written, four articles (a genre of journalism to which she was increasingly committed), and five items of verse including the beautiful and wistful poem, 'But where does the winter go?' Nancy Phelan knew Ethel in her latter years and recalls the feeling of acute melancholy inspired in her by this poem; its final verse as published in *The Lone Hand* of 2 November 1908 gives the flavour:

> *Oh, Winter, Winter, my tears are falling.*
> *Are you glad of the tears of a little child?*
> *Though Spring is abroad and calling, calling,*
> *I cling to the edge of your coat so wild.*
> *And I kiss your hand*
> *And I understand,*
> *And I smooth your poor grey head, low-lying.*
> *Ah, I cannot sing*
> *Just yet with the Spring*
> *While Winter, Winter, is pale and dying.*

One of the articles of 1904, 'How I wrote *Seven Little Australians*', published in the magazine *Life* in March, has already been considered. Her piece for the Christmas Eve issue of the *Daily Telegraph*, 'On Snails: and, incidentally, Christmas', begins with a butterfly goading a snail for its dour and laboured life and suggests that many women make the mistake of deliberately accumulating possessions and cares, 'dragging the whole thing' on their backs and making their lives needlessly complex, most of all in the festive season. On the subject of present giving, Ethel doubted the wisdom of mothers who gave elaborate silver manicure sets to their daughters when a similar expenditure on good books would encourage 'strong, sturdy thoughts that would carry a girl over her difficult age and teach her to cease mincing'. Children laboured like their parents under a congestion of possessions, cupboards crammed with presents 'so complete in every detail there is absolutely no scope for their young imaginings'. It was sensible advice, particularly apt and not without an element of self-interest in coming from a children's writer.[13]

The year had seen important events in the family. Lil had her second baby in November while her elder son Douglas stayed contentedly at 'Avenel'. Later the household was further swollen when Lil and her wetnurse and the two babies came to Mosman for a rest. Herbert had begun to suffer from acute dyspepsia in August and needed attention from Dr Arthur several times and an enforced holiday at the mountain cottage in October. This was the beginning of a disability that had an unavoidable influence on Herbert's outlook and on his disposition towards those who lived and worked with him. Perhaps it was under reasonable control in those early years but by the late 1930s he was perceived by his granddaughter Philippa as formidable and austere.[14]

Dr Arthur's success as a candidate for the Middle Harbour seat in the State elections of August 1904 had been almost a family matter. Ethel cycled with Herbert to Neutral Bay to vote, for she seems by now to have become thoroughly interested in the political process, and at night they went into town with the Arthurs to hear Joseph Carruthers announce the results, which enabled him to form his first ministry. Ethel wrote some children's verses, 'After the Battle', a few days later and in celebratory mood she and Herbert took his sister Dolly to the Matron's Ball and danced till one o'clock as if she was still eighteen. On another night there was a 'great event' when she accompanied the Arthurs to the Town Hall to hear Paderewski and realised 'what music can be'. Herbert had stayed at home to give the children a treat with the magic lantern for he had assured his wife that he 'wouldn't walk across the road to hear him'. The marriage, warm as it was, contained some real differences.

The new year began dramatically with news of the surrender of Port Arthur (now Lüshun in North Korea) to the Japanese, an event that signalled to the world the potent fact of Japan's approach to the status of a great power. So Ethel recorded the news on 3 January 1905 with underlining and an exclamation mark. Next day she took the children for a swim and rested on her return to read *Oliver Twist* and Robbie Burns. Bush fires were raging then 'all over the colony'. Ethel attended a meeting to raise funds for the bush fire sufferers, for in spite of her urban preoccupations as a writer there was a lively interest in the fate of the rural community.

During the final week of January Herbert was busy in town until late every night and Ethel used the opportunity to make progress with a new novel, *In the Mist of the Mountains*, which reflected the family's new commitment to the region. 'Marmee' Curlewis came to 'Avenel' to spend time with Jean and Adrian while Ethel wrote solidly for ten hours. Next day she turned out over 3000 words but felt too 'fagged', understandably, to continue after dinner.

To any lover of the Blue Mountains the story has a sure appeal. Its central theme is the embarrassed friendship which grows into love between Miss Bibby, a governess and would-be writer, and a famous English novelist, Hugh Kinross. Miss

Bibby is looking after the children of Judge and Mrs Lomax while they holiday in New Zealand. Lomax, clearly modelled on Ethel's friend Dr Cullen, had created at 'Greenways' a wonderful native garden which had never 'looked crude and painful as the naked places about did' because he and his wife left the existing eucalyptus wherever possible and planted a wind break of Tasmanian blue gum alternated with silver wattle. The tennis court was guarded at both ends by 'soldierly rows of magnificently grown waratahs' and from the judge's walks through the nearby gullies he would return carefully cherishing some little seedling he had dug up with his penknife, ready for adding to the shade of his plantation. Mrs Lomax, English-born, yearned for the richer greens and colours of English cultivation, so the resulting garden saw ashes and elms 'in perfectly friendly relations with the gum trees and wattles'.[15]

At the end of January, 1905, her diary conveys Ethel's pride in recording a day of varied achievement for she worked for eleven hours with short breaks for meals and children. She did a children's page for *Town and Country*, wrote an article 'Fifteen and her Literature' to preface a group of Dickens' sketches and completed a 'pome', which she said 'gave me extreme pleasure in making; a curious fountain of delight seems to spring up in me after the creation of verse, mediocre tho' mine is. It gives me far more delight than prose'. Significant words, expressing the intimate charm and value of her diary. That poem was 'The Rainbow',[16] which begins:

> *Oh, if that rainbow up there,*
> *Spanning the sky past the hill,*
> *Slenderly, tenderly fair,*
> *Shining with colours that thrill;*
> *Oh, if that rainbow up there*
> *Just for a moment could reach*

Through the wet slope of the air,
Here where I stand on the beach.

So busy was Ethel at this time and so concentrated on *In the Mist of the Mountains* that she had finished it by 25 March, commenting that it had 'come easier than any book I have done, – just rippled off the end of my pen'. Perhaps Herbert and Richard Arthur conspired to slow her down, for in February her husband brought home three books for her to read, one of them George Meredith's *The Egoist.* A week later she was engrossed in a book sent to her by the doctor, *Up from the Slums,* giving further nourishment for her social conscience.

In the midst of all this there was an inquiry by the editor of a new magazine *The Red Funnel,* published in New Zealand, seeking a contribution from Ethel. Despite her intention of taking on no new work she felt that the offer of six guineas an episode for a serial story of 2000 words a month represented easy money. So began 'The Boy who Stole a Voyage', which ran from August 1905 to January 1906, telling of two boys who exchanged places, one to leave shipboard life for a normal child's existence in Darlinghurst, the other to sample life on the ocean wave. It was a fertile and entertaining idea, though Ethel found the commitment to writing episodes month after month a most demanding chore.

St Valentine's Day 1905 brought a crisis for the lonely and despairing Jack Creed. Herbert came home early bringing the sodden lawyer with him to stay at 'Avenel' for a week of drying out, or as Ethel put it 'to tide him over his danger'. That the Curlewises were prepared to take on such a task says much for their feelings of loyalty and compassion. On the same day Herbert had the pleasure of seeing his first article in the 'Mirror of Justice' series appear in the *Daily Telegraph.* After publishing several weekly instalments the editor told him he could look forward to a long run; he was to receive three guineas for each article.

This further source of income encouraged the Curlewises to embark on a redecoration of the house. Ethel went into town several times to buy friezes and wallpaper and soon the place was in 'the wildest chaos' with painters and decorators in every room. Towards the end of March she wrote with satisfaction:

The colourings are very successful, Dining room the studio-shade of terra cotta & 'Silent Pool' frieze. Hall art blue with greenish frieze. Top hall, greenish brown with same frieze. Jean's room, soft blue with almost blossom frieze in pink. Spare room same frieze on white walls. Study not decided on.

Jean and Adrian had been sent off to Leura with Lilian and her children while painting smells and confusion reigned at 'Avenel'. When Ethel finally joined them, walking down to 'Yanalla' from the train in the almost dark, she had the thrill that comes to every parent on being reunited with loved children, 'And there were my darlings heads at the lighted window, watching. A very very happy gathering we were'.

When Jean was seven and a half her gentle lessons with Wynifred Evans came to an end because the teacher went off to England. So began an association with Miss Carter's Church of England Grammar School, Killarney, which Jean liked even better 'for she is public-spirited & very keen about all the games & clubs & so on of the school life'. Soon it was evident that she had not been disadvantaged, far from it, by the absence of pressure which had been the keynote of Ethel's approach to mothering. Both there and at Sydney Church of England Girls' Grammar School Jean worked consistently at a high level and showed imaginative and literary capacities of a high order.

Even from England Miss Evans took the trouble to keep

in touch with Jean and Adrian. Ethel wrote to her in May 1906 saying that the children were laboriously engaged in starting letters to their former teacher, who coincidentally was living not far from Nuneaton, where the Turners had lived before their migration.[17]

Though Herbert had a recurrence of dyspepsia he was soon well enough to take a short holiday with Ethel, going by ship to Newcastle early in July and on to Maitland and Thornton to revisit the haunts of his childhood when his father had owned and managed a coal mine. A fortnight later Jean and Adrian made the journey on a sea as smooth as glass and Herbert had the joy of seeing 'his little son running about on his old playground'. In between these jaunts Ethel arranged a peaceful holiday for Herbert at Jamberoo, lush dairy farming land in the hills west of Kiama, to which they had probably been recommended by William Cullen. He had grown up there on a dairy farm, in a region almost exempt from drought, with emerald green hills, rainforest, and an exciting proximity of mountain and sea coast. Ethel wrote of this visit in terms that might shock the Blue Mountaineer:

It is ideal country, infinitely more restful to eye & brain than the Mts. Such quiet green slopes of hills & a winding creek. And Coral trees in flame everywhere.

At the start of September *In the Mist of the Mountains* was returned from Scribners with a polite note. Most disappointing, for she had wanted to 'get out of the Ward & Lock rut & into the American field'. In October, under sustained pressure to keep instalments going to the *Red Funnel* magazine she suffered badly from insomnia and abruptly terminated the career of 'The Boy who Stole a Voyage', vowing never again to take on such a commitment.

That Christmas the Curlewises remained at home instead

of celebrating at 'Bukyangi' with the rest of the family. Yet it proved a happy day, for the 'chickens' vastly enjoyed decorating the tree themselves and putting the presents on it for the first time. Adversity can be a wise teacher.

chapter
Eleven

The insomnia and general malaise of which Ethel complained at the end of 1905 continued to be a problem in the new year. On 1 January she and Herbert took the children to the Copes at Killara for the gathering of the clans attended by all the sons-in-law except Harold Pockley, who had returned early to his farm on the Richmond River. It was a happy day, enjoyed by Jean and Adrian with their cousins on the broad buffalo lawns of 'Bukyangi', but Ethel found it too much for her depleted strength. A few days later there was an evening of bridge at the Arthurs, when she still felt 'very stupid' and unable to concentrate.

Sydney's humid heat in mid-summer 1906 encouraged Ethel to walk down with the children to Chinaman's Beach, often for a pre-breakfast swim. Herbert's young sister Dolly stayed with the family for a week and there is every sign of a desire to avoid intellectual tasks and concentrate on physical health. On 17 January the diary records a firm decision. Ethel had her first golfing lesson from the champion, Mr Souter, when she wrote:

I am going to take it up & let the brassey be mightier than the pen for a time. I am really going to try to do without writing for about six months & grow able bodied & able nerved again.

Ethel ensured that the family spent a good deal of time at the Leura cottage. Mother and son were both unwell in late January so Richard Arthur prescribed a stay in the mountains, in which Jean did not share because she looked forward so much to returning to school at Killarney. 'Yanalla' was looking smart with its new coat of red paint; some extensions had been made and a tennis court lay ready for use at the back of the house. Pine trees now began to define the front margin of the property; they were *Cupressus macrocarpa*, or large conifers, and ninety years later their huge bulk overshadows the little weatherboard home behind. Balmoral Road was then so quiet and grassy that Ethel was able to spend an hour driving a golf ball along its verges while Adrian played with his catapult to keep her company.

In July Adrian also began attending Killarney School situated in an old home on Killarney Street, Mosman, in pleasant walking distance of 'Avenel'. The year before, when Jean had graduated from home lessons with Miss Evans, it was as important an event for the mother as for her daughter. On that day Ethel recorded in her diary a comment that tells us much about the success of her efforts and Herbert's to inculcate self-reliance and self-discipline:

My little girlie's first day at school. I took her & called for her but after today she begs to go all by herself, not even nurse. 'The girls will think I am such a baby', she said. Well, this starts a new era in the little girl's life, – new interests & so on. I expect I shall come to occupy a less important place now in her estimate of things.

And what of Adrian? Part of the answer to that is given by the charming poem 'Walking to School', which was published in the *Windsor Magazine* of June 1910, about four years after he began his daily walks to Killarney:

Now I am five, my father says
  (And what he says you've got to mind)
That mother's not to hold my hand,
  Or even follow me behind.

To see I'm safe. But down the road,
  And all the way up the next street,
I am to walk now quite alone,
  No matter what the things I meet.

Though horrid horses rear and plunge,
  And cows come trampling, big and bold,
And fighting boys are strutting out,
  I shall have no one's hand to hold.

Still, five is really very old;
  It's pretty close to being a man.
Since I a soldier wish to be,
  I s'pose it's time that I began.

I'll swell my chest right out, like this,
  And swing my books behind, just so
And wear my hat stuck sideways on,
  And whistle all the way I go.

When you were five and walked to school,
  And you met things to tremble at,
Were you as brave as great big men,
  Or did your heart go pit-a-pat?

Freedom from the discipline of regular writing gave Ethel more time for charitable activities. In late July she held a tea party at 'Avenel' to raise funds for the Girls' Realm Guild, a service organization founded in 1900 by the Bishop of London to give women of all ages a chance of assisting young girls with education, training and careers. Ethel became a vice-president when the Guild's work spread to Australia and it was to be a means by which she expanded her social horizons and her involvement in the community.[1] In October she took part in a bazaar at Mosman Town Hall that sought to benefit people who were seen as incurable alcoholics. Here too may be seen the growth of an interest, first stimulated by Richard Arthur, which produced *St Tom and the Dragon* in 1917.

The year is singularly lacking in drama or a sense of literary achievement though towards the end she mentions writing a new book with the provisional title of *Olympian Terrace*. In late November a brief effort was made with the play 'Sundowner'; its third and final act was written on 10 January 1907 when she did 'a war dance with the chickens' who were just as excited as their mother. This being the sixth attempt to bring it to fruition she promised 'if Mr. Williamson thinks it is no good it will be the last'. February brought a prompt but misleading response; he said it was 'well written & full of merit, [but] faulty in construction'. On his return from New Zealand he would discuss with her its merits and demerits, so as to decide if it could be 'shaped into good acting form'. Once again, nothing came of these hopes.

The prolonged rest from creative writing was soon judged beneficial. In two days of late February Ethel gathered the last of the material for the volume of short stories published by Ward Lock as *The Stolen Voyage*, completed and despatched to England the manuscript for the *Ethel Turner Annual* and started a short story which produced 'such a rush of good ideas' that she thought of making it into a book.

At Easter the family had a long stay in the Leura cottage. One of the highlights was a golf match between two professionals for the prize of a block of land; Ethel felt a new eagerness for the game and became a member of the Leura club.

The latter part of April was blighted by the whooping

cough that Adrian developed on his return from Leura. Herbert went off on circuit to Goulburn leaving the rest of the family to succumb; 'we are a charming household & have choruses & duets & trios of coughing all day & night'. Silence descends on the diary till May, when Ethel wrote to Fisher Unwin about a new book she had started. It would go to him rather than Ward Lock, the contract providing for royalties on a sliding scale, 10 per cent on sales up to 2000, 12 and a half per cent on the next 4000 and 15 per cent thereafter, on a selling price of six shillings. But there was no time for dallying for she had already sold the English serial rights to *The Girls' Realm* though the manuscript was only half finished.[2]

That Girl was the title of the story Ethel was now writing, its subject a girl named Marie who had been reluctantly adopted by the domineering Mrs Henderson under the terms of a legal obligation she had assumed when Marie's mother had died of smallpox on a voyage to San Francisco. Marie was 'That Girl', the name expressing Mrs Henderson's angry disenchantment with the task of caring for a stranger's child until she was eighteen.

Like many of Ethel's stories this one was set in a lovely harbourside suburb of Sydney that could well have been Mosman. When Marie was able to escape from the chores imposed by her 'guardian' she frequently visited the children of Captain Curtis, whose mansion 'Roanoke' commanded the heights overlooking the bay. In the opening scene the children were rehearsing a play with the help of Marie and other friends from the terrace houses that lay below on the margin of the bay; it is the development of Marie's talents as an actress that gives continuity to the story and helps her to break free from Mrs Henderson's tyranny. We find in this tale many autobiographical elements: the familiar theme of a blended family; reminders of Ethel's own early but unrealised ambitions as an actress; even the minor detail of a child struck down by whooping cough like her own Adrian.

In an effort to ensure rapid progress with *That Girl* Ethel took the children to a large homely farm cottage at Mulgoa nestled in pretty country with green hills and a river nearby. They had a private sitting room and a 'comfortable enough bedroom', with all meals and services provided. With one important modification, that in future the children would be left at 'Avenel', it was a device Ethel used several times to win freedom from the task of supervising a home while engaged in a concentrated burst of writing. This time it did not work very well, for the children accompanied her and they were still recovering from whooping cough, a malady that was aggravated by the cottage's poor drainage. Yet in the fortnight away from home she wrote six chapters making about 20 000 words, enabling her to complete the book by 1 July and win the reward she had promised herself of a new Broadwood piano/pianola.

Early in 1909 Ethel and Herbert began to plan an extended tour of England and Europe for themselves and the children. Ethel determined to effect savings that would help pay for the holiday and leave a balance for the purchase of pictures and *objets d'art* in Europe.

The wedding of her half-brother, Rex Cope, at 'Avenel' made something of a hole in these promises of austerity. The house was decorated with white flowers and wedding bells and supper was taken on the verandah. Jean, then aged 11, was a bridesmaid for Marie, whom Rex had courted discreetly when visiting the Curlewises at Leura.

February and March were busy months with good progress recorded on Ethel's next book, *Fugitives from Fortune*, which William Steele wanted to secure for the Ward Lock imprint, offering serial rights in the *Windsor Magazine* as an inducement for Ethel to return to the fold after giving *That Girl* to Fisher Unwin. This novel makes a significant break with everything that has preceded it, for there is no domestic comedy, a miniscule plot and little interest in character except as a means of ventilating the author's interest in the relationship between wealth, happiness and virtue. Clearly it is anything but a children's story, for it centres on the attempt of an American millionaire to break free with his family from the trappings and anxieties of a luxurious life which is finally dependent on the vagaries of Wall Street. The novel serves to express Ethel's belief in the merits of a compromise position midway between the extremes of wealth and poverty; in the last resort the primitive simplicity of the life imposed on his family by the millionaire became unacceptable because it denied the basic human need for beauty and variety.

In February Ethel also completed the 'Diary of a Dairy Farm' which ran as a serial in the *Town and Country Journal* and which Cassell described as 'a very pretty piece of work', offering to publish it both in serial form and as a book. Though this did not eventuate, in January 1911 Ethel's newly appointed literary agents wrote to tell her they had sold the English serial rights for 12 guineas to another magazine, *The Woman at Home*.[3]

Society was not neglected. Captain Wilson rang from Government House on behalf of Miss Rawson, the governor's daughter, a patroness of the Girls' Realm Guild, inviting Ethel to come over privately with the children to say goodbye as the Rawsons were returning to England. A Saturday morning visit to Government House was followed by lunch with the Copes at 'Bukyangi' and attendance at the opening of the Killara Golf Club. Early in April there was a reception given at the Sydney Town Hall, where they met the new governor and his wife, Lord and Lady Dudley.

By early May Ethel was again in a 'splendid mood' for work and wrote two chapters of a new novel *Fair Ines* in a day, finishing at 1.30 a.m. With the needs of the overseas trip planned for 1910 very much in mind she went alone to

Merrylands in western Sydney to see what could be done with a concentrated period of writing:

A tiny cottage with a spotless bedroom, comfortable little sitting room, & an old English woman to cook for & mind me. No one I know within miles, but a telephone across the road to ring up & see H and the babes are well. Mrs Curlewis is going to stay with them.

On the first day she wrote till 11 p.m. taking half an hour off for meals and sensibly going for a long walk. Three chapters were produced making 7100 words – a huge output. At the end of four days she had written eleven chapters and contentedly caught the train back to Sydney to be met by Herbert and taken home.

I didn't think it could be done ... But it is the way to work – to get right away with your characters & not to have time to forget just what they might do. Of course it may be poor stuff – but I don't think so – it came easily & happily enough.

Fair Ines was completed at a more gentle pace on 10 June, when Ethel remarked that 'another one stares me in the face if we are to go to England in Jan. *Can* I do another this year'. After a break for six weeks she set off again for her 'quarry' at Merrylands 'to put in five hard days digging at my brain'. By the end of the time she had finished twelve chapters of this new book, *The Apple of Happiness*, and looked forward to 'some leisure & skating & fun'. Both books were to be published by Hodder and Stoughton, since Ethel was disappointed with the performance of *That Girl* in the hands of Fisher Unwin and was on the point of deciding to move away from Ward Lock.

In May Herbert had a recurrence of dyspepsia, which kept him in unstable health for months, often requiring him to spend days in bed on a simple diet with large quantities of the Benger's Food prescribed for babies and invalids. Ethel frequently took writing materials into his room and kept him company without losing her own head of literary steam. On 10 August she corrected the typing of the *Fair Ines* manuscript while he lay asleep on the balcony and noted that it should be ready for despatch to England the following week.

Richard Arthur had sailed in February for a world tour on the *Friedrich den Grossen*. When he returned in October Ethel acted as treasurer of a committee that organized a 'conversazione' to receive him, attended by 250 guests. Next day she embarked on a typical venture of self-improvement, a series of elocution lessons with Jean's teacher, Miss Dumulo, hoping this might reduce her nervousness in speaking at public meetings.

Work had resumed on *The Apple of Happiness* in November and with the family's departure on the *Orvieto* looming close Ethel began inducting Lilian into the ways of the weekly children's page for the *Town and Country Journal*, which she was to edit in Ethel's absence. One Sunday afternoon there was a visit from Dowell O'Reilly who brought his '3 little ones' to say hello, marking Ethel's first meeting with Pixie O'Reilly, whom she was to know later as Eleanor Dark. In the 1930s and 40s she became famous as a writer of historical novels about early Australia and wife of Dr Eric Dark, both of them well known as residents of the Blue Mountains and as contributors to the intellectual life of the area.

Jean and Adrian had begun to attend physical culture classes in the city; it did not save them from turning white as sheets when Dr Arthur came to breakfast and vaccinated the family in preparation for the journey to Europe by way of Colombo and Aden. Ethel had the pleasure of receiving from William Steele copies of the *Ethel Turner Birthday Book*, compiled by Lilian and beautifully bound in pale green padded morocco and in white calf. They came with photographs and a two-page Foreword by Coulson Kernahan, the former Ward Lock reader who had so enthusiastically welcomed the manuscript of *Seven Little Australians* in 1893 and who was to prove such an attentive friend during Ethel's time in London.

Ethel wrote to George Lock in December 1909 shortly before embarkation acknowledging the arrival of the 'dainty & pretty' birthday books and returning to him the signed contract for *Fugitives from Fortune*. It was to be the last such occasion for several years, because a series of manuscripts now went to Hodder and Stoughton, for reasons that she now explained to Mr Lock, troubled by what she described as the 'unpleasant task' of breaking with the firm after so many years:

As you know my great concern for years has been for the books to do better in England & America. Every year I have hoped against hope that they would get a start there, – & each year the hope has been disappointed. I waited again this year before finally deciding for your royalty statement to come in & instead of an improvement the English sales have actually gone back. The only hope of America you seem able to offer me is one that ties me for ten years, at same terms. I feel I *must* see whether this cannot be improved upon.[4]

The comment about American sales refers to correspondence in which Ward Lock had passed on to Ethel a proposal made by an unnamed American house which sought to publish editions of her works in successive years. They were to start with *Fugitives from Fortune*, which had a frustrated American millionaire as its central character, binding her to this firm for ten years. On the face of it, this represented her one great chance of breaking into a lucrative market, though the question remains as to whether she would have been able to suit her writing to the tastes of American children.[5]

Simultaneously Ethel wrote to Hodder and Stoughton confirming the recent exchange of cables. They were to publish her 1910 book *Fair Ines* (the title was as yet undecided) paying royalties of 15 per cent on the English edition and 12 and a half per cent on the colonial. Rates on the American edition could be decided when she visited the head office in London.[6]

A detailed and vivid diary was kept by Ethel which survives as a record of travels in Europe and England from the family's arrival in Naples on the R.M.S. *Orvieto* on 25 February 1910. Ethel's travel book *Ports and Happy Havens*, published by Hodder and Stoughton in 1911, drew on these recollections.

The book opens with an account of the ship's day-long stay at Colombo, which for so many Australians in the age of the great steamships offered the first sight of the colour and heady perfumes of Asia:

And now at last I know why to the west of Australia lie all those wide, grey leagues of ocean; why it takes ten days to traverse them ... It is Nature's profound sense of the dramatic. She takes us by the hand, lays a finger on brown lip, and leads us up the interminable pathway. Then she stops, stops dead, and we hold our breath, for we know that one of the great moments is imminent ... and there we are, gaping and blinking at Colombo.

After an extensive tour of Europe, through Italy, Switzerland, Germany, Holland, Belgium and France, the Curlewises landed at Dover where they took rooms at a big boarding house on the sea front, intending to stay for a day visiting the castle and other places of interest. As Adrian seemed a 'little unwell' he remained in bed while the others did the sights, but by the next day a rash had developed which the doctor pronounced to be measles! 'Fortunately not a bed case but no joke when travelling ... No use kicking against it though so we are making the best of things', Ethel wrote philosophically on 9 April.

Here an unkind fate took a share in the family's plans. Unwilling to take the risk of complications by moving Adrian from a warm home Ethel and Herbert took turns in minding the patient and travelling to London on business. In another twelve days, when Adrian was at last able to come down for meals, Jean was confirmed as having measles, so the process resumed. All told they spent nearly five weeks at the boarding house instead of the intended day.

Herbert saw Ethel off to London ('all my lone self') with some misgivings. She enjoyed the three hour journey through the countryside, got out at Charing Cross and crossed the Strand gingerly 'mindful of my warnings' but found it not so hard as she imagined. 'More wild gazing at the dear dear streets – I could have kissed the pavements', she wrote. Some quick shopping, largely for the 'babes in the Dover wood' and a return to Herbert by 10 p.m.

On her second trip to London Ethel stayed for several days and found herself at last in the office of Ward Lock, 'the Warwick House Salisbury Square of my books'. George and Leslie Lock were 'very nice indeed' to her, as well they might be, in spite of recent disagreements. The latter gave her a cheque for royalties of 259 pounds, took her to open an account at the Bank of New South Wales and entertained her to a lunch of chops, Welsh rarebit and fine old wine 'just as Dr. Johnson wd. have had'. With the help of an address suggested by Mabel Pockley she found the perfect place in Princes Square for the family to use as a London base and next day bought material for an evening dress that was to be made up in time for the Whitefriars banquet on 6 May. Back again to Warwick Square to see Hodder and Stoughton about proofs and serial rights for *Fair Ines*, attempting also to persuade them to take Lilian's book *Fairy*. Time remained before the return to Dover to see a third publisher, Mr Fisher

Unwin, who seemed pleasant enough but gave most unsatisfactory news of sales for *That Girl.*

Pressed by Herbert not to miss the occasion Ethel returned to London and attended the banquet at the Trocadero as the guest of Coulson Kernahan. At last she had met one of the first English literary figures to recognise and promote her talent. Ethel wore a pale blue silk crepe frock, was introduced to the president, Sir Gilbert Parker, who said he'd read her books ever since they first appeared, and enjoyed the brilliant affair exceedingly. Kernahan escorted her home.

While at the banquet Ethel heard that King Edward had died just before midnight. Back in Dover next day she felt 'as if all England is transfixed by the thunderbolt'. Jean, now much improved in health, was able to watch from her upstairs window the proclamation ceremony for King George V which was performed on a platform just below with troops and bluejackets forming a square, joined by the Mayor and councillors in robes of state. When a furious hail storm lashed the official party Jean produced a neat *bon mot*, 'Hail King George, Reign King George'. As the Town Crier read the proclamation:

Dover Castle blinked down on it all with its furrowed grey face & its narrow grey eyes just as it had blinked on all the other scenes in its history.

Since the entire population seemed to be in inky black Ethel bought mourning clothes lest she be arrested for high treason. Leaving the children at home on a cold day to recreate the field of Waterloo with toy soldiers, Ethel and Herbert went on a pilgrimage to the Royal Exchange, the Bank of England, the Monument and the old gates of the Navy House, following the haunts of which Samuel Pepys had written in the diary they enjoyed so often. Lunch at an A.B.C. restaurant, then to Chancery Lane and the Record

Office Museum, which was crammed with 'wildly interesting things', the Doomsday book, letters of Marie Antoinette, Napoleon, Nelson and Washington, followed by afternoon tea at the Old Cheshire Cheese where they sat in Dr Johnson's seat.

Late May brought one of the most memorable experiences of the tour. Lady Tennyson, wife of Lord (Hallam) Tennyson a former governor of South Australia and son of the poet, had noticed a paragraph in *The Times* mentioning the presence of the Curlewises; she wrote asking them to spend the coming weekend at 'Aldworth' in Sussex. Ethel thought 'there was nothing in the wide world' she would like better. Herbert remained in London with Adrian while mother and daughter caught the train to Haselmere to be met by her hostess driving a pair of black ponies. Through a 'dear old village' and country lanes they passed right to the top of a hill on which 'Aldworth' was perched, looking down to a vast plain and beyond it a 'grey glimpse of sea'.

Upstairs in their connecting bedrooms Jean and Ethel found their clothes unpacked and a maid preparing to help them into their evening dresses ready for dinner – 'but what shd I do with a maid' Ethel mused. They dined with three footmen behind them at a round table lit by silver candles with shaded lights. Yet it was 'not a bit stiff' and the conversation flowed easily over travels and books, their host drawing Jean out until she chatted comfortably with him, eliciting the later comment that 'she had quite a wonderful knowledge of books'.

In his study next day Lord Tennyson showed them mementoes of his father including the laurel wreath presented by Queen Victoria to mark his appointment as Poet Laureate. It was a Sunday so they drove to the village church in a landau accompanied by servants; there was a typical English rector and a verger to 'take up the threepenny bits'. After dinner that night, at Ethel's request, Tennyson read

'Inglewood', at Lindfield, where Ethel wrote *Seven Little Australians*

Circular Quay, at the turn of the century. Courtesy of the Sydney Water Board

Louise Mack, Ethel's friend (and rival). Photographed by Elliott & Fry, London, to illustrate 'What Australians are doing'. Courtesy of the Mitchell Library

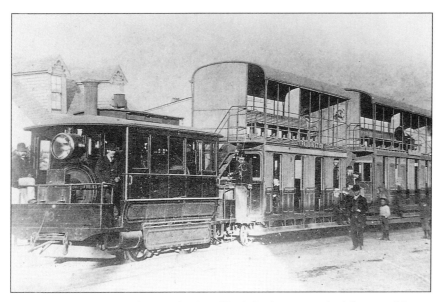

A double-decker steam tram, of the type familiar to Ethel in her journeys to school. Courtesy of the Sydney Water Board

Banjo Paterson. This portrait was published in his *Man from Snowy River and other verses*

Henry Lawson and his daughter. Courtesy of the Mitchell Library

The Mosman Ferry at the time Ethel and Herbert began living at 'Yanalla'. Courtesy of the Sydney Water Board

Military Road c. 1923. Courtesy of the Mosman Library, Local History Collection

Jean Curlewis, aged 3

Adrian Curlewis, aged 2

Family group at Killara on Christmas Day 1906. Back row: Rex Cope, Herbert Curlewis, Mr Cope, Fred Thompson. Seated: Rose Pockley, Ethel Curlewis, Adrian, Jean, Mrs Cope, Lilian Thompson

Family outing with Herbert's father and uncle

Balmoral Beach, showing the 'island'. Courtesy of the Mosman Library

'Avenel', home of the Curlewis family from 1901

aloud several of his father's poems, 'The Revenge', one of the great narrative poems of the English people, 'The Passing of Arthur' from 'The Idylls of the King' and some lyrics. When Jean went to bed and their host to his study Ethel stayed up with Lady Tennyson exchanging confidences like old friends, as one can so often do with a perfect stranger.

On leaving 'Aldworth' Jean was given an inscribed copy of the *Ballads* and Ethel was promised Hallam Tennyson's two-volume biography of his father, while she arranged to inscribe some of her books at Ward Lock's and have them sent as presents to the Tennysons. Leslie Lock introduced Ethel to the editor of the *Windsor Magazine*, who asked her to keep up the flow of stories and verse. One likely consequence was the publication in the June issue of the poem, 'Walking to School' quoted earlier in the chapter. At Fleet Street the following day Ethel spoke to Mr Hodder Williams about *Fair Ines*, which Hodder and Stoughton were to publish. On then to Gay and Bird's making another unsuccessful attempt to place Lilian's collection of short stories and with that rejection sending it promptly to Nelson's.

This was a time of splendid occasions. Ethel barely had time to dress for a reception at the Ritz given by Sir George Reid, the Australian High Commissioner, for Teddy and Mrs Roosevelt. The former president was told by Sir George that Ethel was 'our most famous Australian authoress'. He was very cordial and assured her he had read her books. Lord Kitchener was there, Admiral and Miss Rawson, whom she had known during Sir Harry's term as governor, and G. K. Chesterton.

June 3rd brought a 'budget of home letters at last'. There had been no news for many weeks and Ethel was becoming anxious. Soon there was word from Lil that 'Yanalla' had been sold for 400 pounds, 'the dear little mountain cot we built with such pleasure' in Balmoral Street, Leura. Despite the pang they were relieved at the news for after such a trip they needed the money.

One Saturday in mid-June Jean and her mother were on their way home from Grosvenor Street when they were passed by the

great Women's Suffrage Procession – 10's of thousands watching, & thousands in the procession, – 500 of the 'Prisoners' marching with silver arrows held aloft & bands playing & banners flying. They are certainly in earnest.

Business matters were never far from the top of the agenda. At the suggestion of an acquaintance at the Writers' Club Ethel visited the literary agents, Curtis Brown and Massie in Covent Garden, hoping through their New York office to facilitate an effective entry into the American market. Hughes Massie was to negotiate the best possible terms for her next novel, *The Apple of Happiness*, arbitrating between the rival claims of Ward Lock and Hodder and Stoughton. Into his hands she would put serials, short stories, three plays including the ever hopeful *Sundowner*, and perhaps a book or two. After this meeting Hughes Massie wrote declining 'The New Tutor' and suggesting that he send *The Apple of Happiness* to the *Ladies' Home Journal* and speak personally to the editor about it as a prospect for serialisation while in New York. He closed with a graceful compliment expressing his 'personal pleasure at meeting you today'. Within a year, however, the arrangement was in tatters.[7]

The Women Writers' Dinner at the Criterion Restaurant was a glittering affair attended by 170 women. Long rows of tables were decorated with pink sweet peas and roses and a seating plan was given to each guest. Not unusually Ethel was honoured with a seat at the chief table where Mrs Beerbohm Tree was the chief speaker. Yet she liked it only moderately, adding:

I am not so keen as I was on the Woman Writer – or indeed for the matter of that on the Man Writer either. They lack something – savour – something. And talk shop too much.

Louie Creed, back in London after five years in Italy, had written several times asking Ethel to visit her. Nothing is said in the diary about where she was living but the entry is nevertheless fascinating:

It is nine years since she came from Australia – fifteen since we were such pen and school friends – yet it all might have been yesterday. She has grown stout – developed a marked accent . . . She kept the room almost dark for some occult reason, so I cd not see her too plainly. She has changed in many respects immensely. She spoke of Creed – asked after him etc. Showed me her last two books Sheridan's Husband & In a White Palace. A very curious evening altogether – & a sad – though she seems happy enough & says she is making 1000 a year, writing for Harmondsworth.

Herbert too was not without his publisher-suitors. John Lane called to express an interest in publishing as a book his 'Mirror of Justice' articles, which had run serially in the *Daily Telegraph*, and invited the Curlewises to a reception at which they met some interesting people. Norman Lindsay was there and seemed 'as keen about old London as we are'.

Practical tasks became dominant for a while. Letters from home brought the news that 'Avenel' had been let again for three guineas a week without plate and linen after only six days empty. The tenants undertook to keep up the garden and telephone. At intervals Ethel had bought heavy trunks in which to store the mass of art work and memorabilia which had been collected ready for Cooks to despatch to Sydney. Leaving the heavy baggage in London, the family set out, late in June, to see more of England.

On the way to Kenilworth Castle, going through the ford past thatched cottages and villages, Ethel felt again 'strange memories crowding of going the same drive when I was about seven'. From there by train to Nuneaton, Ethel intending a quest that had been forming in her mind since coming to England of visiting the Attleborough 'Quarry House' near Nuneaton, where Sarah had gone with Lilian and Ethel to live with her second husband, Henry Turner, some time after Rose was born in August 1873.[8]

Significantly, there seems to have been no attempt to locate the far more modest terrace home in Queen Street, Balby, near Doncaster, where Ethel was born in 1870. Not only was it twice as far from London, but she very probably wished to retain undiminished the romantic image of her birthplace that she presented in *Three Little Maids*.

From Nuneaton Ethel took a carriage hoping to find the old 'Quarry House' but there were several structures known by that name, the most likely contender being a home owned by the Brock-Harrises who showed them all over, hoping to evoke sharp recollections. It seemed larger to Ethel than she recalled, but it was pointed out that a wing had been added:

I remembered a monkey tree & an apricot vine on a wall, & it seemed many things in the beautiful old garden. But *not* a tower place built at end of garden & in which they said George Eliot had written one of her books.

The Brock-Harrises insisted that theirs was the original 'Quarry House', so called since it was built in 1760. 'It is a lovely old English home, with such a garden as is seldom seen', Ethel concluded, and 'I hope that it is the right one'.

In London again to do business with publishers Ethel was inveigled to look at 'Dr Marconi's Circulator', advertised as a cure for deafness. Though feeling ashamed to go in because pretty sure the man was a charlatan, Ethel felt the idea was so much on the right lines she simply had to see the machine. But she stayed only a few minutes and left without buying. 'In the noise of London I am not deaf at all, indeed I hear too acutely – but the still places of the earth (like quiet drawing rooms) still are my bane'.

At the Crystal Palace Herbert took the family on an exciting excursion for its first sight of manned flight, 'Grahame White in a magnificent flight as easy & as well governed as the flight of a bird. It gives one a curious sensation to see the upward swoop for "the very first time of ever".' The experience was to give Ethel the idea of putting a flight across the English Channel into a crucial place in the plot of a still unplanned novel, *The Secret of the Sea*, which was suggested two years later by the sinking of the Cunard liner *Titanic*.

Louie Creed and Ethel met once more, the former very fashionably dressed and wearing handsome furs when she came for supper and a long talk before the Curlewises packed for their departure for France on 26 July. Saying goodbye to the Browne-Mason household in Princes Square, where they had been so comfortable, they caught a last glimpse of Westminster Abbey and Ethel felt a tightening of the throat as if she knew it was her last sight of London.

In crossing the Channel the *Brighton* ran into wild weather so that everyone aboard was ill, all but Herbert and

the babes whom it only exhilarated. They are horribly superior people at sea, these same Curlewises. It comes of being coarse-fibred folks, I tell them. A lady travelling in their company of a higher organization & spiritual temperament went under badly . . . H & the chicks had the indecency to be wildly hungry too & were the only people to go down to lunch.

One of the treats during their visit to Paris came when they ran into a cousin of Herbert's from the Transvaal, who carried the whole party off for lunch in the Café de la Paix. The families spent an afternoon together in the Louvre and the adults went at night to hear *Lohengrin* at the Paris Opera House. Everyone made friends so quickly it became a painful thing to say goodbye a few days later.

The events of the voyage to Colombo seemed to Ethel hardly worth recording; the weather in the Red Sea was so hot that survival became the main ambition. Yet a few days out of Colombo Ethel lunched on deck despite a rough sea and big swell and completed a narrative poem 'The Harmless Passenger'.

The story dwells on one of the classic fears that has troubled parents who travel at sea with their children, that one might disappear over the side without anyone noticing, never to be seen again. 'The Harmless Passenger' had lost her little girl overboard, the authorities assumed, when the woman in charge of the nursery gave way to a moment of inattention. An old salt who had been on board when the incident occurred is used as the narrator:

> *Her Mammy thinks she's hiding by.*
> *Thank God the Lord's the Lord, sez I.*
> *And knows why things like this can be*
> *That puzzles folk like you and me.*
> *I'd like to see her die.*
>
> *'And it was all last week, last week?'*
> *I said as soon as I could speak*
> *And turned my eyes from that poor wreck*
> *For ever playing on the deck*
> *Her frightful Hide-and seek.*
> *'Last week?' he said 'She told you so?*
> *It happened years and years ago.*
> *She'd die if taken off the ship*
> *They have to bring her trip by trip*
> *She's harmless as you know'.*

Though Ethel was a remarkably cool and confident mother, able to rejoice in the feats of derring-do her children performed, the diary entry that follows shows her vivid imagination:

Lay on my lounge & finished my poem 'The Harmless Passenger'. It makes my own blood run cold to write it, & I can't bear the children to go near the side of the ship.

All four Curlewises were deposited safely by the *Osterley* when it berthed in Sydney. By 26 September Ethel was sufficiently in possession of her land legs to attend a welcome home, given by her friends at the Australia Hotel and presided over by Lily Cullen. The memento of the occasion was a booklet covered in green suede leather by Mildred Creed, one of Jack's sisters, with a sketch of Australian children by D. H. Souter, the artist who had illustrated *Gum Leaves* in 1899.

On the following day the Woman's Page of the *Herald* reported the amusing speech, which Ethel read 'in her pretty, simple way'. She had been touched on coming through Adelaide and Melbourne to receive telegrams of welcome. To the crowd of women in the Australia Hotel she spoke of the refreshing experience of travel, which she compared with gathering a bunch of a hundred flowers from a hundred spots. Once home, she said, you realise 'that the actual gathering was not the happiest part of all; you realise that you are going to sit and inhale its sweetness, flower by flower, for years'.[9]

or perhaps four years after returning to Australia Ethel sought repeatedly to find the best possible arrangements for publishing her stories. When she visited Hughes Massie of Curtis Brown and Massie, literary agents, at Covent Garden in July 1910 the question was left open as to which of two firms would publish her next book, *The Apple of Happiness*. Very sensibly, Massie advised her to defer a decision until Hodder and Stoughton's performance in selling *Fair Ines* had been assessed.[1]

By November 1910 Ethel was impatient for a result so she wrote to Massie advising that, in the absence of some dramatic success on his part, she would let Hodder and Stoughton have the new book. In explanation, she told Massie that Hodder's Australian representative had taken orders for the book that seemed likely to excel Ward Lock's average sales, and she assumed their efforts in England and America would at least match those of their rivals. Crucial to this decision was the fact that Hodders were offering 12 and a half per cent royalties on colonial sales, at that stage 2 and a half per cent higher than Ward Lock.[2]

Slow Christmas mails and vacation absences delayed action by Hughes Massie until 12 January, when he cabled Ethel in the following terms:

Hodder sale 7,000, no American. Best offer obtainable Ward Lock 100 pounds advance on 12 and a half per cent royalty for colonial and 15 per cent for England for one book or 150 pounds each for three books.

A covering letter described Massie's negotiations with the rival publishers. Hodder Williams had told him a bleak story; colonial sales of *Fair Ines* were only about 6600 – nearly 3000 down on Ethel's expectations – and the English less than 600. Worse still, there were no orders from America and Hodder Williams had been disappointed at the returns on what proved to be an expensively produced book. When he showed little enthusiasm for the new one Massie spoke again to Ward Lock and finally secured an offer that matched Hodder's in royalties as well as giving hefty advances.[3]

Ethel responded with a most ill-considered action. She ignored Massie's cabled advice, though he was the man on the spot, and went ahead with her decision to leave Ward Lock. Her letter to Hughes Massie expressed disappointment that mail after mail had brought no better news of his management of her affairs and regretted that serial arrangements had not been secured in the United States. She concluded by formally giving notice, cancelling the firm's appointment as her agent.[4]

A month later she wrote to Hodder Williams telling him all this and underlining the anxiety with which she awaited the April royalty statement on the sales of *Fair Ines*. She quoted the figure of 7000 given in Curtis Brown's cable, adding (quite erroneously), 'This I feel sure is a mistake or only refers to a certain edition.'[5]

It is difficult to explain, let alone justify, the course Ethel followed in this affair. Her preoccupation with improving her sales in England and America seems to have betrayed her into a serious error, which brought strong protests from Curtis Brown. They wrote in August 1911 regretting that this should be the outcome of our relationship with you, especially as we feel quite sure that had we received a little more consideration at your hands, the result would have been an entirely different one. As matters stand, we feel your statements to be both inaccurate and injurious.[6]

The Apple of Happiness, the novel which lay at the centre of the discord, tells the story, familiar to Ethel's readers, of a family caught in genteel poverty. The lovely Edna Harley had married the young Scot whom her father had employed to remodel his orchards on modern lines and they had been expelled from her family mansion and treated as non-persons. After fifteen years, during which debts had kept pace with the size of their family, the Gillespies were brought back into the fold and an accommodation of sorts was reached making the proud young Scot dependent once again on his father-in-law.

We see again the recipe Ethel used in her first book: a story depending on the interplay and development of character rather than narrative, though it must be said *Seven Little Australians* has a more dramatic plot than any of her later books. Again, there is an arresting opening, immediately engaging and authentic in dialogue and characterization; it shows the wealthy sister calling on the outcast Edna in an effort at reconciliation:

They were at play when Mrs. Imray first came into their lives, and the play was as uncleanly as it was engrossing. [The children were made up as Hawaiians, on the point of assassinating Cook] ... it was a distinct shock to her when the girl, as the eldest of the party at home, advanced towards her and grinned inkily in would-be-politeness. 'This is Clovernook – Mrs Gillespie's?' said the lady, in dismay ...

'I will go up to the house, children', she said almost gently. 'Some one is there, I suppose – a servant or nurse?'

Fonnie shook her head and smiled cheerfully. 'We're the only ones at home', she said. 'I'm minding us'.

'You're not minding *me*', interposed Gil fiercely; 'I'm seven'.

Ethel's main literary task in 1911 was the writing of a series of articles, initially for the Sydney *Daily Telegraph*, about her travels with the family in 1910. Published as a book by Hodder and Stoughton, *Ports and Happy Havens* was dedicated 'To the three others', for Herbert contributed half the photographs, products of a long-standing hobby, and the children appeared in many of the pictures. For a boy, Adrian seems to have dressed with remarkable smartness, though often with a diffident bend of one knee, while Jean faced the camera with supreme confidence.

This travel book illustrates the way in which Ethel found profitable by-products in many of her life experiences. She was able to sell the book to the Sydney *Daily Telegraph*, which paid 59 pounds for the first serial rights, and made later sales to three other newspapers in Australia and New Zealand. Hopes of English sales were not realized, nor did the *Ladies' Home Journal* in Philadelphia take up the offer. As a book it fell flat, perhaps because of a literary and didactic flavour to which her readers were unaccustomed, and its sales fell short by nearly two thirds of her regular novels.

One of the threads in Ethel's professional life that was taken up again on her return to Australia was the editing of 'The Children's Corner' in the *Town and Country Journal*. Her diary for May 1911 has an entry with special significance for anyone who wishes to assess her impact on the thousands of boys and girls who felt their first literary stirrings as 'Corner Children'. Ethel was careful not to give undue encouragement to her young correspondents, lest she cause the pang of unrequited hopes, but when she did feel sure of a child's talent she was prepared to act decisively, as Vera Dwyer, and D'Arcy Niland a generation later, could testify:

At 4 came a girl, Vera Dwyer, one of my Dame Durden girls, to hear my verdict on her ms. I gave it enthusiastically, & am sending her to see Mr Bartholemew to see if Hodder & Stoughton will take it. If not we will try Ward & Lock.

A scrap book kept during these years by Desiree Bertram of Meroo Meadow, Shoalhaven, includes pieces that record Miss Bertram's pleasure in making friends with her Corner contemporaries, one of them being Vera Dwyer, whose photograph was published in *Town and Country* under the caption, A Coming Writer. Vera, a slim and pretty young woman, is holding what appears to be the manuscript of a book and the words that follow show to what effect Ethel had exerted her influence:

The Corner will rejoice to learn that Vera Dwyer, of Ridge-street, North Sydney, whose bright stories were a feature of this page, before she crossed the Rubicon of eighteen, has been using her clever pen to some more ambitious purpose of late ... Her story, 'With Beating Wings', will be published about next September.[7]

Vera's first book was published in 1913 by Ward and Lock; she is represented in the Mitchell Library catalogue by another ten titles, the last published in 1947. From the beginning she was, as Brenda Niall puts it, a member of 'The Turner Circle', using 'the Sydney urban setting, the family conflicts and the problems of genteel poverty with which readers of the Turner novels were thoroughly at home'.[8]

The year after Ethel's return from Europe saw her engaged in a busy range of social activities. With Adrian and Jean at ten and thirteen years of age and aspiring to greater independence in their leisure, the mother could feel more free to indulge her own interests. One expression of this new feeling was her joining the Women's Club; it was to be much used as a place where she could dine in town after a spell of shopping and change into evening clothes for a night function. Late in March she spent an afternoon with Lady Cullen looking at the garden and 'all the alterations necessary to make 'Tregoyd' more fitting for a Chief Justice'.

Gardens and land occupied the Curlewises on their own account. Now that 'Yanalla' had been sold they sometimes resorted for mountain holidays to Lilian's cottage on Hat Hill Road, Blackheath, which had a majestic view towards Govett's Leap, or rented the Doak's cottage adjoining the sixth green at Leura Golf Links. In October they were offered the chance of buying 112 feet of the Doak's land, when Ethel reflected that she would be glad to have her own mountain cottage once again.

Instead of buying at Leura Ethel was suddenly engaged by the prospect of adding a half acre of sloping land to the existing plot at 'Avenel'. Her agent paid 60 pounds more than their limit at auction, making a price of 136 pounds, but she was greatly excited by the thought of laying out fresh garden now that 'Avenel's' precipices and stumps had been tamed, so that it was 'very pretty & restful & running over with flowers'. The new piece, she realized, would have to remain comparatively wild; when she and Herbert dined with the Cullens at Government House a few days later Sir William offered to come over and help with the planning.

The scale of this development together with improvements to the existing garden involved Ethel in heavy expenses on labour and materials for more than two years. A handyman who was hired in December 1911 set up a camp for himself and his family in the bush on the lower level. He made a start on building a low stone wall and a tennis court, which though a source of endless pleasure when it was at last finished, cost much anxiety and expense while a succession of experts gave conflicting advice on the question of making drains to deal with water seeping from higher land. After one

Sunday early in May 1912, in the midst of all this activity, Ethel wrote exultantly:

gardened from morn to dewy eve. Lovely weather. Mrs Armstrong sent me lots of Princess and Red violets, & a boy brought ferns & I had hosts of seedlings to put out. So it was a happy day.

A new gardener, Auguste Heinriche, was added to the 'Avenel' staff, the first one to live there permanently. He proved to be a most willing and efficient worker, responsible for the construction of some 'fascinating new paths' and for laying buffalo grass turf near the tennis court, where Ethel planned to have a sundial and fountain erected, together with ornamental jars sent home from Italy in 1910.

For exercise in winter, Ethel returned after a long absence to ice skating at the Glaciarium, registering her skates there and buying a fur toque and cream knitted coat. In late May 1911 Ethel began a friendship with Mrs Buchanan, a woman of immense wealth drawn from the land, who clearly provides a model for Mrs Calthrop in the wartime trilogy beginning in 1915 with *The Cub*. After lunch at the Hotel Australia with a quartet of smart ladies Ethel was taken about town in Mrs Buchanan's 'most luxurious motor – supposed to be the best in Australia'. Back to the hotel, the lady's Sydney home when she was down from her station in the country, completing 'a very pleasant idle woman's day'.

High culture was not neglected; in June there is a charming reference to a performance of *Marilana* by the Mosman Musical Society attended by all four Curlewises. 'I was brought up on Marilana', Ethel reminisced, ' – Charlie used to sing the songs night after night – & I felt quite a schoolgirl again, doing my lessons'. Soon after, Ethel went to a matinee performance of *Hamlet* by the immortal Henry Irving and though she did not hear well, she was carried away 'by his power'. Ethel later wrote to Irving at his Sydney hotel enclosing a copy of her as yet unperformed play 'The Sundowner'. She wondered if the part of Lawrence might appeal to him, adding 'only for the lurking boyishness of your Hamlet I should not have ventured to send it'. In this action can be seen an almost desperate wish for success in the theatre and a determination which overcame her natural timidity.[9]

For the New Year holidays of 1912 Ethel took a cottage at Freshwater for the first time, beginning a family association with the northern sands that later extended to Palm Beach. Adrian had Max Shaw, a school friend, to stay and Mrs Cope came down too, though Herbert remained at 'Avenel' for by this time he did not care at all for the beach and the crowds it attracted. For most of that week they surfed three times a day, returning to Mosman at the weekend to avoid the press of humanity.

On 18 April news came to Sydney of the sinking of the *Titanic* on its maiden voyage; the accounts were so harrowing and realistic that Ethel felt as if she personally was undergoing the horror of it. Perhaps that was why she wrote and why especially she was drawn to verse – because she felt her emotions so acutely. At dinner the following night they had interesting English guests who were staying with Herbert's parents. No doubt the conversation turned to the disaster, planting the seed perhaps that sprouted four days later in Ethel's diary:

started a new book – the germ of the idea being one of the Titanic cablegrams '7 infants have lost their parents & no means exist by which to identify them'.

Wrote part of a chapter.

Then, two days later:

Finished a chapter, viz Ch ii which is written first. And then did

Ch i in a couple of hours second, – the wreck incident which made me feel positively aquiver as I wrote it.

Several days of intense writing followed before the palpable world reclaimed Ethel's attention. The garden was irresistible that May, first confronting her with anxieties about drainage for the tennis court, then making amends by offering the charm of a Sydney autumn when she noted, 'Wrote a few words. Why can't one write with a trowel in the earth instead of with ink on a desk. I grudge every minute from the garden.'

At last in mid-August 1912 fate gave a hand to the new book when Ethel sprained a muscle while playing tennis with the children. Ordered to stay off her feet completely she went to bed with writing materials 'to let the ill wind blow some good'. That was on a Monday. On the following Friday she exulted:

Finished my book, my Secret of the Sea! – A splendid week's work. Sprains for ever – it would have hung about for weeks yet. And I think it is good – quite good. At all events Jean does if no one else – she got quite excited over it ... Had great rejoicings with the babies as usual.

Of all Ethel's novels *Secret of the Sea* had perhaps the most neatly constructed plot. Its genesis was the fact that many infants, after being saved from the sinking *Titanic*, lost not only their parents but also clothes and other means of identification. In her story two sets of twins, one born to the purple, the other prosaically, were adopted by two sets of English grandparents; its tension comes from the children's attempts as they grow up to find whether they had been taken in by biologically and socially appropriate homes.

As Ethel told an interviewer soon after the book appeared, the story had appealed to her 'as a chance to try to demonstrate that it is the environment and education of the child that mean so much more than birth'. Locating the action in England had enabled her, she said, to enjoy the obsession with which she had returned to Australia, recalling the 'woods, the great trees, the bluebells, the daffodills', which 'crept into the new tale even while I stared out of my study window at gum trees and flannel flowers'.[10]

Not only as a mother but also as Dame Durden of the *Town and Country Journal* Ethel was often involved in entertaining large groups of children. One Thursday evening in June 1912 she and Herbert put on a Sphinx Party at 'Avenel' for 80 children and 20 adults, with the garden illuminated by Japanese lanterns and fairy lights. There were competitions early in the evening and after supper a conjurer; the whole family was pressed into service to make the party go with a swing, though the wind acted as an unwelcome guest, sporadically blowing out the lights. Next day Auguste (the gardener) was busy taking down decorations and restoring the status quo.

One charming echo from those days for which we are indebted to Nancy Brown conveys a strong impression of the impact Ethel made on young people, largely from her sense of fantasy. In a reminiscence she wrote:

Dear Ethel Turner was like a mother to me, or so I felt, when I was young, and when I left Sydney in 1912 she gave me a copy of 'The Seven Little Australians' which she signed. It is one of my most treasured possessions! I spent some of the happiest days of my childhood playing with Jean and Adrian and still have a snapshot of them both. She was a most exciting person to be with, and organised fantastic games both at parties and for us children. She encouraged us all to believe in fairies, and before bedtime in the evening we all had to look under a tree outside the door to see whether the fairies thought we had been good or not. The 'goodest' one would find that the fairies had left a pretty pin, or a stamp, or a sweet etc etc! And I shall never forget one Xmas morning when Father Xmas had come down the chimney during the night with our gifts, and there were two enormous footprints on the newspaper in the hearth, and soot and rubble everywhere!! And her party dishes, to my mind, were 'out of this world'!! Happy happy days.[11]

Adrian had his twelfth birthday in January 1913 and celebrated by going with his mother to stay at Manly in a cottage rented by his Aunt Lilian. In those days the men's baths were kept for women alone until 1 p.m., so Ethel swam there in the morning and at the surf beach in the afternoon. By this time her breathing had improved and she was able comfortably to do 150 yards. Adrian was already showing skill and daring as a diver; he had started at 'Shore' school that year and at his first swimming carnival was so heavily handicapped because of his impressive time of 36 seconds for 55 yards that he did not get a place.

Early in autumn Ethel took the children to Leura to stay in a cottage on the corner of Poplar Street and Russell Road. The place was a little too far from the station and somewhat bare but the verandahs were good. It was buried amongst gum trees, very much to her approval and that year for the first time the family felt the need for mosquito nets in the mountains. The holiday comprised a mixture of tennis, golf – including play with Herbert in a mixed foursome – and a search for a block of land. In this venture they readily succeeded, for on returning to town Ethel signed with Dr Doak's solicitor an agreement to buy his spare block of land near the golf links.

Mrs Buchanan, the lady with the 'luxurious motor', appears often in the diaries at this time. There was a trip early in May to take part in an 'At Home' given by Mrs Jessie Arthur at the Pacific Hotel Manly. Then, twice in as many months Ethel was borne in the Buchanan motor to visit Lady Hay, a fellow member of the Girls' Realm Committee. She lived in a mansion, Crows Nest House, which stood on the corner of Bay Road and the Pacific Highway. When completed in 1850 it had become the centrepiece of Alexander Berry's estate from which the modern suburbs of Waverton and Wollstonecraft have been carved, the latter named after the merchant who had been Berry's trading partner in the closing years of the Macquarie administration. Only the gates remain, at what is now the entrance to the North Sydney Demonstration School.[12]

Ethel's chief literary effort for 1913 was the completion in September of *Flower o' the Pine*, a novel about family relationships, located in Manly and taking its title from the Norfolk Island pines for which the beach suburb is famous. Its heroine was such a sunny, irrepressible character, in spirit not unlike Judy of *Seven Little Australians*, that Ethel felt a wrench at the prospect of losing her. When the work of the professional typist had been checked, copies were sent to the *Lone Hand* for serialization and to Hodder and Stoughton for book rights, since Ethel still believed that this firm was 'really better' than Ward Lock.

With the book finished Ethel turned immediately to writing 'A National Song', which she typed up on her new little typewriter.[13] It opens with the verse:

God of the smiling skies we come before Thee.
Not to the tramp of mailed feet we come,
For sons' and daughters' safety to implore Thee,
Above a rolling drum.

In the penultimate verse there is a clear indication of how Ethel's thoughts would run a year later when Great Britain was drawn into the First World War.

Not England's heart to England throbs more loyal
Than this far land's o'er which the south stars swing.

No English voices cry with love more royal,
God save our gracious king.

Several years earlier the Commonwealth of Australia had
decided, in the light of anxieties prompted by Germany's
challenge to British naval pre-eminence and more locally by
fears of Japanese intentions, to institute compulsory military
training and establish the Royal Australian Navy. Richard
Arthur's had been one of the voices most urgently warning
of the implications of Japan's rise as a military and naval
power. On 4 October, 1913, Jean and Adrian walked down
to Bradley's Head to watch the arrival in Sydney Harbour of
'our first Aust. fleet'. Ethel's foot was still recovering from a
recent sprain so she could not manage to walk. At night
however she and Herbert accepted the invitation of the
premier, William Holman, to view the lighted warships and
the illuminations in the harbour from the comfort of the government's launch.

The State elections were then looming and on 1 December Ethel demonstrated the extent to which she had become
involved in political processes by going to the Arthurs' home
to take part in an election meeting attended by the ladies of
the electorate. On polling day the following Saturday she
helped Mrs Arthur in the morning while Adrian teamed up
with his school friend Rod Colquhoun to work for the return
of Rod's father, also in the Liberal interest. Late that night
it was known that both candidates had enjoyed good victories, Dr Arthur having a majority of 4000 votes, though it
seemed likely that Labour's hold on power would be
unshaken.

Increasingly at this time Ethel was consolidating the family's financial position through investments. Mr Gilchrist, a
well-to-do friend of long standing, had induced her in
February to attend a land auction at nearby Pearl Beach but
neither bought a block because they were aghast at the

wholesale way in which the developers had cleared the native trees. A similar opportunity was considered by her in October in relation to the Kirkoswald estate at Mosman; the idea was to erect a cottage on one of the blocks and then rent it. A few days later she had a long discussion with the Buchanans about stocks and shares; her goal was an investment that would produce a return of 25 per cent, an 'Easier way than writing books'.

Big changes took place in the garden at 'Avenel' in 1914. Auguste completed the summer house by shingling the roof in harmony with the house and the pedestal for the sundial arrived in the care of two masons to erect it. The dial was a copy of Sir Walter Scott's except that the motto was changed from 'For the Night Cometh' (which seemed a cheerless reminder in a sunny garden) to 'Come what come may, Time and the hour runs through the roughest day.'

One of Ethel's most faithful gardening companions, her beloved cat Kim, came home after an absence of ten days:

I had missed her exceedingly – she follows me all the time I garden & sits in the basket, – whenever I go to play tennis she comes too though she doesn't trouble to go when the others do. And half the time I am writing she sits in my chair behind me or sometimes actually on the desk.

D.H. Souter, the illustrator of much of her work, often used the stylised figure of a black cat in his drawings.

Professionally 1914 was an uneven year and spring was well advanced before Ethel started on her annual book. Yet she did write one of her best stories in January, 'Farringdon's Funeral', which was published in *The Australian Soldiers' Gift Book* late in 1917, edited by Ethel and Bertram Stevens as a fund-raising measure to build homes for returned soldiers. The story was a domestic comedy set in a harbourside suburb; it had a superb twist in the tail of the kind we associate with O. Henry, whose work was then at its peak in the United States.

'The Sundowner', almost a hardy perennial, began to reappear in a new guise. Ethel was rewriting it as a novel, for Henry Irving had not taken up the suggestion of a starring role, nor had she succeeded in gaining the interest of Liebler & Company of New York when she despatched it to them, remarking felicitously in her diary, 'Another sea voyage may benefit its poor health.' A more successful dramatic effort started to take shape in April when Ethel had discussions with the theatrical entrepreneur Beaumont Smith about combining elements of *Seven Little Australians* and *Miss Bobbie* into a light comedy that had good runs at theatres in Sydney, New Zealand, Melbourne and Brisbane in late 1914 and 1915.

Soon after embarking on this venture with Beaumont Smith Ethel made a series of attempts to break free from her *persona* as a writer for children. Writing first to Hodder Williams, she said:

I have decided to try to make a new reputation by writing two or three books of an older character, and with more movement and sensation in them. At the same time I am so sure that it would be unwise to bring them out under my name of 'Ethel Turner' which has become associated altogether with young people's books that I have decided to take a fresh name, viz. 'Daveney Daunt'. I send you therefore that new person's first book, a novel called 'The Little Tin Heart', an Australian tale. I by no means think it high art. It is frankly an endeavour to write the sort of story that certainly sells well.

She explained that she was simultaneously offering serial rights to the Northern Newspaper Syndicate (which had asked her for serials) and both publishers were enjoined to keep 'quite secret' the fact of her new identity. Hodders, though finding *The Little Tin Heart* a 'charming story' decided that they could not publish it unless it bore her own name; they kept the manuscript until they heard again from her. She was still trying the same story and the same device with Cassells two years later under the pen name 'Sheila Shaw'.[14]

The years before the war were crowded with domestic and family matters. In June 1913 Ethel went to talk with Miss Badham, principal of the Sydney Church of England Girls' Grammar School, about sending Jean there to finish her formal education. What they saw of the school on this visit and discerned of its spirit helped to decide the question; of course, Ethel was treated by the girls as a celebrity. Soon after, Jean sat for the Junior Public Examination at the University of Sydney, one of only three candidates from Killarney School, and had a creditable pass, with As in English and French, Bs in Latin and History and Cs in Algebra and Arithmetic. In Geometry, a failure, for 'Mathematics don't thrive in the soil of this family'. As Ethel reminded herself, Jean at 15 was competing with much older girls.

Rumours and prospects of war dominated everything from late July to 5 August, when Herbert rang up from the city to confirm that war had formally been declared the day before. That night Ethel walked a mile or two between sunset and moonrise trying to cope with the storm of emotions aroused by the thought of war. Having a German cook, 'my poor little Marie', brought home the fact that there always were two sides to a conflict; she had 'plenty to do to preserve the balance of power in the kitchen just now'.

Ethel now set to work on a series of articles that would look at the impact of the war on women. The first appeared in the *Sydney Morning Herald* on 8 August under the series title 'Women and Wartime'. It depicted a number of possible feminine responses, one of them at a girls' school where the 'fine patriotism of the head mistress fosters that of the eager girls'. Together they sing 'with lusty voices and gleaming eyes' the entire national anthem, giving special vigor to the verse inviting God to scatter and confound the king's enemies. But:

There are two girls there whom they have quite forgotten in their enthusiasm – German girls. These girls keep their blue eyes steadily fixed in front of them.

Before writing again for the *Herald* Ethel noted two reports, that 25 000 German soldiers had been killed in the Belgian engagement and later, that 'they have asked for 24 hrs Armistice'. The second article in the series is a fine example of her craft, typical of the author in the warmth and depth of its human sympathies. Ethel begins by suggesting that the war has already forced women to abandon much of the inconsequential detail of their lives, flinging them 'clean back into our genuine selves'. She then warns of a temptation

that, as a city, we may fall into any day out of sheer heedlessness. This is to illuminate, to make bonfires, to throw up our caps a little too high when cables containing victories reach us.

Victory means bitter misery for both sides. Let us take it with soberness, keeping the thankfulness quietly in our hearts, just as, if news of a defeat at any time should come, let us not be unduly depressed; both are things in the grim day's work of war.

The time to make our bonfires will be when peace is concluded.

After the battle of Santiago and the destruction of the Spanish fleet, 'Don't cheer', said the victorious American General, 'there are men drowning and burning over there'.

Let us be gentle to the stranger within our gates.

On 12 August, the day this article was published, Ethel went to see T. W. Heney, the editor of the *Herald*, for she had developed a remarkable share of self assurance. He told her to continue writing her 'Wartime and Women' sketches as the spirit moved her; she wrote eight pieces between August and late October. It was for Ethel the beginning of an unceasing effort to win support for ideas and policies she saw as essential to Australia's role in the war.[15]

Within days of the declaration of war Lady Cullen, Mrs Arthur and Ethel were planning ambulance classes and making arrangements for bandages, hospital requirements and pyjamas that would be needed before the troops sailed. A fund-raising meeting on 11 August packed the Masonic Hall to listen to speeches by the mayor and Dr Arthur while Ethel and other committee members sat on the platform; names were taken of people to attend ambulance classes and sewing bees. On the surface there was a spirit of urgent enthusiasm and below it, a profound feeling of anxiety that was generated largely by uncertainty, a result of the weight of censorship that allowed unconfirmed reports to be published of a disaster to the British fleet. On 12 September, a Saturday, Herbert had a phone call from an officer at Victoria Barracks to say that Dr Brian Pockley, related to them by marriage, had been killed in action while serving as a medical officer with the British force occupying German Samoa. Herbert broke the news to the family. 'The finest, bravest lad I know,' Ethel wrote. 'It is heartbreaking.'

By late August 1914 the Australian press was condemning the cynicism of the German government in brushing aside its own guarantees of Belgian neutrality and invading this peaceful and prosperous country in order to attack France. The emphasis of Ethel's public comment changed radically and she wrote a sarcastic article for the *Sydney Morning Herald* describing the ruthless killing of civilian as well as military personnel and the destruction of pretty villages the Curlewises had visited in 1910:

The German army has crushed the main defence of this small nation before its friends could get to the help of it, and is placing its booted heel upon the national capital. It will go down to history, indeed, as a victory to be proud of.[16]

For Ethel the Belgian horror had two main consequences: the beginning of another series of articles and poems for the *Herald*, and the sudden solution to the problem of what novel was to be written in 1914. She embarked on one of the most fertile and popular subjects of her literary career, the symbolic and almost mythical figure of 'The Cub', who appears in three books about Australia's part in the war, *The Cub* (1915), *Captain Cub* (1916) and *Brigid and the Cub* (1919).

As a person with an abiding personal and professional interest in children, Ethel was especially responsive to published accounts of the sufferings of Belgian and French youngsters who were orphaned and dispossessed by the war. At one level the problem of finding comfortable and compassionate homes for such refugees caused her to be involved in a scheme initiated by Dr Arthur in September 1914 by which Australian families would adopt Belgian orphans. He came to lunch at 'Avenel' bringing a pile of letters for Ethel, from people offering to take the orphans in. That night she sat up writing an article supporting the appeal, 'Cry of the Children', published in the *Herald* five days later. In mid-October she returned to the charge in another article, 'War Orphans', prompted by the news that Antwerp had fallen to the Germans. There was perhaps a special resonance for her in the knowledge that Louie Mack had been in the city during the artillery bombardment, covering the war as a correspondent for the Harmondsworth press and remaining long after her male colleagues had prudently departed. For Ethel and Louie the challenges set in motion by the war gave each of them her finest hour. Ethel welcomed the chance of service in the cause and wrote of it in terms of self-realization for women.[17]

As well as accepting the opportunity for action on one of the committees set up by Dr Arthur and Lady Cullen, Ethel made the literary responses that were for her a necessary expression of emotion deeply felt. Thus she wrote at this time the poem, 'Belgium, our tears', published soon after in the *Herald*.[18]

> *Belgium, with burning tears our eyes are blind.*
> *The hard-wrung drops lie salt on every cheek.*
> *Belgium, across the seas, adown the wind,*
> *We send those tears unto your heart to speak.*
>
> *Know, in those moments when the guns are still,*
> *And you lie, tense and listening, in the night,*
> *The mists that blow across you, vague with thrill,*
> *Are just the tears that blot us from your sight.*
>
> *Oh, take it, Belgium, as One touched His lips*
> *Unto that sponge with hyssop filled, for mead.*
> *For from a cross, like His, your sweet life drips,*
> *And at its foot, tear-blind, we watch you bleed.*

The chief literary expression of these sentiments was in *The Cub*, which introduces the reader to several refugees from Belgium who were sailing from England to Australia, among them Brigid Lindsay, an English survivor of the Brussels slaughter who was accompanied by the five-year-old Josette, terribly scarred by having witnessed the deaths of her parents. Also on the ship were John Calthrop, the Cub, and his widowed mother, whose cattle stations yielded a vast income, returning to their Sydney home situated in Mosman. Central to the book is the question of the Cub's view of his responsibilities in relation to the war; at first he sees no need to volunteer, preferring to ameliorate social distress in his own patch – Sydney. However, learning of his elder brother's heroic death and of England's increasing peril he attempts to enlist but is accepted only after submitting his once sluggish and inefficient body to a regime of intense physical training. So he sails through the Heads in time to take part in the Gallipoli landing, watched proudly by Brigid in much the same way as Betty Curlewis watched twenty-six years later from her Mosman balcony when her husband Adrian sailed in a troopship for Singapore.

Brenda Niall compares the approaches to the war as a literary subject of the rival Ward Lock writers, Ethel Turner and Mary Grant Bruce. She begins by going back to look at *The Wonder-Child*, which was published in 1901 at the height of the Anglo-Boer War. The passage that follows reveals Ethel's impression of the Bush Contingent in camp at the Sydney Showground before embarking for Durban:

It was an odd, unmilitary spectacle ... Here a sunburnt fellow from 'out-back' drilled in a tattered flannel shirt and a pair of ancient moleskins ... Next to him was some wealthy squatter's son in a well-cut light grey suit ... None of the pomp, the 'eclat' of militarism – not even the discipline ... They were a fine independent-looking lot, and you knew at a glance that they would think no more of carrying their lives in their hands than most people think of carrying umbrellas.[19]

On the eve of the twentieth century, Ethel was writing about the essential classlessness and informality of Australian fighting men in terms which anticipate the work of C. E. W. Bean in the *Official History of Australia in the War of 1914–18*. The Cub, as Dr Niall points out, preferred to enlist as a private, since 'Plain fighting's all I want', intending to fight alongside his friend Harry Gale who had worked in a Sydney bottle factory. She continues:

That the Cub, unpopular at school and a domestic misfit, with 'stooping shoulders' and a strong dislike of football, should turn into a first-class officer is proof not only of Ethel Turner's preoccupation with the anti-hero but of her belief in the justness of the war and the transforming power of sacrifice.[20]

Something of the enthusiasm with which Ethel took up these causes may be gathered from the huge output of articles and poetry flowing from her pen in the final quarter of 1914. Simultaneously she set a new record for speedy writing with *The Cub*, which was completed on 21 November about eight weeks after she began. All this against a background of work on two committees and the continued management of 'Avenel', not omitting attendance at Shore's Belgian concert in which Adrian Curlewis played the part of a girl named Cicely, looking as his mother remarked 'quaintly like what I remember myself at 13'.

With the publication of *The Cub*, contracted on 4 January 1915, Ethel came back to Ward Lock after what seemed to William Steele to have been seven lean and frustrating years. She had given the contract for *That Girl* to Fisher Unwin in June 1907, *Fugitives from Fortune* to Ward Lock in 1910, then a succession of books to Hodder and Stoughton, starting with *Fair Ines* in December 1909 followed by *The Apple of Happiness*, *Ports and Happy Havens*, *The Secret of the Sea* and *Flower o' the Pine*, the last contract being dated 16 February 1914.

Gradually Ward Lock bought back the farm. When *That Girl*, for all its merit, yielded poor returns, producing royalties of only six pounds ten shillings in 1911, George Lock arranged with Fisher Unwin to take over its publication in January 1912. At the same time they spiked Hodder and Stoughton's guns by putting together collections of Ethel's short stories on which they held copyright and issuing them as what purported to be her regular books for 1910 and 1911. *An Ogre Up-to-Date* and *Raft in the Bush* were published without Ethel's knowledge and as the Hodder and Stoughton representative complained, they adversely affected sales of legitimate new material by giving booksellers the impression they had already placed orders for the current Ethel Turner volume.[21]

Ethel's anger at being placed in a false position by her old publishers stood for some years in the way of reconciliation. She told William Steele in October 1911 that the unauthorized books, for which she received no royalties, touched her honour as an author:

Last year I was continually being mortified by hearing of children who had bought or been given the newest Ethel Turner [and] being greatly disappointed on opening it & finding they already had read it all though not under the title 'Raft in the Bush'.[22]

Ethel herself contributed to the estrangement from Steele. For years she had objected to the uniform presentation of her books and was delighted by the 'distinction and individuality' of *The Secret of the Sea*. Tactlessly, she wrote to Steele praising Hodder's readiness to gratify her every request with regard to appearances and accused his firm of being 'positively afraid' of individuality, putting out the work of half a dozen authors in a uniform way 'until they all look as much alike as tins of jam'.[23]

Hodder and Stoughton's sales, however, remained a subject for anxiety. For a time Ethel made allowances, partly because she liked the look of their product, partly because she recognized the disability of their having to compete with 'pirated' work by their own author. By August 1914 she could contain her disappointment no longer. Acknowledging a half yearly cheque for 113 pounds she exclaimed, 'I am simply horrified at the amount'. Sales of three of the older books seemed to be 'practically dead':

This has not happened in the case of any other of the books held by Ward and Lock. Mr. Steele, the Australian representative, managed always to obtain steady orders for every one of the books, even those published 18 and 19 years ago. They never lapse like this, but are continually going into new editions.[24]

Even before this Ethel had complained to Hodder Williams that he was still far short of Ward Lock's English sales and reminded him that it was with the idea of improving performances in England and America that she had come to him. As 1914 drew to a close she wrote to Steele, hinting that *The Cub* when complete would go to his firm. When that commitment was finally made on 9 December, on the basis of a 15 per cent royalty and a style matching that of their competitors, Steele was fulsomely grateful. He compared the joy of her return to the fold with the 'bright ray of gladness' he had felt in 1893, after a period of deep commercial depression, on receiving the manuscript of *Seven Little Australians*.[25]

Any lingering ill feeling between Ward Lock and their star Australian writer had been dissipated by the end of 1915 when *The Cub* was stimulating strong sales and generous reviews. Ethel was delighted with Harold Copping's illustrations and with presentation in general, a subject on which her views were consistently sought. For the firm itself there was the satisfaction of receiving an approach from Hodder and Stoughton offering to sell their rights and sterotype plates on the five Turner books. Ethel readily consented, for she was offered the same terms as she had won with *The Cub* and had learned at last to value the relationship with Steele and his firm. No one could match the efficiency and enthusiasm of his work in marketing and promoting books; the other Australian managers, such as E. R. Bartholemew, were simply part-time agents.[26]

That she appreciated her good fortune was shown clearly enough by Ethel's letter to Steele of 11 November 1915, acknowledging some reviews he had sent her of *The Cub* and adding the potent words, 'I really appreciate being in touch again with someone who keeps me posted in all the interesting things about the production.'[27]

chapter
Thirteen

ithin days of the outbreak of war Ethel had embarked on a range of activities as a publicist and volunteer worker which seemed to imply a belief that it would 'all be over by Christmas'. The magnitude and intensity of her effort, most of all in writing for the *Herald* on the theme 'Women and Wartime', would have been difficult to maintain. Yet Ethel kept going right through to the armistice of 11 November 1918 and even beyond that date so as to complete *Captain Cub*, the third novel in the trilogy that had begun publication in 1915.

Early that same year Ethel made a revealing comment on a 'frightful' book she'd just finished, *Ragged Trowsered Philanthropists*, 'I feel excused for always being more than a bit of a socialist'. This remark is somewhat surprising in view of Ethel's almost lifelong friendships with Sir Joseph Carruthers and Dr Richard Arthur, senior members of an essentially conservative political party, and her efforts in 1913 to prevent the re-election of the Holman Labour Government. Nor does it sit easily with her intimacy with the government house set in Sydney, which began long before her close friend and gardening confidante Sir William Cullen became Chief Justice and Lieutenant-Governor of New South Wales.

An immense variety of individual beliefs is embraced by the concept of socialism. At Ethel's core there was a tender and compassionate heart, deeply moved by an awareness of individual and group sufferings, notably, though not exclusively, of the women and children who seemed most vulnerable in the then state of society. That social conscience had first been aired in *The Little Larrikin*, in Ruffy's anger at a system in which 'half the race work like horses – so that the other half can have carriages and *culchaw*'. It furnished the theme of *Fugitives from Fortune* and was expressed repeatedly in the *Cub* wartime trilogy and *St Tom and the Dragon*, so that John Calthrop's initial reason for not enlisting was his concern to 'stop this rich-and-poor business'. He wanted to 'build things up in the world, not destroy them'.

Her socialism involved an attempt to ameliorate injustice and curb evil, invoking in some cases the legislative power of the State, as in the campaign for the early closing of hotels, which had implications for the more effective prosecution of the war and for families that were shattered by intemperance. At the same time, both for philosophical and practical reasons, she would not rely wholly on state action in the causes she espoused. A great deal of her energy was spent after 1914 in voluntary organizations that worked for the comfort and health of Australia's fighting men or to provide homes for disabled soldiers and war widows and orphans. Even more of her time and strength was taken up by trying to influence public opinion and government action by means of a flow of articles, poetry and novels.

Inevitably, the balance and impartiality of Ethel's early reaction to the war succumbed to the often sensationalist reporting of atrocities committed by the Germans. The Curlewis family and its friends seemed to make a disproportionally heavy sacrifice to the demands of imperial solidarity. Her diary for 8 May 1915 records the heart-stopping news of the sinking of the liner *Lusitania* with the loss of 1500 lives. Ethel commented, 'The horrors deepen'. In September she noted with anguish the deaths of three of the four Curlewis cousins from Western Australia.

On 14 May, when news of Australian losses in the Dardenelles was almost at its worst, Ethel wrote, 'Afternoon – result of the week's paper horrors wrote some verses "Bayonet".'[1] There is a spiritual contradiction apparent in some of Ethel's poetry – the extent to which she invokes God's name long after she had ceased to be a church-going Christian. This, perhaps the most powerful of her war verses, begins and ends:

BAYONET
When He had made the earth,
Breathed on and brought to birth
Lands and the main,
When He had made Him infinite races,
Infinite hearts and souls and faces,
God sat hushed in His secret places,
Fashioning Pain.

Any escape is vain
Pain is upon us, Pain
Bayonet chill.
This be the thing left now for asking
Let us be equal to our tasking
And coward souls with courage masking
Bear and be still.

Though 'Bayonet' seems to have remained unpublished, so much of Ethel's verse was printed during the war that she must have been one of the best known and most influential Australian poets of her time. On 2 March after an afternoon in the surf at Manly she wrote, 'Night the moon moved me to verse, – war verse of course, – 'Full Moon'. Though a

month too early it emerged as 'Easter moon'. The Darda-
nelles campaign continued to stimulate her imagination;
while staying at the Cullen's property 'Tahlee' on the water
north of Newcastle she completed her poem, 'Oh, Boys in
Brown' which was published in the *Herald*. It quickly joined
'Belgium Our Tears' as a piece for elocution on patriotic
occasions, being recited for the first time in public by
Lawrence Campbell before a huge Town Hall audience that
roared its applause and demanded encore after encore.
Campbell had earlier told Ethel the Belgian poem was the
most sought after of his patriotic pieces.[2]

When it came to expressing profound emotion Ethel
always preferred the vehicle of poetry; at the end of June
1916 she had the distressing news of the death of Captain
Arthur Ferguson, son of one of Herbert's fellow judges and
the second of his boys to be killed. Though in bed at the
time with a high temperature she was clear-headed enough
to write some verses as a tribute to the young man. After
the poem 'Sed Miles, Sed Pro Patria' was printed on the
leader page of the *Herald* the editor wrote to tell Ethel that
'a man who is a good judge said to him "Sed Miles" was
the best war poem yet published in Sydney'.[3] The poem
begins:

God's gift to youth, fair happiness,
And Fortune's gift, a life of ease,
He flung aside for battle stress,
For toil, for peril overseas.
Hearing above the drums the Voice
That leaves the valiant heart no choice.

Contributing to Ethel's reputation at this time was the production by Beaumont Smith of *Seven Little Australians*, a children's play taking its title from the classic novel but drawing
its characters from *Miss Bobbie* and the story from a

combination of the two. Bertram Stevens wrote of the production in *The Lone Hand* that it was the first play, as distinct from a pantomine, intended for children in Australia and depending entirely on the ordinary lives of youngsters for its interest.[4]

The play opened in Sydney at the Palace Theatre in Pitt Street on 26 December 1914 and had its closing performances there on Saturday 6 February, going on to short runs at Manly and Katoomba followed by a season in New Zealand. For the final matinee Ethel, accompanied by Jean and Adrian, took a box when they saw a performance by Edward Landor as the ineffectual widower, Jack Radford as Bunty, Vera Spaull as Miss Bobbie and Cecil Haines, the champion child elocutionist from Wellington, New Zealand, as Suds. In both countries it was Cecil Haines who stole the show in the part of the irrepressible Suds.

Cecil Haines, now Mrs Cecil Parkinson, regarded Ethel Turner as 'one of the greatest influences in my vivid, & . . . somewhat incredible childhood'. She still treasures a memento of that time, a heavy-gauge silver photograph frame with a koala nestling in one corner, inscribed with the words, 'For Cecil Haines. The best "Suds" that I can possibly imagine. Ethel Turner, Sydney Feb 1915'.

Every Saturday morning while the play was running Ethel took the ten-year-old Cecil to morning tea at Farmer's Roof Garden in Market Street. It was here Cecil, accompanied by her doll Isobel and her pet tortoise Jiddyboo in his own little carrying case, first heard the words of Ethel's poem, 'Belgium our tears'.

From the Sydney and New Zealand performances of the play Ethel received a total of 51 pounds, not a handsome return for the effort she had put into it.

Bertram Stevens interviewed Ethel for *The Lone Hand* after the Sydney season finished. The piece that emerged was penetrating, witty and well-informed; it made the point that she was highly irregular in her method of working:

An idea for a story may simmer in her mind for months before she begins work upon it, and then it may be written in three months or twelve. She has no regular hours for literary work, but writes whenever inclination coincides with opportunity.[5]

The long sustained success of the two leading Ward Lock writers at this time – the other one being Mary Grant Bruce – both turning out a book a year, bears out the truth of Ethel's remark to Stevens:

There is no audience so loyal and faithful as the young. Once a writer has caught its ear – it is not, by the way, the easiest matter in the world to catch it – it listens to you year after year so long as you do not begin to speak to it in a voice different from that with which you first won its affections.[6]

Ethel continued to give her time and literary skills to public causes associated with the war, not ceasing till the armistice was declared. She was an enthusiastic supporter of an appeal for funds to endow and furnish the house and garden that had been donated as a rest home for Australian nurses. This was to be a memorial for Nurse Edith Cavell, who had stayed on in Brussels after the German occupation to look after the wounded on both sides, only to be executed for assisting Allied soldiers to escape to Holland. Ethel's article in support of the plan stressed the aptness and utility of such a memorial, compared with tablets and towering marble monuments.[7]

Ethel's other big project at this time was to promote the early closing of hotels. As early as May 1915 she had written an article entitled 'Twenty Thousand a Day', this being the sum which she said was spent on drink throughout the State. She typed it and sent it by hand to T. D. Heney, the poet who for decades served as editor of the *Herald*. Its central point was that resources were being wasted on alcohol which should be directed to the war. However it was not published, the editor lecturing her on its impracticability and she muttering darkly about the leverage exerted by the liquor interest upon newspapers through 'whisky advts'.

One of the best articles was published in the *Herald* and *Telegraph* in September 1915. Responding to the use of the term 'fanatic' to describe people who used the wartime emergency to push their temperance barrows she began:

Will you permit me to subscribe myself a fanatic, too – Mr Fitzgerald's choice term?

A year ago I could not claim the honour of being one. I saw wine on my dinner table daily and felt no stirrings of reproach; I even once, out of sheer thoughtlessness, sanctioned the purchase of some brewery shares ... And I am still of the opinion that a golden age will see, not the total prohibition of the soured temperance advocate, but light, sound wines, lightly taken.

What she would like to see one day was the provision of open-air drinking gardens where men could have a glass of wine or beer over a smoke or enjoy the company of wives and children while listening to good music or watching good pictures. But in the present emergency, quoting Lloyd George, she believed there was 'more to fear from alcohol than from the German submarines'. She wanted the government to seize the nettle, declining to cringe for votes and legislate for early closing.[8]

Late in November she attended a dinner given by the Institute of Journalists, of which she was a 'brand new member', in honour of W. M. Hughes. As president, Mr Heney took Ethel to the top table and she was most courteously treated by Fitzgerald, the minister with whom she had crossed swords in the press. 'At dinner Mr Braham of the *Telegraph* & Mr Fitzgerald both lifted their glasses to me

& signalled 'Water', which I was greatly pleased with & drank back in lemonade'.

When the referendum was held in June 1916 Ethel worked all day at the polling booth in Mosman with Mrs Arthur, whose husband had been one of the principal speakers in favour of early closing at many public meetings. By ten o'clock it was known that the vote for 6 o'clock was winning in the suburbs and next day she wrote triumphantly: 'Practically certain 6 o'clock has won an immense victory: only some country returns not yet in.'

John of Daunt was Ethel's writing task in mid-1915. On 26 May she wrote in her diary:

Spend day in the sun trying to think out – & succeeding – new book, a story of a small boy. And to be a jolly one!! At night did a few pages of it, – call it 'A Man's House' at present.

The Harold Copping painting on the cover of the first edition, published by Ward Lock in 1916, shows Ian, a plump eight-year-old boy in a grey school blazer and white cricket trousers, stretched out on a lawn chatting with his khaki-clad uncle who had been sent back to Australia to recuperate from his wounds. Ian's father is a suburban doctor who lives and practises in a four-storeyed terrace that sounds very similiar to 'Leonidas', the former Cope home in L'Avenue, Newtown. There is a gentle romantic interest linking the soldier uncle and the lovely Barbara; much of the action stems from Ian's attempt in company with a school friend to make a contribution to the war by poisoning a dachshund belonging to a German neighbour named Schwarz. Ethel finished the manuscript in late August, inspired at the last by having seen the wrapper and illustrations for *The Cub* and feeling 'extremely pleased' with Copping's drawings.

Commonwealth Day was celebrated as a public holiday in 1916 on 1 January, when Ethel motored down to French's

Forest to inspect progress on Dr Arthur's latest project, a scheme involving voluntary workers in building homes for ex-servicemen or widows on five-acre farmlets. At work on the site they found about 150 volunteers including the Minister for Lands with his coat off, clearing the plots and preparing to start building. One way in which the Voluntary Workers' Association planned to raise funds was by commissioning Ethel Turner and Bertram Stevens (of *The Lone Hand*) to edit what was to be called *The Australian Soldiers' Gift Book*; it was to be made by the Government Printer at no charge and the income from sales would add to the Association's coffers.

Ethel wrote the Introduction and Richard Arthur the final chapter 'Home Building for Heroes'; he warned readers that a generation would arise which might turn a dull ear to the claims of those who bled and agonised that the Empire might live, 'Let us strive now, when our hearts are full of gratitude, to place these men ... in a position where penury and neglect will not embitter their later years.'

Editorial planning for the book began in March over lunch at the 'Civil Service with Mr Bertram Stevens'. More detail emerged a fortnight later and Ethel went home to start typing letters to the writers and artists who were asked to contribute stories, poems, paintings and sketches. Famous people took part, headed by Madame Melba who wrote 'My Home-Coming' to open the book. There were several poems by Mary Gilmore, Henry Lawson's 'A Letter from Leeton', his story from the Murrumbidgee Irrigation Area, a poem by Ethel Turner's friend Dorothea Mackellar. Virtually the whole of the artistic community sent sketches and paintings, ranging from B. E. Minns and May Gibbs to Julian and Howard Ashton, the Lindsays, D. H. Souter and Sydney Ure Smith, for whom Jean Turner later wrote in *Art in Australia*.

By Ethel herself there was the highly amusing story 'Farrindon's Funeral' which opens with a game of besique in progress at the home of Mr Peter Mason and describes with an observant and sardonic eye his reactions to a telephone message carried by the maidservant, which he took to be a summons to yet another funeral, a rite of passage which he was finding ever more tedious in its demands on his valuable time. Not the least interesting sidelight of the story is the emphasis Ethel gives to the rudeness used by an autocratic employer of the day towards his domestic staff.

Prominence in the *Gift Book* was given by Ethel to Lilian Turner's weak and melodramatic tale of a husband and wife who went their separate ways in search of freedom but came together in a final sunset while an angel with a fiery sword whispered, 'These whom I have made one have at last learned they can be twain no more.' The inclusion of such material could have contributed to the book's failure when it was published late that year.[9]

Where her sister Lilian was concerned Ethel suffered a suspension of critical faculties and of the normal claims of self-interest. Many times during this period when she was stretched to the limit by the accumulated demands of committee work, family, journalism and creative writing, she took up one or another of Lilian's chores to help her through a difficult time. On 14 April, for example, she started work at 11.30 one night, writing Lil's regular feature for the *Herald* under the pen name of 'Penelope' rather than let her miss a deadline. The same happened on 1 September when Ethel was desperately trying to finish 'Captain Cub' before going into hospital for an appendix operation of which she said not a word to her mother or sister.

A likely reason for Ethel's generosity to Lilian, continuing childhood habits, was her discomfort at realizing that her sibling had always been forced to struggle for popular and critical rewards while she herself succeeded from the outset. The writings of both sisters exhibited melodramatic tendencies, relieved, however, in Ethel's case by psychological subtlety, and a well-developed comic sense. Accentuating differences between the sisters in practical terms was the fact that Herbert Curlewis was about to become a judge whereas Fred Thompson seemed always to be struggling for financial survival.[10]

But at Easter that year, while Ethel was at the Doaks' cottage in Leura intending to play golf and begin writing a sequel to *The Cub*, she received a long letter from Lil, conveying the news that she was to edit a new children's magazine planned for the *Mirror*. Jean was also to be involved, writing 'legends & native stuff' at a guinea a week 'so she is to grow independent early – as I did', Ethel wrote in her diary.

This comment about Jean's 'independence' takes us close to answering the question of why Ethel's highly intelligent daughter did not go to university. Ethel herself did not appear to regret the life she had chosen. Though bookish and of a literary bent she frequently revealed an impatience with the more formal aspects of her craft and shied away from gatherings that ponderously attempted literary criticism. Literature to her was something to be done rather than talked about and it is likely that Jean followed her in this and so felt unattracted by university. Ethel's attitude to formal literary studies had been recorded uncompromisingly in her diary after attending a meeting of the Women's Club to hear a paper on Dorothea Mackellar in May 1914. It seemed such

a solemn & ridiculous waste of time that it is amazing such scores of women sit through every Tuesday afternoon – why can't people read the books – & have done with it. But to take your literature in public, in silly little doses at Women's Clubs – heaven protect me from a repetition.

Confirming this interpretation is the evidence of the Baby Book in which Ethel recorded Jean's progress. Her approach was child-centred from the first, seeking to promote the child's sense of its own identity rather than use the procrustean approach of the Victorian educationalists. Far from pushing Jean by formal lessons to become an aspiring prodigy, Ethel allowed her to set her own pace and read eclectically for pure enjoyment. Seen from such a viewpoint the university may have had little to recommend it.

Jean was now in her eighteenth year, an intelligent, popular girl with light blonde curls and fine features reminiscent of her mother's. On a sunny Saturday afternoon late in June a tennis party was held at the 'Avenel' court to which six young men from 'Shore' were invited – 'prefects who seem to like young Adrian – or Jean – enough to condescend to his tenderer years. Most of them going to the war after Xmas'.

In spring, after clearing her desk and completing the manuscript of *Captain Cub*, Ethel was admitted to a private hospital in Paddington to have her appendix operated on by Sir Alexander MacCormick. Herbert and the children waited outside the hospital till it was all over, after which Ethel had the feeling her 'mind & spirit were clearer & better than ever in life, – rather wonderful experience the spiritual side of this – unforgettable – as if spirit & body were entirely dissociated'. One night when she could not sleep she began to write some verses in favour of conscription for overseas military service; a national referendum on this question, the most divisive in Australian history, was to be held in late October.

Those verses were published on the leader page of the *Herald* on 4 October under the simple title 'Yes'.[11] They were as stirring as anything she ever wrote. Here are the first and fifth stanzas:

Land that leapt to arms,
As a warhorse leaps to the fray,

When the deep drum's first alarms
Rolled from a world away –
Land with the flame-lit eyes,
With its passion of love set free,
Not by high victories,
But the blood of Gallipoli –

Stifle the lie, O Land,
Leap to thine arms once more,
Spurning the petty band,
That would smirch thy fair name o'er.
Leap swift, nor count the cost,
Leap, honour knows no bars,
Shouting, though all be lost,
'Yes', to the tingling stars.

With the referendum on conscription only a week away Ethel addressed the agonizing question of how any person in a free society could cast a vote that might send a man to his death on the other side of the world. Her article 'The Other Woman's Son' identified those men who might be legitimate subjects for compulsion, invoking the image of battle-weary soldiers dying in the trenches because they were inadequately reinforced.[12]

A story that Ethel published in *The Windsor Magazine* in 1916, 'His Wonders to Perform', has a rather more literary flavour. It alternates between glimpses of the hero, a lance-corporal stationed in the Egyptian desert, and his family back on a dairy farm in Australia. In the first scene he is opening cases of jam, the aroma of which carried his thoughts back to the farm, when Ethel uses a striking image:

But Cape Gooseberry! As he opened the tin, and the golden fruit, swimming in a syrup full of infinitessimal seeds, met his eyes, and the faintly pungent smell assailed his nostrils, his soul dipped and rose again, as does a seagull at the sudden sight of a floating morsel.

The boy died at Gallipoli and the mother was inconsolable until the moment when she saw her son on a newsreel film, opening cases of gooseberry jam and smiling the 'crinkly' smile for which he was famous. She knew then God had answered her prayer by giving her a sign that all was well with her son.

On preparing to leave hospital Ethel arranged for twelve copies of her books to be delivered. She autographed them for the nurses and was driven home 'cushioned up in a motor car' to be welcomed at 'Avenel' by a blaze of spring blooms and a placard made by Jean, 'Oh frabjous day, callool, callay'. Ethel's first venture out of doors after returning from hospital was on 28 October, when she went to the Mosman Town Hall to vote in the referendum on conscription. By the next day it seemed clear that the 'no' vote was winning, which she found 'unbelievable'. When feeling strong enough she went with Jean for a fortnight of quiet country living in the meadows of Bowral, staying at 'Arrankamp', a big comfortable boarding house run by a Miss Brennan.

From here Ethel wrote a note to Adrian, sitting on the grass behind the tennis court, addressing him as 'Dearest old Boy', and telling him of the green hills and meadows and pine trees of Bowral, which she found 'infinitely more refreshing to the eye & spirit than the cruder mountain surroundings. At the same time I fancy I get a keener sense of exhilaration from the mountain air'.[13]

The healing process at 'Arrankamp' was aided by the arrival of a healthy cheque from Ward Lock which prompted an appreciative letter from Ethel to Steele. The cheque marked a good advance on the previous year and reflected the popularity of *The Cub*. There followed a comment which showed how perceptively she had responded to the mood of the time when writing the sequel, *Captain Cub*:

You will see it will be one of the favourites; the young girl of today, with the world upside down & partings always in the air, really demands her love story. Already Cub 1 is in high favour & letters have poured in demanding 'more Brigid and the Cub'.[14]

Now very much restored, Ethel travelled with Jean by train to Yanco in the Murrumbidgee Irrigation Area, which was part of the setting of the second and third novels in the Cub trilogy, *Captain Cub* and *Brigid and the Cub*. Here it was that Brigid Lindsay's father lived as the newly appointed surveying engineer of the irrigation works, here that he was joined by his once fashionable wife and family. Ethel was shown around the region by Mr Evatt, the minister's secretary, looking at experimental farms, butter and bacon and fruit canning factories and visiting the Burrinjuck Dam. They were hardly back in Sydney before it was time to pack again for Bowral, since the family planned this year a quiet holiday in restful country, playing golf and riding horses by day and bridge at night. Ethel attempted no writing; the closest she came to creative activity was on Boxing Day when she enjoyed a fancy dress dinner at the boarding house, appearing as the Pink Witch and telling the fortunes and characters of her fellow guests. Jean took the part of Lady Teazle in a powdered wig and Adrian performed as Charlie Chaplin.

The popularity of the Cub trilogy ensured for Ethel a massive share of the juvenile market in Australia, which she retained until the mid-1920s. From 1910, however, an increasing portion of that market had been won by Mary Grant Bruce, the fourth child of a land surveyor who had married the daughter of a Gippsland cattleman. Mary grew up with an intimate knowledge of horses, cattle and pastoral stations on which she drew to good effect in the 'Billabong' series.[15]

Like Ethel, Mary Grant Bruce showed an early talent for writing and had edited a school journal while at Sale High School. Unable to afford university, she left home in 1898 to live in Melbourne and run the children's page on the *Leader*, at the same time as Ethel was cast as Dame Durden on the *Town and Country Journal*, invaluable training for an aspiring children's writer. The similarity was carried further by Mary's use of pathos in her early stories; 'Dono's Christmas' published in 1900 employs a falling tree to kill an heroic child. Yet they differed in locale and emphasis in that while the 'Billabong' stories were set in the bush and concentrated on manly narrative, Ethel's used city locations and relied on homely domestic comedy and characterization.

A more substantial difference between the two Ward Lock authors lay in their market aspirations. Whereas Ethel became less interested in writing novels for young children and sought to meet the desires of young women for stories with a love interest, Mary Grant Bruce concentrated on books for juveniles. A related point was Ethel's growing interest in social issues, which found no place in Mary's work.

Increasingly, Ethel was made aware of the younger writer's high place in the Ward Lock camp. Late in 1916 Steele suggested that she might follow Miss Bruce's lead by having an abridged version of *Miss Bobbie* published in conjunction with E. W. Cole of Melbourne and circulated in large numbers to Victorian school children. Rivalry became explicit the following year when Steele wrote to Ethel about her current manuscript, *St Tom and the Dragon*. Anxious that she should make it a full length book, he said booksellers had been complaining of the brevity of *Captain Cub*, disguised though it was by large type and wide margins. What followed must have been acutely galling, though the problem of 'short weight' went back to the beginning of Ethel's dealings with Steele, a product perhaps of her habit of writing at speed in concentrated and exhausting bursts:

Compare in this respect with 'Possum', and you will see how you appear at a disadvantage, and frankly, let me tell you, Mrs Bruce's newer books are selling better than your own ... The name of Ethel Turner helps us considerably, but I am sure these shorter length books will be noticed by reviewers before long, and it will have a tendency to prejudice sales.[16]

Anzac Day was celebrated in Sydney for the first time in 1917. Ethel went with Jean to the Town Hall to help with the War Widows' 'Entertainment', as she quaintly describes it. There were flowers and speeches and tea but the really unforgettable and macabre sight was a parade of 400 of the black robed widows in a startling hangover from the Victorian taste for morbid display.

A few days earlier Ethel had decided on the subject of her new book, *St Tom and the Dragon*, which was 'to make at least an effort to help kill drink'. Tom St Clair, the schoolboy hero of the book, like Adrian Curlewis, was a champion diver noted for the daring and grace of his performances from the high tower. Writing to offer the book to an American publisher she expressed the hope that the novel might to some degree do for drink what *Uncle Tom's Cabin* had done for slavery. Dr Arthur arranged for her to gather local colour by visiting the Central Police Court, 'it was a really severe experience' she wrote ' – I shall never forget it'.[17]

A good deal of this emotion was conveyed in a melodramatic plot well suited to a nineteenth-century novel. The tragic figure of the alcoholic Godwin, who eventually kills himself, gave purpose to the life of the crusading Tom St Clair, who persuades a locally residing whisky manufacturer to abandon the making of hard liquor and take up philanthropy and light ale. Associated with this theme is another of Ethel's abiding concerns, the quality of working-class housing, which had grown from her childhood in Paddington and Newtown. The book was finished in a rush on 21 October 1917, the last six chapters being written in less than a week. It ran as a serial in the *Daily Telegraph* from 23 February 1918.

Dowell O'Reilly, a friend since the *Parthenon* days, was a frequent visitor to 'Avenel' during the war years. After the death of his wife, who had suffered a long illness, he continued to visit, sometimes with his children.

When O'Reilly remarried in May 1917 he received from Ethel a touching, heart-felt letter, with an evocative quotation from Yeats to introduce it.[18]

Dear Mr O'Reilly,
I am so very glad.

> *'The wind blows out of the gates of the day,*
> *The wind blows over the lonely of heart*
> *And the lonely of heart is withered away'*

I knew the wind was blowing, & it hurt me often, as it must have hurt all the friends to whom you mean a great deal.
And now it is to cease.
I think if there is one thing more than another of which I am absolutely sure it is that the human heart cannot be alone. Somewhere, somehow, there has just got to be another, speaking the same tongue, & dreaming the same dreams. – The anatomy of that may be a little mixed but indeed the sense is sure.
I am so very glad.

The second referendum on conscription was held on 20 December 1917 and Ethel registered her vote on the way home with Jean after shopping in town for Christmas presents. 'It is going to be no,' she accurately predicted; she noted in her diary that 'no' was leading by some 100 000 votes in New South Wales alone. 'It is a land without a soul,' she decided.

The first of two parties for the children of soldiers had been held the previous day in the Agricultural Hall at the Showground. After two days of work preparing thousands of toys for distribution Ethel turned up early in the morning and laboured till 6 p.m. in what proved one of the most distressing days of her life:

Applications were made by 8000. We provided for 9500. About 15000 came so there was tragedy after a time – children crying, hot, weary women clutching at us & begging for toys. A long time before I shall be able to wipe it out of my mind.

During the final year of the war Herbert was in poor health intermittently suffering from jaundice, and his weight fell to 8 stone 6 pounds making a gallstone operation inescapable by the end of 1918.

At this time when Herbert's indisposition made him less available as a companion for Ethel, it was evident that mother and daughter took much pleasure in each other's company and in their shared interests. The impression of Jean is of a young woman of charm and intelligence who enjoyed an easy balance of family, friends, sport and the arts. In April she went to tea with Dorothea Mackellar who encouraged her to keep writing; two months later her poem 'Italy's Day' appeared on the leader page of the *Herald*, identified only by her initials. With Adrian for company she attended the Light Horse Ball and could have filled her programme several times, as her mother proudly remarked.

From July 1918, especially with news of American victories at the Marne, the people of Sydney gave almost their first expressions of hopefulness about the war in France, blowing whistles and flying flags. In those final months Ethel became involved in the 'Purple Packet' fund-raising scheme. Mrs Garvin, the headmistress of Sydney Girls' High still situated in Elizabeth Street, took a stall with the girls in a room made available by David Jones. That period is still spoken of by very old girls of the school, 'Elizabethans' as they are now described, who remember seeing Ethel, a most familiar and honoured visitor, calling on Mrs Garvin for a chat over afternoon tea, wearing hats and dresses of striking elegance.[19]

Ethel tried hard at this time to complete *Brigid and the Cub* but her energies and spirits were so depleted, perhaps by concern over Herbert's health, she felt she simply could not finish the manuscript. On 8 November came the first rumours of peace, received with the wildest scenes of enthusiasm. Verification of the armistice came through to her on the twelfth and next day the two maids and 'both chicks' went into town to celebrate. Herbert lay prostrate on the sofa downstairs while Ethel flogged herself along, determined to get the book out of the way so as to be free for work on the War Chest and the Children's Christmas Committee. As she succinctly put it, 'Victory does not spell much to widows and orphans.'

The manuscript was finished on 16 November after what had seemed a nightmare for the final two months. Some of the accumulated tension and agony of that period is reflected in the last three chapters of the book. Both Brigid and the Cub, with Mrs Calthrop, were on holiday in Devonshire, safe at last after the young captain's heroic labours in the trenches. To everyone's astonishment, now the way was clear for them to marry they both seemed to have second thoughts, much to the anguish of the Cub's mother and his friend Harry Gale, who had also emerged from the war as an officer.

Not until the final scene is there a happy resolution of personal and public anxieties. Unable to sleep, the two lovers walked independently to watch the sunrise and 'ran straight into each other's arms and kissed and clung'. A speck appeared in the distance, an excited girl in a red sports coat riding a white pony, waving a banner as she came. Since telephones had broken down in the region she'd gone to wake the countryside with her heaven-sent news.

'Victory!' she shouted when she saw the boy and girl running towards her, 'Victory! Victory!'

ℱourteen

William Steele, the publisher who had wept over the death of Judy, died in September 1918. C. S. Bligh, his successor in the Melbourne office of Ward Lock, had written to tell Ethel of her friend's passing.[1] She wrote immediately to Steele's daughter, who replied saying how much she had appreciated the 'kindly interest & hospitality you have always so cordially extended to my dear Daddie & myself'. A visit from the daughter the following January reminded Ethel of this and she wrote simply in her diary, 'I feel his loss very much.'

As well she might. Steele had guided Ethel's fortunes for more than twenty-five years. He had recognised her talents from the moment he had seen the manuscript of *Seven Little Australians*, feeling so certain of its quality as to negotiate a contract before consulting his head office. Able from the first to stimulate in his new author a sense of confidence in her abilities he encouraged Ethel to produce good manuscripts at high speed, enabling her to gain firm hold of the children's book market. Yet with or without Steele, Ethel was bound to succeed as a writer since her abilities were outstanding and her determination and qualities of organization exceptional. She was a keen business woman, well aware of her own market worth and able to use the newspaper press not only to augment her income from novels by having them serialized but also to extend the currency of her name. She was one of the great publicists of her generation, involved in many causes that touched her sympathies including not only big popular issues like conscription and early closing but also those which exerted less leverage upon the public mind. During the war she had become one of the best known and most respected journalists, given virtually *carte blanche* by the editors of major Sydney dailies. As well as using these outlets she responded to appeals from an impressive range of organizations. The issue of the health and education of children was of great concern to Ethel. An article she wrote for the Child Welfare Conference emphasises the consequences for the individual and for society of childhood experiences. Introducing her piece 'A Larger Motherhood' she imagined using field glasses with a retrospective lens to focus on the childhoods of various citizens so as to discover

in a very great measure, just what that childhood had lacked or been supplied with to give it those good, bad or indifferent qualities that are marking its career at the present moment.

Focussed on the men who would burn or murder or rob, or seek selfish profit from the war, she felt sure the lens would bring to sight childhoods so deprived and starved in soul if not in body that we should be ashamed to go on living in a world in which such things were permitted.

Ethel's sense of relevance as an artist to the issues and events of her day had another form of expression. Her 1919 book was *Laughing Water* – its title came from the name of Professor North's family home at Katoomba – and like many of her stories it grew naturally from recent experience. Three weeks before she began to write it the first mention had occurred in her diary of the Spanish influenza epidemic which had caused huge losses of life around the world and was about to bring chaos and suffering to Australia. This new story used as a turning point the quarantining of the North residence when the professor's hospitable wife was struck down by the dread disease. As so often happened with Ethel's novels that responded to specific events – another example being *Secret of the Sea* in relation to the sinking of the *Titanic* – *Laughing Water* was written at a fast pace. Though not finished till 15 September the manuscript was completed in a writing time of about five weeks, including an opening burst when she wrote eleven chapters in as many days.

In the first chapter, 'Catastrophe', we are introduced to naval cadet Humphrey Bligh, who missed his train from Katoomba to Sydney and so failed to board his ship when it sailed on training exercises. Nea, the shallow and selfish temptress who had deflected young Bligh from the path of duty, made some amends by telephoning the ship's captain to make the cadet's apologies and finding a place for the lad on the North's crowded verandah. In this there were some echoes for Ethel of her own experience of the way in which mountain cottages were treated by some people as a limitless fund of accommodation and hearty food.

The story is simple but well constructed, depending for its appeal on situations that allow the interplay and growth of character. It has good realism and suggests Ethel's belief that the people who enjoy the greatest chances of happiness are those who have only a modest share of the world's goods. Mrs North's best pleasures came from her unfailing generosity and hospitality, from the love of family and friends, and from a lively concern for the less fortunate.

The Spanish influenza epidemic caused widespread fear and concern. The Curlewises were inoculated and began avoiding engagements 'taking us to the uncertain city'. Soon there was an edict requiring people to wear gauze masks in public places; schools and theatres were closed at the height of the panic early in April with reports of 167 cases and 22 deaths. Volunteers were now called for, and Jean insisted on offering to serve. Her post was a distant one, at the Walker Hospital in Parramatta, where there were 55 cases producing 2 deaths on 10 April. Next day an anxious but proud mother wrote, 'Very limp. But 2 letters from my girl, full of courage – even fun, pulled me up. At night also she rang up to say all was well.'

At twenty-one years of age Jean had several serious suitors, the most prominent of whom was Leo Charlton and by the end of 1919 he was regarded as a likely husband.

Meanwhile Adrian completed his Leaving Certificate year, and delighted his mother by being awarded the Brian Pockley Memorial Prize, which remembered one of the first Australians to fall during the war. It was, Ethel noticed proudly, 'the best & most honourable of all the C.E.G.S. prizes'. Though far from being a natural student, and needing to cram to matriculate for Law, Adrian performed well in many fields of school activity, not just as a swimmer and footballer but as a contributor to plays, to cadets and above all as an acknowledged leader.

This was the year of Mrs Garvin's retirement after thirty-six years as Headmistress of Sydney Girls' High School. As one of the first intake at the school when it opened in 1883 and the most illustrious of its old girls, with a record of consistent involvement in its public activities, Ethel was inevitably concerned with plans to honour her old teacher. A committee was appointed and a reception held in October with the Lady Mayoress in the chair when Ethel presented a cheque for 365 pounds. Some weeks later, Mrs Garvin accepted the position of principal of the Church of England Girls' Grammar School, Cremorne, which Jean Curlewis had attended.

In January 1920 Adam McCay, editor of the new Joynton-Smith publication *Smith's Weekly* asked Ethel to write a vignette, for which he offered the handsome sum of ten guineas. It appeared at the end of the month under the title, 'Paradise' and tells of the relationship between 'Little

Anne', a maidservant of 17 from the bush, and her young mistress. The latter had tried on several extravagantly beautiful dresses before going out for the evening but being bored had come home early. Anne meanwhile had taken a number of two shilling pieces from her weekly wage, for it was Friday night and the money needed to be paid off her lay-bys at the shops in town: the silver tea pot for her mother; the Winchester rifle for her brother Jim; the kewpie doll for her little sister and the georgette dress for herself. Ethel's achievement is to reveal the contrasting values of the two people, the indulged young woman of fashion and the unspoilt girl from the bush, supremely happy with long-deferred pleasures, whose bliss lay in 'waiting for Paradise on earth'.[2]

Young women had furnished copy for Ethel since the publication of 'The Little Duchess' in the *Bulletin* in December 1894. When she visited France on the way home from England in 1910 she had been drawn to compare the midinettes of Paris with the working girls of Sydney. Both could be seen emerging into the sunshine of the city after long mornings cooped up as needlewomen or shopgirls:

Their lives are spent in hard work, in the service of imperial fashion. The luxury of others and the triumph of beauty in costume is at their expense ... Some way, somehow, we must pass on to them some of the better things of our own life.[3]

Experience of public life during the war had given Ethel a better idea of a possible solution. It was expressed in her article 'The Sun is on the Hill', which appeared in the *Herald* in June 1919. Drawing its title from the refrain of an old song, 'Though the rain is on the river, Yet the sun is on the hill', it celebrated the contribution made to the life of the city by the 'cheery army of its working girls'. Ethel's concern was to publicize the tiny margin that remained to these girls after paying for board and lodging and urged the setting up of a chain of hostels where friendly and less costly accommodation would be available.[4]

Even more remarkable was the next piece, 'The Seeing Eye', which included one small evocative vignette:

In a determinedly sordid street in Woolloomooloo. One blistered front door opened, and then, a little distance away, another still more blistered. Out from each came a tiny girl – eight years was probably more than their joint ages. They suddenly saw each other, their feet became wings; they flew to each other as two birds might have done – they twined their tiny arms round each other and kissed and kissed again. There was purest joy on each of the little faces.[5]

While this story was being written Ethel had the plot of a new novel simmering in her mind. *King Anne* saw the return to her pages of Tom St Clair who had fought the good fight against whisky some years earlier and now faced the choice between marriage to Anne and a commitment to philanthropy. Since one of the characters was a pioneering pastoralist in South Australia Ethel felt obliged to do background reading with some care, consulting the anthropological studies by Spencer and Gillen and discussing a point of aviation with the redoubtable flyer, Captain Gordon Taylor. Perhaps this was why, when she posted the completed manuscript to Ward Lock in November, she demanded an extra penny a copy in her royalties.

By this time Ethel was a member of both the Women's Club and the Journalists': the former gave her a place where she could change and eat in town before going on to a show; the latter, which met in those days at different restaurants, gave contacts with editors and senior politicians and offered regular opportunities for lunching with celebrities. Thus on 19 February, 1920:

To Journalists lunch at Sargents to meet the heroes of the day. Was put at the charmed table with them; Mr Fairfax – who was next to me – introduced me to Mrs Andrew Smith & she brought both her boys to shake hands – she told me she had read all the books. Sir Keith [Murdoch] came back after shaking hands & said, 'I'm going to shake hands again because I've read & liked your books so much'.

The event of the year for imperial patriots was the visit in June of the Prince of Wales who sailed through the Heads in the battleship *Renown* watched by the Curlewises from a headland and by a flotilla of small craft on the harbour. At night they went to the ball given by the governor general and after a long delay in Macquarie Street had the pleasure of shaking the royal hand. Much the same happened the following night except that the scene was even more brilliant; from Government House with its coloured lights and fountains the eye was drawn to the illuminated warships nearby in the harbour. Stirring stuff, though Ethel felt jaded after several days of dense crowds and late hours and thought what a frightful strain it must be for the man at the centre of it.

Ethel felt rather 'crook' in the final run to Christmas in 1920 and was relieved soon after to arrive with the family in a car packed to the gunwales for a surfing holiday at Palm Beach. Their shack for the fortnight was a Californian-style bungalow with the surf rolling in a few minutes' walk away. She found that the sea stimulated her imagination and when they packed to leave after a 'final glorious surf before brekker' there were two new short stories to be sold, 'Gift Horses' and 'A Prophet's Honour'.

The new year which had opened with such healthy promise continued in productive vein for both mother and daughter. Jean had the thrill in February of hearing from Ward Lock that her first manuscript had been accepted, 'The Ship that never set Sail'. At the same time Ethel wrote to

Campbell Jones, managing director of the Sydney *Sun*, reviving a project which she had put before the board in July 1919. Just before the war started she had planned to bring out an Australian penny weekly for young people, aiming at a circulation of 50 000, on similar lines to *St Nicolas* in America and *The Scout* in England.

As she saw it in 1919:

Young people want specialising for in their sports, their school matters and their leisure and are omnivorous readers ... and very faithful ones ... of matter that really has an appeal and interest for them.

Part of her motivation was to offer the rising generation 'without any preachiness', some 'higher and broader ideals'. She stressed the inexpensiveness of providing copy for such a paper, saying that her experience with the *Town and Country Journal* had taught her that 'young people prefer their own and their contemporaries' efforts in print to the best professional matter'.[6]

Campbell Jones and the board of the *Sun* felt unable to act in February 1921 because of industrial trouble and fluctuations in currency – in 1919 the difficulty had been with the shortage of newsprint. Yet they made clear their interest in the idea of 'The Rising Sun', and in mid-September Campbell Jones wrote to say the omens were now propitious and asked Ethel to make a detailed proposal. The management's initial thinking was that she would simply edit a single page to begin with until new machines arrived from England enabling the production of a separate colour supplement. A meeting was held at the *Sun* office on 4 October with the editor Mr Tonkin and the well-known illustrator, D. H. Souter, in addition to Ethel and Mr Campbell Jones. They decided to call the page 'Sunbeams' in order to use Ethel's 'Rising Sun' motif.

But she added:

Am starting disappointed, though – they say it wd be impossible to give me shares in new paper when it comes. So it only means 500 pounds for new editorship with increases as circulation goes up.

'Sunbeams' made its first appearance on page 16 of the *Sun* on Sunday 9 October. Ethel, who soon became the Chief Sunbeamer, wrote a welcoming piece 'From A Chair In The Sun' which captures nicely her easy approach to young readers:

Dear Boys and Girls, –
Let us shake hands with each other and say we hope we
find each other quite well, as it leaves us at present.
   'The Sunday Sun' has sent over a comfortable basket-chair for
my sunny verandah, and asked me to sit in it and catch
sunbeams for you in between planting silver bells and
cockle shells in my garden.
   When first I saw the chair I was quite alarmed. I thought
they meant me to write their leaders in it, or their sporting
columns, or their fashions, or similar serious things. But
when I found it was merely a matter of catching sunbeams!
And for you, whom I have known so long! Well, I simply
laughed and sat straight down in it.
Ever yours,
Ethel Turner

In that first issue of 'Sunbeams' Ethel included a literary competition asking children to 'Glance at something – anything in the world, your dog, an old boot, the Post Office clock, anything'. Prizes were offered to children in two different age groups for the best humorous descriptions of the chosen subject, five pounds for those under ten and ten pounds for competitors between ten and sixteen, with sixty consolation prizes of half a crown. Imagine the work involved in reading the hundreds of entries before the results were announced on 18 December!

The promised four-page children's colour supplement with comics began on Sunday 13 November. It introduced 'Us Fellers' drawn by Jimmy Bancks, which soon developed into the best-known comic strip in the country. Next day the *Sun* printed a news item describing the enthusiastic welcome given to the colour supplement; it was said to mark a departure in Australian journalism 'which challenges comparison with any in the world'.

Within a week or so of the beginning of the supplement Ethel was becoming anxious at the tone of some of the comics. That feeling was reinforced by a paragraph in *Smith's Weekly* on 24 November

about the company of 'Domain dossers' & such figures being on my Children's Page – which precipitates what I have been practically deciding to do – resign or have the pics taken away.

Next day she wrote to Mr Campbell Jones saying she could not go on if the Sunbeams page was 'covered with "Weary Willy & Drink Comics".' On 6 December there was a meeting in the *Sun* office with Messrs Campbell Jones, Tonkin and Deamer which seems to have made progress with the question that was worrying the Chief Sunbeamer.

By Christmas 1921 Bancks was drawing in 'Us Fellers' a new boy called Ginger who was soon given a mother and father called Mr and Mrs Meggs, a girl friend called Minnie and an older antagonist named Tiger Kelly whose unpleasant behaviour underlined the essential goodness of the hero, larrikin though he almost was.

Years later in an undated note, intended perhaps as the basis for a talk, Ethel recalled the genesis of Ginger Meggs, who became the best-loved figure of children's comic lore in Australia. After telling Campbell Jones of her uneasiness at the tone of pictures then being used she spoke of her hopes for a new style of Sunbeams:

The director groaned – the paper was making splendid headway, why disturb things? What was it I wanted?

I wanted, I said, something in the shape of a boy half imp, half angel, who did mischievous & funny things every week from the top of the page to the bottom; who even if he purloined the last tart from the pantry with his left hand, with his right presented it to his mate or some hungry child; a very small boy – in socks preferably.

The Chief rubbed his chin ... 'There may be something in what you say', he said grudgingly. 'Well, I'll see what I can do about it, though it won't be easy to find the right man'. But there, he could always find the right man! In a few days there came an urgent telephone call. Could I go to town to see the Chief? He had something to show me. All over his desk he had ... Ginger!

That was a moment of purest happiness. Moments of purest happiness are very rare.

I remember saying later on to the artist who came in – a young man with a shy yet eager manner & eyes with a glint of laughter in them. The young man, the famous 'Jim Bancks', who is still a young man & always will be, – I remember saying to this young man at our first meeting 'But how do you know all this about small boys & their haunts & habits?' And I pointed to sketches of Ginger on a billycart, Ginger falling in a pond, Ginger fighting.

'Well', he said modestly, 'I rather like boys, & in the street where I live I often watch them from my window racing their billycarts down the hill after school. Great fun they are. I used to have a billycart myself once'.[7]

Ethel's birthday in January 1921, her fifty-first, was shortly followed by an attack on the accumulation of papers in her study. Even after this tidying operation there was need for more space so she really cleared the decks, 'casting out mss. of several books & hundreds of articles that I shd have burned long since'. (What a tragedy for librarians and scholars!) Within a year, which included six months of editing 'Sunbeams', she realised that a larger and more sophisticated filing and storage system was needed. Her half-brother Rex Cope was called in to design a new study and work began on the foundations in July 1922. A month later the new 'Sunbeam desk' was finished and Ethel enjoyed putting her papers in the pigeonholes.

Need for extra space was not the only factor in this development. Ethel's income from writing had been strong and steady during the war averaging about 700 pounds a year until 1920. In 1921 it rose to 1059 pounds, which compared favourably with Herbert's judicial salary of 1500 pounds, and then climbed to a peak of 1543 pounds in 1924, reflecting the growing popularity of the Ward Lock books and the new income from the *Sun* of 364 pounds a year. Mr Bligh, now in William Steele's place at the publisher's Melbourne office, told Ethel in March 1921 that *Seven Little Australians* had sold over 100 000 copies and that her books, and those of Mary Grant Bruce, had such a devoted readership 'that the booksellers will order quantities of these & only very few or none of others'.[8]

Such news encouraged Ethel a few days later to take Jean into town to look at the autumn fashions. She bought two frocks at David Jones, made from Jersey material, hers being cream with black touches and Jean's old rose and white. Already a programme of refurbishing had begun at 'Avenel', with painters busy downstairs and the verandah being remodelled to make it more suitable for dancing. New carpets were bought from Beard Watson's, a creamy Indian for the drawing room and a plain mauve art felt for her own dressing room; as she explained, she did not like 'gloriferous carpets'. 'By request no flowers' was her motto.

Of course the family was not without its worries. For some time Jean had been losing weight and Ethel asked a Dr Clark to see Jean for a follow-up visit since this was continuing in spite of their best efforts. Though she seemed as well as possible she was down another pound to 7 stone 3 pounds. Adrian was now at the university but failed in first year Law; because he was borderline Professor Peden was prepared to allow him to carry first year subjects and take the two years together. A daunting prospect, one would have thought, yet the challenge was successfully met in the year that followed. Completing that circle of disappointment, Jean's suitor Leo Charlton failed in fourth year Medicine, which was likely to mean a long postponement of wedding plans, but the family celebrated their formal engagement in June with the clinking of wine glasses.

In March 1921, Ethel began writing her new book for the year. Though she circled Friday 11 with a relieved flourish it was not till 9 May that the manuscript was given a title, *Jennifer, J.*, and substantial progress was made. It was completed in two bursts, the second coming to an end on 24 September when she wrote: 'Finished Ch 25 & last in afternoon. And really finished with more breath left than any book for years. So much for Jennifer J.'

One nice touch, very much in character, was the dedication 'to the girls of the Sydney High School of 1921, who migrated then from the old, much complained of historied buildings known by myself, to their shining new ones'.

Familiar as many elements of the plot may be, the book was deservedly successful when Ward Lock published it in 1922. Most of the action takes place in the harbourside home of Andrew Firth, a newspaper editor, and in a boarding house in the Blue Mountains. The choice of Mount Wilson, which Ethel had discovered in the late spring of 1919, enabled her to write a wonderful chapter, 'England in the mountains', evoking the striking contrast between the different types and conditions of vegetation the region affords. On the drive they passed through scrub blackened by the fires of the previous summer, then insensibly the character of the ground changed from sandy soil to a darker and warmer loam which supported wild tobacco, wild raspberries, clematis and grevillea. Further off, mountain ash and stringy barks towered to the sky

with tree ferns, graceful as gazelles, rising everywhere from a green foam of undergrowth ... the foam being luxuriant vines that, having smothered and killed the young trees they had used as ladders, had flung themselves into the tall tops of the giants.

At last they came to the 'arched roof of the serried rows of chestnuts and walnuts that had just uncurled their pale green leaves' and saw gardens ablaze with rhododendrons and azaleas, when there was a lively debate between the relative merits of Australian and English scenery. Some time earlier Jennifer had made clear her own identity (and that of Ethel herself), 'With two English parents and an English aunt, I remain Australian'.

The Firth family, like so many in Ethel's novels, was managing without its dynamic mother, Fidelia, who had gone back to Oxford from whence she had come, to complete a degree. Andrew Firth's sister Amy had volunteered to fill her place but the real work was done by the housekeeper, Mrs Sams and the female children. The book has much to appeal to readers of all ages, a gently developed love story that blossoms in the leafy glades of Mount Wilson, the detection by Jennifer of the housekeeper's regular thefts from the Firth pantry and most of all the depiction of character and personality.

Especially moving is the early chapter in which Jennifer reflects, with all the gravity of her fourteen years, on the personalities of her parents:

Fidelia was much older than their father, albeit some years younger. Fidelia, grave, tall, slender, with that little pucker between her brows that told she had always tasks too many and too heavy on hand, did not know how to play, – had perhaps never known how to play or roll with laughter ... [while her father] despite all his dignities and responsibilities was still at heart a boy and a lonely boy.

The book expresses Ethel's essential belief in the over-riding value to a woman of the role of wife and mother; Fidelia is made to realize by the blue-stocking who tops the honours list at Oxford that she would have chosen motherhood in favour of academic success, if only it had been available to her.

Harold Copping was again chosen as illustrator. He wrote to Ward Lock in June 1922 suggesting they use his drawing of Jennifer seated on her favourite pillar as frontespiece, adding:

I have taken some trouble in endeavouring to make this a successful realization of the character, which seems to me one of Mrs Curlewis' most attractive creations, and hope the authoress will feel I have succeeded.[9]

Now in their fifties, both Ethel and Herbert found that the passing years touched with increasing severity the lives of parents and older friends. 'Marmee' Curlewis required constant nursing and was restricted to a wheelchair. The family moved from Stanmore to a cottage in Manly, where Dolly (Herbert's sister) seemed to have been marked out to stay at home with her mother; her lot, Ethel thought, was 'very hard'. So many families of that day called on one of the daughters to sacrifice her prospects of happiness and independence. In September 1922 Ethel's mother was discovered to have an inoperable malignant growth.

Walter Jeffery and Bertram Stevens, two men who had meant a great deal to Ethel over the years were the subject of obituaries on 13 February 1922. In her diary she wrote of the 'very real shock & grief' she felt at the news of Mr Jeffery's death, after collapsing at his desk. As managing editor of the *Evening News*, he had been 'a real figure in my literary life for 30 years'. The *Herald* made a point of Jeffery's 'honest kindliness which he extended to all men' and stressed the keenness of his interest in imperial relations and the early maritime history of Australia. Bertram Stevens was a much younger man, whose death on the same day came as 'a double shock' to Ethel. He had taken over the editorship of the red page of the *Bulletin* from A. G. Stephens, that is, after Ethel's contributions to that magazine terminated, perhaps from concern with its republican emphasis and the disapprobation of Ward Lock. But he had much to do with Ethel as editor of the *Lone Hand* and as co-editor of the *Australian Soldiers' Gift Book*. Common to the two men was a deep interest in Australian literature, and in the case of Bertram Stevens, an almost unrivalled knowledge of the subject through his work on the collection of David Scott Mitchell.

In September of that year Henry Lawson died. There is no sign in Ethel's diary of any direct contact having been made after his return from England in July 1902, and he was once again drinking heavily and estranged from his wife Bertha. Yet he contributed substantially to the *Australian Soldiers' Gift Book*.

The summer vacation at Palm Beach came a little early in 1921, which was just as well since Ethel had been badly frazzled by the weight and variety of the tasks that confronted her. On 12 December she spent the morning at the *Sun* office and then attended a matinee at the Palace Theatre to raise funds for the Matraville Soldiers' Homes. For the next two days she was again busy at the *Sun* packing scores of 'Sun fairies' that had been sent in by the children who read 'Sunbeams', intended as presents for distribution to children in hospitals and the back streets of Sydney. There were visits to be made to the ailing Marmee Curlewis and to see Charlie and Sarah Cope for their joint birthday at 'Bukyangi'. On the way home from Killara, which took two and a half hours, by public transport she felt overcome by the events that pressed upon her: there were 'too many things in every day for any mortal woman'.

As always Ethel was her own worst enemy. On 16 December she waved her daughter off to Newport for a surfing holiday, taking on the responsibility for Jean's children's page as well as her own 'Sunbeams'. Next day was a Sunday, the day of rest, but when it was over she wrote:

10,000 things & H very put out of sorts & cross – feel like breaking down. Sense of fighting obstacles all time. Packed Xmas presents – hang all Xmas presents.

When the car came on 22 December to take the family to the cottage at Palm Beach it was none too soon. The place was a stone bungalow built by two returned soldiers on rising ground close to the beach. The whole party surfed before breakfast each day and late in the afternoon, lying about on lounges in the heat of the day and playing bridge at night.

Refreshed on Boxing Day by two 'lovely surfs' Ethel felt so much better that she was inspired to write some verses. Her diary entry for 30 December shows well the workings of her mind when the plan for a novel was being formed:

Bade my 'sub-conscious' go hunt for new characters for a book for next year among all the impressions roughly gathered. And lo', I woke with the thing shaping amazingly & several characters standing ready – Nicola Silver – Alec – the father – the stone house slipping down a hill. 2 days ago had not one notion in all my brain for one. Idled all day.

Although the beach was closed for days early in January because of a wild storm Adrian was able to keep up a programme of regular training for his lifesaving certificate. An exhibition of life saving was held on 8 January 1922 at which Adrian won his award; it was to be the beginning of an interest and a commitment that made the name of Curlewis known to generations of Australians.

*E*thel's practice of drawing inspiration for her books from day-to-day experiences was brought out nicely by the outcome of a visit late in February 1922 to Leura in the Blue Mountains. She had gone with the Cullens by car to see 'Clifflands', their new garden at the bottom of Morven Road, returning on the same day. The house itself, like 'Tregoyd' at Mosman, is comfortable and rambling, with a good deal of the decorative use of dark stained timber mantels and picture rails that were characteristic of the period. A week later came the beginning of a literary off-shoot, 'Wrote quite happily at a new sort of garden book "The Ungardeners".' It was put aside to await further inspiration and when published in 1925 was dedicated to the Cullens, whom Ethel described as 'the two most dauntless garden makers and truest garden lovers I know'. From Sir William she drew a warm appreciation for native Australian trees and shrubs that she first acknowledged in the character of Judge Lomax in *In the Mist of the Mountains*.

After a few days work on the new manuscript Ethel was invited to join Lady Cullen in a motor trip via the mountains to stay at the boys' sheep and cattle station 'Inglewood' near Mudgee. Coincidentally, the property bore the name of the house in which Ethel had written *Seven Little Australians*. She accepted, feeling it would be good to experience some dry country air after what seemed like the 'hot fomentation' of Sydney. The chauffer-driven car collected her at 4 p.m. and the party reached the mountains as the sun was setting – 'twas as if all the scenery had been freshly painted since last week's run'. It was 9 p.m. before they got to 'Clifflands', suggesting that the journey took at least twice as long as it does seventy years later. Ethel was back home in time to record her vote in the federal election; though regarding herself as 'more than a bit of a socialist' she was glad to record that the Nationalist/Country Party coalition was practically assured of victory.

Farmer-Whyte, the new editor of the *Daily Telegraph*, arranged in April for *Jennifer, J.*, the new Ward Lock novel, to appear serially in his newspaper. As well as paying 50 pounds for those rights he inquired about Ethel's readiness to write articles and poetry as well and suggested the possibility of selling serial rights in New Zealand. Jean was already having the pleasure of seeing her story 'Drowning Maze' appearing in *Pals*, where she was billed as 'one of Australia's finest writers'.

Perhaps so. But she lacked some of those qualities of character her mother enjoyed in abundance. Ethel's diary entries in May tell an all-too-familiar story of an essentially unhealthy dependence within the extended family:

Sunday 14 May 1922. Felt very unwell again – like flu. Did Lil's Herald article for her. She down with flu.
Wednesday 17 May 1922. Felt very off for a time – rush of work too great – had done Marie an article to help her, Rex one, Lil's 3/4 column. Then Jean couldn't do her 'Sunshine' chapter & I had to take that on suddenly. And do my editorial & all the page today. Worked till 1/2 past 12 at night.

It seems clear that there was unfortunate aspects of this relationship on both sides, the less obvious being Ethel's increasing tendency to make a martyr of herself and to draw satisfaction from that role. Herbert was perhaps the chief sufferer since he now seemed to be powerless to stop Ethel taking on too much; she became less and less available for the range of shared activities that had been such a feature of their early married years. His name occurs seldom in the diary during this period and it is often difficult to know if he is present or absent in a family situation, notably when they were on beach holidays, which Herbert enjoyed little, largely because of his distaste for crowds.

Jean shared in her mother's life at every level, sometimes doing the very kinds of thing Herbert had formerly helped with. On 24 May, for example, by which time Ethel was feeling brighter and full of energy, Jean helped her cutting out from the columns of 'Sunbeams' the 39 chapters of a light-hearted serial story, which was to be published by Ward Lock as *The Sunshine Family* in lieu of a new novel for 1923. It was Jean who provided company at garden parties and shopping expeditions, she who enjoyed the waves at Palm Beach or who provided the stimulus for dinner parties and dances at home. When Dorothea Mackellar came to dine in June it was her friendly patronage of Jean's literary career that would have prompted the invitation, though in her diary Ethel makes it clear that every one in the family enjoyed their charming guest.

For their annual speech day Sydney Girls' High again invited Ethel to present the prizes. This time she read a long and controversial talk entitled 'Too much to do, High School girls', arguing that, as in her own day, the demands of the curriculum and the standards set in the examinations were far too severe. Girls were the chief sufferers because of the difficulty of keeping them 'free from the incessant demands of domestic and social life, that the boy escapes'. She often spoke to old school friends who felt there should have been a greater margin left to them in a day 'for joy, for fun, for beauty, for pure idleness'. Such latitude might have made a difference to the whole of their lives, 'might have made healthy, radiant, well-balanced women of them, as well as well-educated ones'.

This speech, which was given a headline and full report in the *Daily Telegraph*, was received by the girls with 'immense applause' though Ethel was careful to absolve Miss Campbell and her teachers of any blame since they were obliged to follow directions from Mr Peter Board and the Department of Education. The latter, who was present, was concerned enough by the criticism to assure his audience that any possible danger from exhaustion was met by the precaution of the three-monthly health examinations of the girls made by departmental doctors.[1]

There is a mood of ennui about Ethel's diary for the start of 1923 that is partly explained by her entry on 22 January noting that it was a 'sorely hot day' with a humidity of 81 per cent. Lilian had gone to the mountains for a short break and Ethel added, 'We all really should have gone away for a change but H so hates leaving home we stay on & on year after year'. Little trace was left of the active and adventurous young man who had sailed with the Macks on Sydney Harbour, glorying in the challenge of a brisk wind and often providing the cool decisiveness that got his party through a tight situation.

Making Ethel more than usually susceptible to the nor' easters that ravaged the maritime suburbs in mid-summer was a toothache that soon needed surgery. She hardly slept at all on 8 January, so fearing an abscess she consulted a dentist who arranged for X-rays, her first such experience. Four days later the tooth was extracted with a gas anaesthetic by Dr Marshall in Macquarie Street.

For her birthday Herbert bought Ethel a Polar Cub electric fan/punkah that promised to be a great boon in 'these weary hot days'. Next day began just as oppressively but in the afternoon came the rain the garden had needed for an eternity, prompting her to find a catalogue and write out a seed order for autumn sowings.

Several times that January Ethel had visited her mother at 'Bukyangi'. Since December Sarah had been looked after by a live-in nurse but Charles Cope seemed to have revived his capacity for being disagreeable and Ethel felt 'very heavy hearted' on returning to 'Avenel' after a long day. Soon Sarah began relying on the services of a Christian Science healer, Madame Aurangi, whom Ethel met on 31 May when she spent a day relieving the nurse on her day off.

On one of her relief visits in June Ethel was told by the nurse that Mrs Cope might be kept going by her indomitable spirit for perhaps a year, though a heart attack could carry her off at any moment. Her dependence on morphia had increased; on the 9 July soon after the injection she began to talk again of the old days, opening up a subject that has particular interest for any student of Ethel's writing. The theme of the beautiful child adopted out by an impoverished parent for financial reward occurs in *Three Little Maids* and *Mother's Little Girl*, so it is almost certain that Ethel had known of Tom Turner's offer from so long ago:

Told me how Tom Turner [presumably her dead husband's brother] had offered her 1000 pounds to let him & his wife have Ethel to bring up instead of letting her come to Australia. Said he would bring her up like a little Queen. He was very wealthy – roll top desks in Coventry. Odd to wonder now if Mother had thought two children were enough to bring over the seas.

On 12 May 1923, the very day after Ethel received her record royalty cheque from Ward Lock she had along discussion with Herbert over the question of buying a car, possibly brought on by the increasingly frequent trips to 'Bukyangi' and visits to Lilian and other members of the family. And as on so many matters it was now Ethel who took a modern attitude to things and Herbert who tended to stay-at-home conservatism.

Next day Ethel wrote triumphantly, 'Car – a Buick 6 cylinder, 5 seater, 1923 model is acksherly ordered & will arrive in 6 or 8 weeks'. The big day for delivery was 2 July:

Up very betimes. With H & Adrian to receive our car – & pay for it! £517 + 8 regist. + 14 insurance. Was at first disappointed in colour – more Adrian's choice than mine – a warm chocolate. I had chosen a softer greenish khaki, H & I went with Adrian round Lady [*sic*] Macquarie's chair to christen it.

The car was not actually driven to 'Avenel' until 4 July, since no one in the family had a licence. On that day, accompanied by an instructor provided by the retailer, Adrian drove his mother to 'Bukyangi' to show the machine to Sarah, who came to the bedroom window to see it.

Not having enjoyed her usual surfing holiday in January, Ethel went with Adrian, by tram and motor bus to Palm Beach on the first weekend in February. Together they had a 'glorious surf' at 4 o'clock on the Saturday and returned to 'Kookaburra', the little boarding house they had used in 1922. On the Sunday, without benefit of clergy she had a 'before brek, surf & lounged on beach breakfastless till 11'. Adrian caught the early bus to return to his law studies on Monday, and Ethel followed later in the day.

Both Adrian and Leo Charlton had academic hurdles to negotiate this year with final examinations in Law and Medicine and much hanging on the outcome. Leo had begun the ordeal on 26 February and felt, as it proved with good reason, he had not done well. Jean made a point of going into town every day to give support as each session concluded but when the results were posted on 5 April his name was not on the list, so the young people had to postpone their plans for marriage and postgraduate work in England till October.

At the beginning of March Adrian was given the best possible incentive for success when Sir William and Lady Cullen came to 'Avenel'; in the course of a stroll in the garden the Chief Justice said how much pleasure he took in the thought of having the young man as his associate when he was through his exams. A very relieved mother wrote in her diary 'my good old lad is through' on 7 April, towards the end of an Easter holiday in the Blue Mountains.

This year, 1923, saw the height of Ethel's income from writing. Ward Lock's royalties amounted to over 1158 pounds, the largest in her career. With salary from editing 'Sunbeams' of 364 pounds and earnings from *Smith's Weekly* and the Religious Tract Society, there was an all-up income from writing of 1543 pounds, a shade more than Herbert's judicial salary.

In February Ethel decided to give more attention to the share market as a means of enhancing her income. On the 20th she had withdrawn money from the bank and called on her broker, A. B. S. White, to discuss investments and arrange for the purchase of a further 199 Pedriau Rubber Company shares. More than 2000 pounds of her War Loans were to be sold with the intention of seeking more profitable investments. One project that emerged from all this was the idea of building four speculative cottages on land in Central Avenue, Mosman for which she paid 600 pounds, so giving effect to a dream she and Lilian had formulated thirty years earlier when the Copes had bought their land at Killara. Rex Cope, her half-brother, was to be involved as architect, for the scheme was largely designed to put business in his hands at a time when his fortunes were at a low ebb. Rex came to 'Avenel' on 13 July with a builder who signed up to build the first cottage for 984 pounds; the roof was on and rough casting of the walls completed by early December but progress was slow in the new year and it was not till May 1924 that it was offered for sale through a local agency for 1650 – 1700 pounds.

Ethel's work on 'Sunbeams', which provided a basic and stable income, had lost some of its early excitement and became at times, as she noted in her diary on 26 April when contemplating the weekly accumulation of related correspondence in her study, a 'frazzling job'. It was almost as bad as having a dairy farm, though it was possible to escape the toils for a week or two by preparing editorial matter in advance. A young man came out to 'Avenel' on Mondays with a huge pile of letters and competition entries; the record was set on 23 June 1924 when 'George fairly staggered over with entries – 3960 this week'.

As Chief Sunbeamer, Ethel had overall responsibility for the *Sunday Sun's* children's supplement but she had quite a fight to prevent the intrusion of vulgarities of the kind she had complained of at the outset. There was, as she recorded on 24 November, 'a sense of obstacles all the way', so she wrote next day to Mr Campbell Jones after seeing the latest edition, explaining that Mr Colles often failed to act on her requests to remove the offending material. A reply came almost immediately upholding her authority.

Yet there were compensations, not the least being the stimulus Ethel derived from preparing her Chief Sunbeamer's letter on subjects that enjoyed vogue or current interest. The letter written on 22 February for example was on ancient Egypt; as she explained in the diary, 'the Tutenkhamen discoveries have sent me delving into Egyptian lore which is very fascinating'. The following year she had the thrill of attending a lunch given by the Journalists' Association to two remarkable Australians who had become famous for their contributions to archaeology and medicine, Professors Elliott Smith and John Hunter. Ethel was at the table of honour and enjoyed being recognised by Elliott Smith from their schooldays when the Sydney Girls' and Boys' High

Schools shared the old building in Elizabeth Street. She took the opportunity of having the professor autograph a copy of his work that Herbert had given her years earlier.

A similar occasion took place in July when Herbert, now the proud possessor of a driver's licence, took her to Devonshire Street to see Miss Rivett's 'beautiful library for slum children – all its devices warmed my heart', she wrote. They gave presents to the children, including fifty golliwogs that had been sent in by the Sunbeamers and Ethel resolved to write a special letter and interest her members in the enterprise.

The novel for 1923 was in fact a revival of *Nicola Silver*, a story that had taken shape during the summer of 1921–2 but had been put aside. It concerns a family that lives in a farmhouse perched on a stony hillside, where Dunstan Silver, the tyrannical father, requires his children to carry a daily darg of 100 stones from the paddocks to contribute to farm terracing. Nicola, a spirited girl of 15 with a passion for literature, declines to do so on her birthday and is given 500 as a task next day for punishment. While she is engaged in this labour the family is visited by a rich young man named Conan whom Rhys Silver had rescued from No Man's Land when they had been serving in France. Rhys persuades Conan to carry Nicola off in the car for her first sight of the world of fun and fashion, living with his family in the heart of the city. Inevitably they are drawn to each other and it is the girl who really has the greater influence in this exchange for she inspires Conan to make something of himself and be of service to his fellow man. Like Ethel thirty years earlier, Nicola requires her suitor to wait four years. The story works very well and offers glimpses of Ethel's ideals on social problems and their solution. Some of its interest today comes from noticing her approval of smoking tobacco as a relaxing pastime. Even Nicola at fifteen years of age is taught by her elder brother how to enjoy a cigarette. She drew the air through it 'and soon had the luxurious wreath of smoke about her face'. Herbert's pipe smoking was an invariable accompaniment to his conversations on the verandah with his men friends.

In resuming work on this book Ethel had drawn inspiration from a familiar source. On 25 July, needing to have a garage constructed for the new Buick, she signed a contract that called for 143 pounds more than the original quote, and concluded, 'Time I wrote again and made some more money – it is running away like water just now.' The manuscript was completed in less than seven weeks, the last few chapters being written in trying conditions on holiday in the Blue Mountains, without a proper table, in the light of two flickering candles and a 'cold – warm – hot water bottle' to keep her from freezing. With the manuscript finished she wrote firmly in the diary, 'That ought to clear the decks for the wedding.'

One further hurdle remained to be negotiated before the manuscript went to the printer. In April 1924 Ward Lock wrote to Ethel advising that they had altered the manuscript by deleting the reference to Nicola's half sister 'because it turned upon marital unfaithfulness and divorce, subjects which, by general consent are absolutely banned from discussion in books for the young'.

This change must have reminded Ethel of a similar intervention nearly thirty years earlier, in relation to *The Little Larrikin*; apologies were offered for the absence of consultation but publishing deadlines had prevailed.[2]

The lead up to Jean's wedding, set for October 1924, was more than usually harrowing, with Ethel's mother and both of Herbert's parents dying in a short space of time, Sarah Cope only two days before.

Ethel and Herbert had a late call from Sarah's doctor saying that she could not last past midnight. Adrian drove his mother to Killara, collecting Lilian on the way just in time for them to say goodbye to their mother, in the company of Charlie and the nurse.

On 22 October Ethel and the immediate family took part in a private funeral ceremony at the Northern Suburbs Cemetery when, as she put it in her diary, 'Buried my poor brave little Mother'. Sarah's courage and sense of humour had equipped her to be a great survivor; both qualities were possessed in good measure by Ethel, though she chose a more reliable route to security than did her mother, seeking that precious commodity in her own capacities rather than in the more hazardous expedient of marriage.

But even darker shadows were gathering for the Curlewis family. Jean's health was continuing to trouble her mother. On 9 April that year Ethel had taken Jean and Leo off to the mountains and Jenolan Caves in the valley beyond to give them a holiday after the stress of Leo's exams. Yet, safely back at 'Avenel' with 10 000 words of 'Nicola Silver' behind her she admitted a continuing anxiety about Jean 'who still looks ill'.

On Friday 13 April:

Took Jean for an examination by Dr Ritchie – she very angry because I insisted and made the appointment. He justifies my anxiety – says she has chronic tonsilitis, is anaemic etc.

Off they were sent for an X-ray, Ethel feeling upset, yet sensing an important step had been taken in finding what was keeping Jean thin. However, in a move the parents must soon have passionately regretted, they sought another opinion from Dr Mills, Dean of Medicine.

And everything Ritchie says he says no to. Says her chest is perfectly sound, no trace of tonsilitis. Just needs to readjust her diet & play a little more. – Never felt such relief – though in my bones I sort of knew she was quite sound.

The full consequences of the family's decision to act on this second opinion were not apparent for several years. In the meantime, Leo passed his finals, and he and Jean were married on 23 October, at an evening service at St Luke's Mosman. The Woman's Letter in the *Bulletin* described Jean's gown ᵃˢ ᵃ 'fairy-tale confection of shimmering satin'; Ethel 'wore a frock, mostly glistening black sequins, that flew a wing-like effect in gorgette as blue as her own eyes'.[3] 'Avenel's' roses were in full bloom for the reception, Sir William Cullen proposed the toast to the bride and groom while the bride's mother was torn between her hopes for the couple's future and a consciousness of her own mother's life having just ended. Jean and Leo were booked to sail for England on 17 November in the *Port Campbell* after a round of parties and a sad farewell from Charlie, who knew he would not see his granddaughter again.

During four splendid weeks in August 'Avenel' had the services of a butler, Barclay, who filled the place of his friend Jenny who had gone to Brisbane. Ethel had felt dubious about the experiment but decided to make the trial because he had been an enlisted man and was 'out of a billet'. Within a week she knew she would 'like to always keep a butler' but it was not to be.

While this experiment was in progress 'Avenel' had another unexpected accession in the shape of Ethel's niece Theo Pockley whose mother Rose had gone to England leaving the little girl for her sister to care for. Ethel's anger at this imposition came to full flower on 22 August when Dr Barnes was called in to check on some alarming symptoms and pronounced measles:

Words fail. [*she wrote*] Mothers with children jolly well oughtn't to go to England & dump their youngsters on other people. We took ours with us. Of course I'm sorry for the poor kiddie & won't let her see what a frightful infliction it is.

For the first time in ages Ethel was impelled on New Year's Eve to review recent events and look towards the future. Thinking first of the death of Herbert's parents and her own 'Little Mother' she wrote:

This has been the fullest year & the saddest & the happiest I have known. My girl has gone but it is all for her happiness & the future promises very brightly for her. But I shall be glad when she is this side of the world again ...

Lily's troubles affect me deeply – no hope of Fred's recovery.

With that & with Leo & Jean likely to need lots of help for some years, my pen must not give up.

So I am glad I have done next year's book Nicola Silver. Must keep Sunbeams on too.

Rex & Marie, living so close, must have help & interest – life is very hard for them.

She felt thankful for 'excellent health' and 'comfortable circumstances', but even with the record earnings of the past year concluded that it was 'not enough for the calls on me'.

Family matters dominated the start of 1924. News came of the *Port Campbell*'s arrival in Dunkirk; some weeks later came a packet of letters that Jean and Leo had posted in Suez, where they had been healthy and in good spirits. A farewell lunch was given at the Metropole, a comfortable and gracious countryman's hotel near the gardens, to Harold and Rose Pockley, who had returned from England and were now planning to stay indefinitely in New Zealand. Lil's husband Fred was very ill with cancer, necessitating injections of morphia several times a day. He died in late January, when Ethel accompanied Lilian to the interment in the family vault at Waverley Cemetery, remarking later that her sister was 'marvellously brave' and well supported by her two boys. 'Poor old Fred – a thwarted life, never doing the work he wanted & then cancer as an end'.

As a writer Ethel would not have thought 1924 a good year. Admittedly William Bligh had told her he thought *Nicola Silver* was her best work and it was readily accepted by Mr Prior of the *Bulletin*, who had written to ask if she had anything suitable for serial publication in the projected new *Women's Weekly*. But Nicola was a product of the previous year and in the search for a new and profitable venture Ethel was driven back to very old material. The manuscript of the play 'Sundowner' was exhumed in June and made up into a parcel to send to Hugh Ward for consideration; in October *Ungardeners* was sent to Ward Lock for publication as the 1925 book when it failed to interest American publishers.

Yet, even in this year of modest achievement, with Ethel's royalties from Ward Lock 500 pounds less than in 1923, she and Herbert had managed to save 1415 pounds in spite of some heavy expenses, as she recorded with some surprise after doing the accounts at year's end. This, despite a continuing inability to sell 'Gresmere', the speculatively built cottage in Central Avenue, which had been offered for sale by auction on 14 November. It was a relief to Ethel when a buyer turned up the following June with an offer of 1500 pounds.

Three notable achievements should be mentioned. In late September she wrote versicles for her leader in 'Sunbeams' 'on guarding the beauty of the bush & beaches, from picnickers traces & so on', which helps to show that a commitment had developed, much under the influence of William Cullen, and later of Amy Mack and Florence Sulman, to appreciate and conserve the unique flora of Australia.[4]

In mid-October Ethel attended a meeting called by the Mayoress of Mosman to establish a branch of the District Nurses' Association. Dr Guy Griffiths spoke but very few people attended so it was agreed that meetings should be held in private homes to generate a local consciousness. Since no one else offered, Ethel took on the task herself; it was the beginning of a significant and valuable commitment. In March 1925 she wrote an article about the Association for the *Mosman Daily* and in August when she gave a tea party at 'Avenel' to promote it there were forty people attending to enjoy asparagus sandwiches and fruit salad.

Apart from the constant commitment to 'Sunbeams', Ethel's life at the start of 1925 was occupied by domestic and social matters. A new mole-grey Queensland maple bedroom suite was ordered for 'Avenel'; the cushions were covered with purple silk, making a striking contrast. The study carpet was taken up, and the books were rearranged, with Herbert's large collection of foreign novels being set up in a long cupboard. A new carpet was laid, a thick, soft grey Axminster, plain but for a trail of coloured flowers in each corner. Soon there was a further trip to town to buy an 'Electric Vacuum Cleaner' which cost over 13 pounds, hundreds of dollars in today's currency.

At the end of January, when she had finished her stint with 'Sunbeams' for the week, Ethel was 'full of energy & getting on with everything splendidly'. The following morning, a Sunday, was wonderfully cool so she worked in the garden, which was in abundant flower; in the afternoon she went in the car with Herbert and Adrian to Mona Vale, where they found an empty paddock in which she drove her car for the first time: 'they said my steering was quite good. Did figure 8 a dozen times, started, changed gears etc.'

Work on the manuscript of *Ungardeners* approached finality in late January when Ailsa Cullen brought over some photographs from 'Tregoyd' that were to be used as a basis for some of the illustrations. William Bligh called in for a long discussion after he had seen the manuscript, which he said he liked as an enthusiastic gardener, but had little confidence in as a commercial proposition. His judgement was soon vindicated by the cool response of Ethel's readers; though intended to celebrate the achievements of two unconventional gardeners, the book fails as a narrative and lacks conviction in all but one of its child characters. The middle ground of the story is cluttered by the names of plants that would be unfamiliar to anyone but a botanist and there are long, tiresome stretches of philosophy and reflection on the meaning of life.

Nicola Silver, on the other hand, had sold well, though Jean's *Dawn Man* had been a disappointment. Ethel had learned from recent letters that the young couple had spent Christmas apart because Leo had taken on work as a locum. Yet there was an understanding that they were to return by December via New Zealand in a ship on which Leo would be employed as a doctor.

Charles Cope, in his remaining months of life, was looked after at 'Bukyangi' by a nurse, Fanny Grundy, whose task was much exacerbated by the patient's susceptibility to delusions. When Herbert and Ethel drove over on 17 March 'something had infuriated the poor old fellow & he would barely see us'; on 3 May he told them the nurse was trying to kill him. As she explained 'it was morphia raving'. So it was a relief to everyone when he died of heart failure on 30 May. His estate was sworn for probate in October, for a sum of 13 047 pounds; most of the money went to his son Charles Joseph (known as Rex) together with the bulk of the furniture, though Lilian received the drawing room suite and plate, linen, glass and china, as well as specific paintings and ornaments. There are two puzzles about this will and that of Sarah Cope who had died in 1923. One is the size of the property, given the fact that Charlie had been left out of the wills left by his father, Joseph Cope of Windsor, who had died in 1862, and also by his mother, Mary Ann, who had died at North Sydney in 1905. The other surprise is the fact that Ethel Curlewis was only a minor beneficiary in the estates of both her parents, receiving only a few specified paintings and pieces of jewellery, while Lilian got a block of land owned by her mother and all her personal belongings as well as cash. Perhaps that had been Ethel's wish, communicated to her parents long before their deaths. Her diary recorded nothing but approval of these arrangements.[5]

The Curlewis family now acquired a new pleasure made possible by an uncharacteristic extravagance of Herbert's, the purchase in September 1924 of a wireless set. It was Ethel who was most interested in keeping in touch with technological change but his awareness of her difficulty in hearing programmes on his crystal set may have prompted the action. Mechanics from the Home Electric Company came to instal the new instrument together with an aerial. She heard 'really splendidly' from the beginning and now rushed home early from engagements in town to listen to classical music concerts and plays.

Four years later she listened, enthralled, to direct messages from Kingsford Smith and Charles Ulm on board the *Southern Cross*, making the first air crossing of the Pacific.

On the first day of spring 1925 Ethel went into town to buy hats to go with some frocks she had chosen the week before, 'a nice French little model in orange & navy' and another navy frock, 'different but well cut'. On the second trip she remarked, 'Heavens. The time one wastes over clothes. But the spring things are very alluring.' And after all she had some big moments in prospect, with delegates coming from England to attend a Sydney gathering of writers and journalists which started on 2 September with a garden party at Government House. There she met Lord Burnham and was taken in to lunch by A. P. Herbert, whose conversation she found most stimulating. Next day at the university reception she was disadvantaged from sitting behind the speakers on the dais, where she was unable to hear the flow of Herbert's wit that so delighted his audience. At the end of the conference a meeting was held at the Mary Elizabeth to form the Women Writers' Association. To Ethel's disappointment few of the fifty women present were book writers and she came home 'feeling frazzled to death – all one's vital forces seem dissipated at such things'. A few days later Ethel took a number of her friends in the car to a meeting of the Feminist Club for which she and Mary Gilmore represented the Women Writers.

Inspired perhaps by her recent meetings with celebrities, Ethel had Adrian drive her to Blackheath on 12 September where she spent time at Lilian's home but stayed at the Ivanhoe Hotel, refreshing her soul with the cool, clear air and blue mists and working hard on her current novel, *Funny*. There in a quiet room, seated at a desk in front of a cosy fire 'the end of the story ran gently & easily off her pen. Magnifique', she exclaimed. 'Now the decks will be clear for Jean's return.'

Ethel impatiently followed the progress of the ship to Panama and New Zealand, where the Charltons changed to the *Manganui* for the final stretch across the Tasman Sea. When the letter had arrived saying that Jean was packing her mother had written 'It makes me very restless – feel *now* I cannot wait any longer.'

One of the outings that filled those days of waiting was an exhibition of paintings by Theo Proctor and Margaret Preston; Ethel bought a woodcut by the latter, whose still life pictures were marked by the bold designs and strong colours that characterized the twenties. She was driven for this occasion by the chauffer Smith, who was coming to 'Avenel' on trial to drive two days a week. On the night of 30 November the three Curlewises sat up playing the new card game, Rummy, to pass the time. Predictably they were waiting at the wharf soon after sunrise, long before the Charltons were through customs. Again there is a note of undefined menace in the diary entry:

J looked as fragile as when she went away – & sad – though gay – which worried me. Leo very well & grown broader. A long day of talking & happiness. Leo to his home so we had her to ourselves.

Ethel delighted again in the pleasure of Jean's company, taking her to lunch at Farmer's, having her help with Christmas shopping and sharing with her in presenting the prizes at St Thomas's Memorial Church. Herbert became involved also when the decision had been made for the young people to live in a cottage at Pymble, for which Leo's parents paid the first year's rent. With Christmas only days away and the house badly awry the family spent a whole Sunday there working 'like happy niggers – waxing floors, lining cupboards – anything that turned up'. Even on Christmas Day, when Ethel and Herbert took the family's meal to Pymble with sensible presents such as a carpet sweeper and wine, they helped in painting and making the house straight.

he new year of 1926 began for Ethel with her usual fortnight's holiday in a cottage at Palm Beach starting on 4 January when the Sunbeams proofs had been disposed of. With a hired driver she arrived in the Buick in late afternoon feeling 'clean used up'. A surf before breakfast next day 'washed much of the weariness away' and by the time she'd had a third swim before nightfall she felt like a new woman and slept contentedly in a stretcher on the verandah 'among the stars all night'.

Adrian came down for a week of surfing and study, for he still had final year Law to negotiate, so the household was 'quiet & peaceful beyond all telling'.

Ethel was still concerned enough about self-improvement to practise her overarm stroke in the rock pool.

She returned to 'Avenel' on 18 January to find matters in something of a rush. Jean needed advice; she had been invited by *The Home* to do their dramatic criticisms and edit the children's page. When her first piece came out early in March Ethel thought it excellent, a view she was confirmed in by the publisher, Sydney Ure Smith, when she spoke to him over lunch at the Institute of Journalists.

While at Palm Beach Ethel had seen an article of Jean's published in the *Herald*.[1] Entitled 'Lights of London.

Harvest Moon', it was set in the amber twilight of rural Buckinghamshire, evoking a picture of:

Pink hollyhocks stiff in windless golden air before the cottages ... church bells ringing far away.

The golden heart of England, and at the village pump, like a sob of blood, flies the Red Flag.

In what followed, Jean contrasted the socialist view of the evils of the capitalist system and a society drained by the recent war with the satisfied assumption of an old conservative standing on the edge of the meeting who had a vision of hollyhocks and quiet harvest fields. Jean seems to be saying that while the spirit of John Hampden, the great parliamentary leader of the 17th century, walks abroad in Great Missenden, England can be confident of her long term future.

Late March was taken up with Ethel's preparations for a holiday with Rose in New Zealand while the Pockleys were living there. She wrote an enthusiastic letter of acceptance, remarking that the invitation forced her to 'dismiss my qualms about being wanted'. She wrote a sufficient number of Sunbeams editorials to cover a month's absence and found time to entertain Mary Gilmore to lunch. A few months earlier Mary had sent a copy of a newly published volume of poetry, *The Hound of the Road*,[2] inscribed to Ethel with the verse:

She hath a child's heart still,
For all the pile of books
That show her constant will!
And hers the manner mild
Of some dear child, – who pitying saw
The horror of life's naked claw,
And wept above the fallen stooks

Ethel in the garden at 'Avenel'

George Robertson (of Angus and Robertson), London 1900. Courtesy of the Mitchell Library

Dowell O'Reilly, a long-term friend of Ethel's and father of Eleanor Dark. Courtesy of 'Varuna' and the Eleanor Dark Foundation

Ure Smith, publisher of *Art in Australia*, for whom Jean wrote until shortly before she died. Courtesy of the Mitchell Library

A. G. Stephens, literary critic of the *Bulletin's* Red Page. Courtesy of the Mitchell Library

Manly, the Corso 1929. Courtesy of the Sydney Water Board

A motoring picnic at Palm Beach 1926, including Ethel and Adrian and probably Lil and
Eric. The Buick was the first car owned by Ethel and Herbert

Ethel at her window in 'Avenel', photographed by Cazneaux

Herbert Raine Curlewis on appointment as a judge, June 1917

Jean, aged 13

Jean as a bride on 23 October 1923

Lifesavers in action, Adrian at the rear

Dorothea Mackellar c. 1920. Courtesy of Jyoti Brunsdon

The young Miles Franklin

Adrian and Betty's wedding at St Philip's Church on 12 December 1928

Ethel in her chair by the window

Captain Adrian Curlewis in uniform before going to Singapore in 1941

Ethel, Betty, Ian and Philippa while Adrian was in captivity

Ruth Park, who shared many of Ethel's views about writing for children

which war, in its dread might,
Shook down in one fell night.

It was a calm and uneventful trip from Sydney to Wellington on board the *Manganui*, where Ethel was welcomed by Harold and Rose Pockley and taken by car to their home on a hill overlooking the harbour. Inevitably there were interviewers and photographers to capture her words and images for various newspapers and a would-be writer seeking advice on the manuscript of a play, unaware that this was a medium which had so far resisted Ethel's efforts.

The Pockleys took Ethel on the long drive that circles the edge of Wellington's spectacular harbour and then to the high peak at Newtown where lived Sir Truby King, the man who had done so much for the health of New Zealand babies. Rose and Ethel boarded the *Maori* for an overnight trip across the Straits to Lyttleton, port of Christchurch on the South Island. Their brief stay included a coach journey to Akaroa and a visit from Mr Whitcombe of Whitcombe and Tombs who asked Ethel to write a book for him.

Back in Wellington on 28 April Ethel said goodbye to Rose and Harold and set off on her journey north as a lone traveller. From Hamilton she wrote back to the Pockleys describing the parlous condition of the road north which had been torn up by a washaway but praising the Plunkett Rest Room where the female travellers refreshed themselves in the warmth and read *Vogue* and the *Ladies' Home Journal*, 'And free! N.Z. *does* look after its women folk'. A proud railway porter sternly declined the two shilling tip she offered, regarding it as an insult to his country's wage system.

From Brent's Bathgate House at Rotorua Ethel wrote one of the best intra-family letters that has survived her general tendency to 'clear out and burn'. It suggests that her time with the Pockleys overcame any lingering reserve between the half-sisters that might have remained from old differences: the consciousness of having different fathers; conflicts within the thrice-mixed Cope family; and more recent resentment at Rose and Harold for going off to England and leaving Theo to be minded at 'Avenel':

Dearest little Sis,
That letter to Prince's Gate warmed the middlingest part of my heart. I had all that feeling to you – & yours . . . while with you & simply couldn't . . . & can't express it. Will you just take it that I have loved you all so much while I was with you . . . & understand you so much better than ever before . . . & been so grateful for all the sweet little acts of kindness from all.

She went on to describe a wonderful Maori guide who showed her the tribal village at Ohinemutu, which took its name from a rock at the lakeside (meaning 'the girl cut off from the world'), named by a chief who lamented his daughter's death at the hands of his enemies:

I cd write pages about it I got such a good guide . . . And yes – now are my doubts set at rest, I am a truly celebrated person. I made a few notes here & there as she talked & she asked what for. I said – oh a book. She. Will you tell me your name? Me. E.T. She. Wringing my hand & practically falling on my buzzom. 'I am the mother of seven myself – Seven Little Maoris'. That's honest Injun.[3]

Ethel's first sight of Auckland was from her room at the Grand Hotel, gazing at the dismal sight of warehouses and wet shipping on a Sunday pouring with rain. Wishing to escape from the 'tedium & yawns' in the hotel lounge she tried the Museum and then the Public Library only to be told that the opening time was 2 o'clock, so she concluded that 'a wet Sunday in a strange city is a frost & shd be cut out'. But on Monday the gloom had disappeared for she was busy once again being entertained royally at the Penwomen's Club where she read a speech and signed autographs. Her eye was pleased by the sight of a chocolate cake for morning tea, decorated with a map of Australia on which Sydney was marked in silver. Next door's shop had its window entirely filled with books by Ethel, Lilian, Jean and Mary Grant Bruce.[4]

Some of Ethel's time in Auckland was used profitably in a visit to the Museum, 'a vastly interesting place', where she took notes about the Moa and the great war canoe of Maori mythology, intending to use the material in a newspaper series just as she had done with the European trip in 1910. Medical friends drove her to the Karitane establishment which had pioneered infant nutrition and training and in the last night at the Grand she worked on a talk she was to present at the Lyceum Club. 'Home,' she wrote, 'grows sweetly near.'

It required all of Ethel's stoicism to dress for dinner each night on the voyage back to Sydney for the ship pitched and rolled all the way. As she put it in a letter to Rose on arrival, 'my dead aunt, I was glad to be on terra cotta again'. Herbert and Jean had been on the wharf for hours, the former thinking perhaps of his pent-up emotions thirty-two years earlier when waiting for his fiancée to return from Tasmania. Home they drove in the new Chrysler 'shining with Duco & spattered with mud' to find 'Avenel still there. Same maids. House in first class order', prompting the reflection, 'Mothers aren't all they imagine they are.' A fine dinner had been prepared on Herbert's instructions with asparagus, roast chicken, forcemeat balls, bread sauce and vegetables, and jellies and trifles washed down by two bottles of champagne. Then a big fire in the drawing room where 'the returned hero recounted her moving tales by flood & field'.[5]

Within a month of her return Ethel had made a good

beginning with the New Zealand articles. The third one, on the coming of the Pakeha, was in the hands of the typist. Meetings with the District Nursing Association had resumed and in her study the decks had been cleared with a ritual burning of Sunbeams correspondence into which all manner of other material no doubt found its way. Adrian's friend, Betty Carr, was now increasingly included in family dinners and bridge games especially at weekends. A pretty and athletic young woman whose family had initially migrated from England to Western Australia, she was growing ever closer to an understanding with Adrian, at a time when the family was poised to receive its sharpest blow.

In July 1926 came the shocking news of Jean's tuberculosis:

J's housekeeper rang up that J was ill & H & I went up ... Telling me what was the biggest shock of my life that she had had a haemorrhage & Leo had taken her to Dr Sinclair Gilles – Influenza, & overdoing. Stayed arranging things till late. She is to go to Mts at once, to give up all work & rest well.

Making matters more difficult was the departure of Jean's housekeeper, perhaps in fear of infection, which led to Ethel and Herbert's driving to Pymble to do the housework and cooking, after which Ethel brought back to 'Avenel' the material on which Jean's columns in *The Home* would be based. Jean was soon packed off to the mountains by car, wrapped in furs, with Adrian driving and Leo in the back seat. After lunch at the Carrington Hotel in Katoomba Jean was with Nurse Tobey by 2 p.m., so beginning a long and tragic battle to resist the inroads of the disease.

From this point a great deal of Ethel's life was shaped by a concern to help her daughter. Her own work on Sunbeams needed to be completed quickly in order to make time for doing Jean's articles for *The Home*. On 19 July she saw Sydney

Ure Smith in his office; he was much concerned about Jean's illness and accepted Ethel's undertaking to do her work, at least the children's page and the Clearing House for the next month. Ethel's own commitments were substantial as her New Zealand articles had begun running in the *Herald*, intended also for serializing in Victoria and New Zealand, so involving her in a weekly task in addition to the work for the *Sun*. After the meeting with Ure Smith she went to bed 'very cold & shivery' but was determined to be well enough by the following Sunday to drive up with Adrian, Leo and Betty to see Jean at Katoomba. Only ten minutes of conversation with the invalid was permitted and after a brief visit to the land at Leura they returned to Sydney.

In the midst of this crisis Ethel had the disquieting news that Rose was sending her daughter Marcia by ship to stay at 'Avenel' until the rest of the family was transplanted to Sydney. As always Ethel bowed to the wind, reflecting 'My heavens my hands are going to be full, my own extra work, all Jeans & now my poor little Marcia.' Collecting her at the wharf on 3 August she brought her new charge home in a taxi, remarking in her diary later, 'My heart aches for her.' Why the child should have been separated from her family in this way is a complete mystery, but it will be recalled that a similar thing had been done with Theo years before when Rose had gone to England.

Jean put on five pounds in weight during the first five weeks at Katoomba but in mid-September, when she was brought down to Sydney for a few days to see Dr Sinclair Gilles, he warned that she must expect to remain in the mountains for a further six months. 'Felt very cast down' her mother wrote, for she had been greatly heartened by the apparent improvement in Jean's health and spirits and her enjoyment of lunch in town and a sight of spring fashions at Farmers. Towards the end of that month when Ethel took her niece to town for an X-ray she despatched Marcia home early and dined alone at her club, remarking 'a rare thing for me but I get a little tired of someone in house all the time'. Yet Marcia offered engaging company, and several times accompanied Ethel to Mr Leach's film studio at Bondi to watch the shooting of the courtroom scene in Marcus Clark's classic novel on the convict system, *For the Term of His Natural Life*. Inspired perhaps by this experience they went to watch Herbert preside in court for a whole morning after which they lunched with him in his rooms. 'I loved seeing him in it all,' she wrote. Her article, 'The Big Picture' was typed and sent in to the *Herald* on 5 November.

Ethel was now having her own health problems and began consulting Sir John Macpherson for neuritis in the neck and arm in late October. No improvement having occurred by the end of November it was arranged that she should go to the Wahroonga Sanitarium for a week's rest cure and electric baths, taking the precaution beforehand of seeing the optician so as to secure better reading glasses, for she took with her a pile of current books. Even after the second electric bath she 'Felt very cheap still'; on day four she was a trifle better '& my spirit is getting broken to the no tea & coffee & meat', this being the dietary regime at the Sanitarium.

Adrian's engagement to Betty Carr was announced in early 1927 though it was to be kept quiet till he was through Law. At the thought of 'losing' her son Ethel was philosophical. 'He is nearly 26 so it had to come & I think we shall grow very fond of her – she has plenty of sweetness as well as beauty'. Adrian felt decidedly pessimistic about his final exams which began on 21 February but on 9 March his mother exclaimed in her diary, 'Oh frabjous day! A is through his final!' Two days later Ethel and Jean sat in the Banco Court that Francis Greenway had designed to house the beginning of modern legal institutions in Australia and saw Adrian admitted to the Bar, looking very like his father at the same stage. He went off with his mother to choose a carpet and other furnishings for his chambers, a present from Ethel, just as Herbert's had been three decades earlier. Betty missed the celebrations as she had gone to Adelaide for a year as sports mistress at the Methodist Ladies' College, a well-paid resident position that gave her a chance of repaying the fees incurred for her training by the Australian College of Physical Education.[6]

With the approach of Betty's departure her mother had called to see Ethel, when Betty dined at 'Avenel' and went with Adrian to see *The Pirates of Penzance*. Two days later Ethel wrote:

Last night left it to my 'sub-conscious' to make a song of Sydney. Sat & walked the verandah & one came singing in my head & the lines very soon & then made up an air on the piano that seems to fit. H & A went to see Betty off & I was on piano stool till about 9 when I finished it. But must get a musician to write it out more elaborately.[7]

It concluded with the verse:

O, slopes, O spires, O sands so fair,
O childlike city free from care,
O magic of the salty breeze,
Magic of eucalyptus trees!
O youth that went with flags afly,
Gladly for England's sake to die,
You ask what city's set apart?
Sydney's the city of the heart!

Several times in February and March, 1927, Ethel took advantage of the splendid concrete road that had been built to Palm Beach the year before at a cost of 30 000 pounds, driving down with Adrian of whom she had said, 'Like Queen Mary's "Calais" you would find "Palm Beach" engraved on little A's heart.' One of the special attractions of the place had been the feeling of privacy and exclusivity that was engendered by its remoteness from Sydney. While appreciating the road Ethel noted, 'Of course 'twill ruin Palm Beach from our point of view. Everyone will come now.'[8]

Soon after completing her 'Song of Sydney' Ethel had one of her regular sortings through the accumulation of paper in her study. The shortage of space in her bookshelves that had developed as Herbert increased his own purchases, especially of French and Russian classics in translation, was remedied by having him remove them to his dressing room. Dorothea Mackellar and her mother came to lunch on 2 March; they were planning to sail to England a fortnight later. This was at a time when Dorothea regularly had verses published in the *Herald*, long before there was a separate literary section.

Jean's illness made Ethel even more concerned about her finances, for she saw both children as likely to need assistance. On doing up her share book at the start of 1927 she found rather to her surprise that she and Herbert had put away about 1500 pounds in spite of heavy expenses including the new car and the trip to New Zealand. Nevertheless in June she wrote determinedly, 'I *must* make money faster for Jean – & Adrian too.' She went into town to withdraw 1000 pounds from War Loans and put it in the hands of J. Palmer & Sons for a more remunerative investment.

Another response was to get started on a novel that would take up one of the themes of *Seven Little Australians* by telling the story of Judy's time at boarding school and her nearly disastrous flight that ended in the barn of the family home at 'Misrule' on the Parramatta River. With Betty now in Adelaide Adrian could be pressed into service for a weekend trip to the mountains, visiting Mount Victoria and the school that had served as a model for the Misses Burtons' establishment, where Judy had been a reluctant scholar. *Judy and Punch*, published by Ward Lock in 1928, represented an attempt to halt the downwards slide in her royalties from the firm, which had gone from the 1923 record of 1158 pounds to 556 pounds in 1924, 624 pounds in 1925, 469 pounds in 1926 and 356 pounds in 1927. It is significant that the remark, 'I must make more money' had been made on 8 June 1927, just after the royalty cheque for the period to 30 May was received.[9]

In the event, *Judy and Punch* was not a success. The whole concept of restoring Judy to life over thirty years after her death at the foot of a gum tree was probably found a little suspect by Ethel's faithful readers and the dialogue is unconvincing. Ward Lock royalties fell to 222 pounds in 1928, recovered to 327 pounds in 1929 under the brief impact of *Judy and Punch* and resumed the downwards trend in 1930. It was for Ethel a sad way to end her career as a novelist but the thought is inescapable that her sense of the joy of life, her genuine enthusiasm for the human condition, had been sapped by Jean's illness.

Jean was again living in the mountains and on the fourth anniversary of her marriage her mother wrote hopefully 'it seems as if better things are ahead'. Jean's condition appeared stable and Leo had been appointed as medical superintendent of the St George Cottage Hospital with good prospects. Jean occasionally came down by train to spend a weekend with Leo at a city hotel and just before Christmas after a fresh X-ray Dr Gilles gave an encouraging report while insisting that the patient should remain in the mountains for the hot weather.

As a mark of faith in life's prospects at the start of 1928 Ethel bought herself a much larger diary than the tiny ones she had been content with for several years and proceeded to record her activities with something like the old enthusiasm.

Betty Carr was back from Adelaide and for Adrian's birthday on 13 January Herbert took the family to the theatre to see *The Girl Friend* completing the night with supper at the

Hotel Australia. During this hot summer Adrian's career as a barrister really took off. A proud mother recorded his three wins at Redfern Court on Monday 6 February; there were another two briefs on Wednesday and a jury case given him on the Thursday. Each day the heat was so oppressive that Herbert tried to get home early and take Ethel for a surf at Manly, which restored her greatly, though she sighed at the thought that her husband did not share in her pleasure.

But they were again enjoying an active social life that recalls the adventures of thirty years earlier. On the following Saturday, after finishing her Sunbeams chores:

At night with H, Betty & A to a party at Wahroonga at the Braddocks beautiful home, Rippon Grange. Had not been there since the Sargoods had it. Party was a 'Back to Childhood' one & very amusing to watch. Betty & Marjorie were twins in little spotted frocks & anklestraps. Marcia & Rob [Rose's children] sailors – & so on. All the girls barelegged & in socks – the boys too, some of the young married ones too. Mrs Fitzhardinge looked 13. Home at midnight.

On 5 April, when Adrian had finished a long day at the bar the family set off in the dying light of Easter Thursday for the mountains, stopping at the Log House at Penrith for a cold chicken tea and calling on Jean briefly at the Ritz, a private hotel/sanitorium, before going to their own rented cottage. When the others had returned to Sydney Ethel spent most of her time writing and walked one afternoon to visit Lily Cullen at 'Clifflands' in Morven Road, Leura, making a round trip of four and a half miles. Her friend spent most of her time on a sofa on the verandah confined by a disabling illness but was 'very bright & well otherwise'. Ethel took her a sealing wax outfit to give her a change of occupation.

At the beginning of June, when Jean was down from the mountains for a short holiday at 'Avenel' with Leo, it was decided that a new cottage should be built on the family's land near the golf links at Leura so as to establish a base there during the remainder of Jean's illness. As Ethel put it, Herbert 'nobly withdrew his objections to building ... & said go ahead'.

Plans for the new cottage occupied much of the latter part of this year. Ethel signed the contract on 17 August. A week later she had the now unusual experience of travelling by train to Blackheath to stay with Lil, for whom she drew up a list of articles for use in her children's page of the *Daily Telegraph*. Already excavations had been done, timber and bricks were on the site and foundations under way. There was much pleasure in planning the garden and buying linen and furniture for the cottage, which gave an excuse for installing at 'Avenel' a new gas stove with an elevated oven and exiling the old one to the mountains. Ironically, it was in the midst of this activity that Jean decided on renting a flat at the St James apartment building in Kings Cross. Situated on the ninth floor it sounded rather splendid, with access to a roof garden, ballroom, and a restaurant with facilities for meals being sent to rooms. Ethel was anxious at the thought of Jean's being alone there at times and the doctor likewise but she was so eager she simply had to try.

For Adrian and Betty, however, it was a time of new beginnings. He had come back jubilantly on 11 October after winning a big case relating to a bridge contract in which he had acted without a senior barrister to lead him. The week's work had earned him 45 pounds, turning his thoughts quickly to new chambers and matrimony. In November he went with his mother to look at a cottage for rent on Spit Road; it had six rooms and offered 'glorious views' through the heads. Betty went to see it at night and liked it just as well. Ethel organised a pre-wedding party for Betty and the bridesmaids, each of whom received a spray of lily of the valley. A linen tea followed, and the mood of largesse came to its climax with the decision by Herbert and Ethel to give each of their children a new car, a Ford Tudor sedan, financing the gift by the sale of shares.

In the first week of December the move into the new cottage, 'Garth', was made. With Rose for company and support Ethel made an early start in her car and enjoyed the first sight of the almost finished home. She found the contrast of the dark blue paint on the doors and guttering very effective against the cream of the walls, but there were many details to be seen to, wet paint everywhere, floors unwashed, curtains to be hung and electric light not yet connected. In spite of all this she was thrilled by the prospect of having a mountain cottage once more, 'Have rarely felt so happy', she wrote simply. Just a few days later Adrian and Betty Carr were married and came to live nearby in Mosman.

In March of 1929 Ethel was having a quiet holiday at 'Garth' with Betty, after having said goodbye to a contingent of guests which included a golfing friend of Herbert's. She and Betty played an occasional round of golf together but the idyll came to an end when the news came that Jean had suffered another haemorrhage and had been taken to hospital in Sydney. Feeling terribly cast down Ethel put the cottage right and set off by train for Sydney. An X-ray on 25 March gave promising results but Jean's weight was down to 6 stone 12 pounds and she was to be sent back to the sanatorium at Katoomba as soon as she could travel.

By July, after yet another haemorrhage, Jean became a patient at the Molong Private Hospital in Darlinghurst. Ethel wrote on 11th, 'To Jean – very irritable, poor little soul, but looking well – or fairly well.' Her room was full of lovely flowers and friends Ure Smith and Leon Gellert had given her a beautiful jade water holder and glasses.

One of the consequences of Ethel's preoccupation with Jean's struggle for life was that she could not give much attention to the pregnancy of Betty Curlewis, who produced a beautiful plump boy weighing 9lbs 10oz on 22 September. A month later, as Ethel described it, she and Herbert went on a Saturday night 'to mount guard over Ian' while the parents went to bridge for the first time since the birth. So began an association that was to have increasing significance for the two grandparents in the years that followed.

There was little time that summer for swimming but on 27 December Ethel did have a day in the surf at Palm Beach: 'They do me an extraordinary amount of good,' she wrote, 'take all the fever & fret away for a time.' The following day she worked on Sunbeams 'throughout a hot & killing day. Took me slow hours to write a rotten leader'. Never had the responsibility of children's pages seemed so onerous a task as during the final summer when Jean's life was slipping away. In February Ethel spent a day in book-shops and in the Mosman Library looking for books on tuberculosis – mentioning the awful word for the first time in her diary – and on Christian Science. Ethel's mother had taken an interest in Christian Science when her death was approaching; on 18 February Ethel spoke again to Jean on the subject and though sceptical she said she would try it. A few days later Jean spoke briefly to Mrs Holdship, then a leading exponent of the faith in Sydney, but she remained doubtful.

During these last few weeks at the Molong Hospital Jean was extremely reluctant to receive any visitor but her mother. For Ethel sleep became increasingly elusive and on 20 March she had a dream about Jean where she seemed to be looking over a balcony 'watching for Nellie Pockley then falling to ground in bedroom – long hair flying round her – water froth-ing from her mouth – "They are taking my life" – oh a vile dream'.

The following day Ethel noted:

To Jean. Felt stronger myself – more able to help her – She likes me to stroke her spine – says it wonderfully helps to stroke her. She seemed better. Mrs Holdship went later. Simply had to switch my mind away & went to pictures, St James "Paris".

Jean died on 27 March 1930.

chapter

Seventeen

or months after Jean's death Ethel was driven regularly to the grave at the Northern Suburbs Cemetery where she left flowers from the 'Avenel' garden. Her daughter-in-law, Betty, most frequently drove Ethel to the cemetery, and it was Betty's first baby, Ian, born on 22 September 1929, who gradually filled the emotional chasm in Ethel's life, and equally in Herbert's.

Ethel forced herself to reply to the hundreds of people who had written to express their feelings about Jean's death. In mid-June the task of composing those 'terrible letters' hung over her 'like a great cloud' yet she could not leave a single reply unwritten. One who had been close as a friend and fellow writer was Dorothea Mackellar, who told Ethel in May that she was writing an appreciation of Jean for *Art in Australia*, the Ure Smith magazine that had published in 1929 her last piece of prose, 'Sydney Surfing', with photographs by Harold Cazneaux, a remarkably joyful celebration of Sydney's love affair with the surf and sunshine. Very much her mother's daughter and Adrian's sister, Jean had written of the 'extraordinary glow of well-being after a surf' and defended the Australian predeliction for pleasure before industry.

The poem which begins with the line, 'I love a sunburnt country', for which Dorothea Mackellar is universally remembered, qualified her well to write of her young friend:

I suppose she was about seventeen when we first met: very pretty, with the colouring of a Fortune's Yellow rose in her smooth cheeks, and curling hair. One noticed most of all the beauty of her dark-lashed green-grey eyes, and her swift, dazzling boyish smile. But it was her voice that enchanted me, a sweet, soft voice with unexpected modulations in it, and an odd little deliberateness singularly individual. This deliberateness was not the result of slow thinking, but rather that, much more quickly than most people, she had surveyed several sides of the subject (that perhaps had only just arisen), and she wished to present them all with scrupulous fairness. For she had a grasp, a breadth of vision, amazing in one so young and rare enough at any age. It is not easy to estimate how much Australia lost when Jean Curlewis' long gallant fight came to an end in that hospital room some weeks ago. Her love of life, her sane and humorous outlook, and her quick, warm power of observation were reflected in all she wrote.

Gradually Ethel became better able to cope with the loss. Early in August she sent her daughter's green writing table, with a memorial tablet on it, for her old school at Darling-hurst to retain as a memento. Soon after, Ethel wrote to the headmistress describing her awareness of the proximity of the school and how it affected herself and Jean in those final months at Molong Hospital across the road:

The School's loving sympathy was very dear to me.

For months in some strange way it has often seemed to me as I stood at Jean's window and watched you playing in the grounds and working in the classrooms where she had played and worked, as if a wave of your young love washed right across the road to us. Jean felt it, too, and it often cheered her.[1]

At the end of the month she wrote in her diary, 'With flowers for Jean with H. Very calm, peaceful'.

Adrian and his family, who lived within walking distance of 'Avenel', occupied an ever larger place in Ethel's life and thoughts. At the end of the financial year in 1930 she went with Herbert to visit their son, of whom she later wrote proudly, 'He has made 940 pounds at the bar this year without his allowance or dividends – really excellent for such a beginner.' One mark of the acceptance of new functions as a grandmother was the purchase in September of a cot and go-cart that were to be kept at Leura for Ian. By January 1931 when she and Herbert joined Adrian's family on holiday at Palm Beach, the sense of a renewed commitment to life was clearly growing. On seeing her grandson's enthusiasm for the ocean she wrote, 'Our babe grown surprisingly in the fortnight. Runs most eagerly into the sea quite alone ... I surfed & swam in pool & even H had a surf.'

Ethel and Herbert also spent the last week of January with the young family at 'Garth', buying a new ice chest to cope with the summer heat. It was there Ethel celebrated what was in fact her 61st birthday, attended not only by the family but also by her own two maids and Betty's one, prompting the remark, 'bizzy – 3 maids in so small a place is worse than 1 only'.

Back in town Ethel confided in her diary an increasing alarm at the economic crisis into which Australia was drawn by reverberations of the Wall Street Stock Exchange crash of 1929. World trade suffered a general decline, with Australian primary exports being disproportionately affected. In 1930 the national income had fallen by 100 million pounds; import restrictions were imposed to restore the balance of payments, making for a steep fall in federal customs revenue, to which the Scullin Labor Government responded by adopting a heavy sales tax that hurt industry and commerce. After September 1929 national statistical figures revealed the dimensions of the human cost as unemployment rose, quarter by quarter, from 12.1 per cent to 13.1 per cent to 14.6 per cent and to 20.5 per cent, eventually reaching 30 per cent.[2]

In October 1930 Jack Lang had led the Labor Party to a decisive victory in the NSW elections, campaigning against Tom Bavin's Nationalist/Country Party coalition on a States' Rights policy which involved withdrawal from the Loan Council and the Financial Agreement, and emphasizing what he chose to see as a 'gigantic conspiracy hatched amongst the London financiers and British manufacturers to drag down Australian wage standards'. Ethel thought Labor's sweeping victory an 'appalling result' of the election.

Worse was to follow. At the end of January 1931 Ethel celebrated news of the Nationalist victory in the Parkes by-election, commenting that it 'may be the saving of the country' by marking a rally of conservative forces. But ten days later, referring to the Federal Treasurer's implication in a mining scandal and Premier Lang's threat to default on the payment by New South Wales of interest due to British bondholders on 1 April, she wrote, 'Between Theodore & Lang's repudiation one wants to hang one's head in shame.'

'Avenel' itself was not untouched by the deepening depression. In common with other public servants, judges had their salaries reduced, Herbert losing a quarter of his 1500 pound annual gross. Lilian had told Ethel that the entire staff of the Sydney *Sun* had received dismissal notices. On 10 February the two sisters attended a meeting of shareholders at which the chairman, Sir Hugh Denison, came in for 'some harsh speaking' because of the decision to stop publication of the *Guardian* and the *Pictorial*. In June another shareholders' meeting received the resignations of several directors, including Ethel's old friend, Campbell Jones. Eric Baume, the new managing director, called her in for an interview. 'Shorn of polite words', it amounted to her compulsory retirement from the direction of 'Sunbeams' and being asked to write a token 200 words for two guineas a week. She declined, so bringing to an end her long and immensely fruitful association with the *Sun* which had seen the start of 'Sunbeams' and the birth of Ginger Meggs. It terminated also a career in managing children's pages and magazines that had begun in 1889 with her work on the *Parthenon* and led almost without a break *via* the *Illustrated Sydney News* and the *Town and Country Journal* to the Sunday *Sun*. It was with relief she reflected quietly on 6 November, 'Thankful Sunbeams is done with'.

Within a year, the Curlewises lost two of their oldest and most intimate Mosman friends, Lily Cullen and Richard Arthur. At Sir William's retirement he and his wife had moved permanently to 'Clifflands' in Leura where Lily was virtually immobilised by illness. On 10 June 1931 there was a telegram from Ailsa Cullen saying that her mother had died, so the following day Ethel was driven by Adrian to the funeral at Wentworth Falls. There she was engaged in writing for the *Herald* an appreciation of her 'very dear lost friend', which she dropped into the editor's box on 16 June for publication on the leader page next day. It tells a great deal of both writer and subject, showing Ethel's capacity for ardent and sustained friendship and her precious skill in conveying incidents and scenes that were charged with emotion, notwithstanding the drying up of her inspiration as a novelist:

LADY CULLEN. Some Memories.

There has just gone from us a woman whom many loved. I remember her from a day more than thirty years ago, when I went as a bride to return the first call she made on me. Tregoyd, that rare garden, that smiling, unassuming home among the trees at Mosman, was still quite young then, its six acres of native bushland coming friendly and fearless to the very verandah. The blue sparkle and splendour of the bay broke in through the trees and through the casement windows to insist that here was a shrine to beauty, not made so much as left undisturbed.

Two tiny light-haired boys breathlessly hosing each other at a standpipe lent life to the scene as I went up the gravelled path. Round a corner came impetuously to their aid a very tall, very slender, girl-like figure. Intensely blue eyes she had, with a gleam of fun in them, soft brown hair, under a garden hat, a skin soft and pink as her children's.

There had to be towels and rubbings and dry garments before social amenities could be attended to. And so began a long unbroken friendship between two homes that loved the trees, the pale sands, the blue curving bays, and the simplicity of wave-surrounded Mosman.

Not so very many weeks ago, and I was with her in her mountain home at Leura. Despite the harsh thrust of fate that had made walking impossible for several years, the same woman of my first visit was there. Out of her eyes, that seemed more blue than ever, looked the same young indomitable spirit. She sat erect and slender as ever; her cheeks were as soft and pink, her laugh as happy, her interests, world-wide or domestic, in no wise abated. She was engirt, as at Tregoyd, with the native bush. Her canaries came out of their cages, hopped on to her chair, her arm; her cockatoo, become almost human, obeyed every movement of her lifted finger.

Ethel wrote of her friend's unfailing knowledge of the animal, bird and insect life of the Australian bush, much of it gathered at 'Tahlee', home of her girlhood near Port Stephens, where the 'bush became a real thread of her, woven in with the most intimate strands of her nature'.

On 27 March 1931 Ethel was able to face the reality of Jean's death for the first time. As she expressed it in the diary:

To Jean's school. Saw the tablet & table. To the hospital after & talked a little with the matron. Impossible before. Then with flowers to where she lies. Just a year.

About five weeks later the power of a new grandchild to rekindle a zest for life was suggested by the diary entry Ethel made after minding Ian for the day when his parents were away at a boat race. 'I minded my little boy. They say he often cries to come to me, calling "Nan, Nan, Nan".' In the following February, when Ethel and Herbert were sharing a cottage at Palm Beach for a fortnight with Adrian's family, Ethel wrote of regular swims 'before brekker' and of being woken up each morning at daybreak by 'my tiny boy ... pouring out my morning tea, eating my bread & butter for me. Great joy'. By the time Ian was four years old he would often be left at 'Avenel' for days at a time, causing some loss of sleep to his grandmother, whom he awakened at half past five 'by gently stroking my cheek & asking me to read his book'.

In this new spirit Ethel chose at the approach of spring 1932 to buy some blue silk material to be made into a coat, since she had decided to leave off wearing black clothes in mourning for Jean. The year had begun eventfully with the 'sensational episode' of Captain de Groot prematurely cutting the ribbon to open the Harbour Bridge and soon after, the dismissal of Premier Jack Lang by Governor Sir Phillip Game for breaches of federal law, arising from his earlier decision to default on interest payments to holders of state bonds. The depression was worsening. In June Ethel was obliged to buy her husband a new warm overcoat because he had given away his own topcoat to an ex-digger whom he had found in rags on a cold day. The day before, Ethel had herself cooked a hot lunch for a man who had come to the door begging for food. Such was the feeling of crisis in Mosman that Adrian decided to stand for pre-selection as a candidate in the state elections for the newly formed United Australian Party. His nomination by the former member was one of Dr Arthur's last actions before he died on 21 May. Ethel went to the Sydney Town Hall to hear her son campaign; though she thought he spoke well he was unsuccessful but soon after, the UAP recorded what she described to her immense relief as a 'smashing victory'.

Yet there were signs of hurts what would not go away. Weddings, even that of Betty's sister Marjorie, usually provoked the comment, 'Don't like weddings' and the anniversary of Jean's in October 1931 had seemed a 'cruel cruel day'. More subtle and less readily explicable was Ethel's reaction to the birth in December 1932 of her granddaughter Philippa, which was not mentioned in her diary at all, in part perhaps because of her preoccupation for several months with Herbert's ill health, which confined him to bed with a full-time nurse to care for him. The child's very existence was not noticed in that immensely important chronicle until 11 February 1933 in a general family reference to 'Betty & the Babes'. And for years Ethel persisted in misspelling Philippa's name. When a photographer came at the end of April to record pictures of Betty and the children at 'Avenel', a special portrait was taken of Ian and his grandmother. Unlike Philippa, he was not seen as competing with the memory of Jean.

'Garth' offered Ethel during these years a continuing outlet for energy and imagination. In March 1933 she and Herbert were driven up by their chauffeur/handyman, to find the garden choked with weeds. A builder was commissioned to erect a verandah and outside room to house the chauffeur and provide storage space, Herbert looking on with much interest and making valuable suggestions. The next long visit occurred in January 1934; Ethel was in excellent health and spirits, gardening, reading and working with her old zest and pottering about on the golf links across the road. But there is almost an audible sigh as she writes, 'If only H cd find more to do, he wd like it too.'

In the spring of 1933 Ethel began writing again for publication in a modest way. The BP (Burns Philp) magazine accepted what she described as 'my queer verses, "Book at Midnight",'[3] which she had begun twelve months earlier while sitting at her desk in a lonely vigil beside Herbert's sick bed. It was dedicated to Flynn of the Inland, whom she saw as one of the forerunners who had 'passed the torch along since ancientest of days'. Soon after receiving this encouragement she wrote an article intended for the *Herald* to mark the fiftieth jubilee of her old school, Sydney Girls' High, entitled 'Featherweight Recollections'.

Another writing commitment, of an unlikely character, came in January 1934 with a request from Miss J. L. Ranken for Ethel to contribute the final chapter to a crime story with a total of sixteen contributors. It was eventually published by Angus & Robertson in 1936 as *Murder Pie* and used the work of many distinguished writers, among them Professors Walter Murdoch and George Portus, and also C. H. Bertie and Bruce Pratt. Each writer was asked to take up the story where a predecessor had left off; it was Ethel's task to write the penultimate chapter, 'The Death Ride'.

Such commissions offered little financial reward. Royalties had declined to a tiny fraction of the dimensions of the midtwenties so that Ethel's continuing interest in financial independence needed to be pursued through the stock market rather than her profession. But dividends had also declined and in early 1934 she decided reluctantly to instruct her broker to sell her 544 ordinary shares in Associated News at 31s 3d, which represented a heavy loss in view of the fact that there had been no dividends for years.

During this period Ethel recorded the disturbing news that Leo Charlton's second wife had died, apparently, like Jean, from tuberculosis.

In February came the happy news that Adrian had been elected President of the Surf Life Saving Association of Australia, a position he held for decades, making his name synonymous with the voluntary work of this great movement.

Adrian had been bred early to a sense of public service by both Jean and Ethel, perhaps imperceptibly by his mother's novels and poems of the war period. As to his sister's influence on the formation of the young man's character, Ethel made a memorable comment after watching the Pageant of Nationhood that was held on 26 January 1938 to mark the sesqui-centenary of British settlement, which the family watched from seats in front of the Mint Building in Macquarie Street:

Felt proud & touched at the spectacle of the growth of this land which is nearly mine. I liked the Surf parade best, perhaps because of Adrian's share in it – & Jean's for in a great measure it was she who stimulated him to it – daring & service.

At the great surf carnival at Bondi on 24 March 1934, Adrian's first as President, Betty presented the prize pennants watched by the proud family. A year later, when medals were issued to mark the 25th Jubilee of George V's reign, all three surviving Curlewises were honoured, Adrian for what Herbert called 'good surface', Herbert as a judge and Ethel receiving one of the few federal awards for literature.

There was a shock for Ethel in late November when she picked up the *Herald* and saw the headline, 'Louise Mack Dead':

Poor little Louise – I hadn't seen her to speak to for about ten years [*when she settled down in Sydney and remarried after a wandering life, following the excitement of her work in occupied Belgium during the war*] – but she was just the little schoolgirl friend again all in a moment.

Gathered flowers, made a beautiful wreath, & went to the crematorium Funeral Service. Arthur made a mistake & took me to the wrong chapel first, with the harrowing result that I attended two services.

In March 1936 the first copy of *Murder Pie* reached her from Angus & Robertson's. On 27th she had an appointment with a Mr Crick, manager of Fox Films, to receive advice about an offer made by another firm to produce *Seven Little Australians* as a movie. It was generally agreed that this was a valuable property which would repay a mature and well financed production. Encouraging her to think along these lines was a visit with Herbert to see the movie *Mutiny on the Bounty*, using a Western Electric hearing aid which transformed her enjoyment. It was, she thought, the 'Most powerful & best filmed picture I have seen – swept me off my feet – made me miserable that such misery cd ever have been'.

From Melbourne, Ward Lock passed on the news that the parent firm agreed to Ethel's contracting to use her film rights in *Seven Little Australians*. At the same time the Broadcasting Commission was adapting *Bobbie* and *That Girl* for production on air. In June there was a cheque from Ward Lock for more than five pounds being royalty payments for the Finnish translation of *Bobbie*.

In July 1936 Betty and Adrian had a brief holiday in Queensland while Ian and Philippa were looked after at 'Avenel'. When they returned Ethel remarked sadly 'we had to hand back our little boy who has made us both very happy'. A few weeks later she joined Marjorie Barnard, later to become famous as an historian of early New South Wales, as guest of honour of the English Speaking Union. Ethel felt awkward at the praises that came her way on such occasions. Far more enjoyable were the regular lunches put on by the Institute of Journalists or the Society of Women Writers, of which she was a founding member. In June 1933, for example, she sat between Mary Gilmore, a very old associate, and Ion Idriess, one of the most prolific writers of the thirties and forties.

Though Ethel had for ten years been using a small diary

of the kind often employed simply as an appointment book, its pages were crowded with domestic and foreign news in the late spring and summer of 1936. On 5 November she reported the outbreak in the Blue Mountains of the worst fires on record. For days fires raged at Springwood and Glen-brook and even at Leura they had been severe, arousing anxieties for the safety of 'Garth'. But another kind of conflagration was taking place overseas, in the Spanish Civil War – 'Madrid tragedy worse than ever'.

In the next week, 'Everything [was] swept from the canvas but the news about the King & Mrs Simpson & the probable abdication.' At the end of it all she listened to Edward's final broadcast as King, writing simply, 'And that's that.' It would be fascinating to know more of her thoughts as an expatriate but intensely loyal Englishwoman as she watched her monarch putting sentiment before duty.

*C*onveying the essence of Ethel's life during her sixties and seventies is the image of a tiny woman, secure in the love of her son and his family, yet struggling at times while performing grandmotherly duties.

Philippa started in the primary department at Wenona in June 1938 and looked 'such a darling in her tiny school uniform of navy and grey'. Though she was proud of the new possession, by the time her parents went off for holidays in July, leaving the two children at 'Avenel', fears and uncertainties about a rapidly changing personal world made her a handful for a grandmother who revealed the slightest want of resolution. She was in tears on Tuesday 19th at the thought of school and as she had a cold Ethel kept her at home. By Thursday, duty could no longer be denied, giving rise to a charming and evocative diary entry:

Philippa broke me all up – trying to do her curly hair, getting her off to school – an endless business. She is not naughty exactly, but very trying indeed.

However, Philippa was winning a bigger place in her grandmother's heart and the diary references become increasingly affectionate, with the name at last spelt correctly. In April 1937 Ethel arranged to have Philippa's playhouse re-erected in the lower garden at 'Avenel' beside Jean's Hereward Rock, a garden landmark that had been invested by mother and daughter with special links to the hero of the Saxon resistance. The bonds between grandparents and grandchildren were very strong.

One family legend concerns a time in October 1937 when Ethel and Herbert arrived at 'Garth' feeling rather frazzled after the drive to find that young Ian had made nearly every lock in the house unusable. As Lady Curlewis tells the story, Ian had his friend Charles Brown staying with him for the day while his mother went with friends for a picnic. For a while they indulged one of their naughtier pastimes by climbing onto the roof of the house and watching the golfers playing along the ninth fairway, waiting for a moment when a ball was lost in the long grass and later swooping on it. Tiring of this they became more imaginative in their play and used Herbert's tools to take apart the locks from virtually every door, collecting the springs, screws, handles and other parts in an indiscriminate pile on the floor that defied interpretation and replacement. It is said that Ian was told he must fix the locks if he wanted supper but his mother's impression is that Herbert was able to persuade himself that the adventure was more inventive than mischievous. Where Ian was concerned there were no limits to the grandfather's tolerance.[1]

During these years, until his death in 1942, Herbert moved out of the shadows and became once again a figure of significance and remark. The change had to do partly with the almost complete cessation of Ethel's activity as a writer and the consequent reduction in the hectic pace of her life. From August 1931, the weekly chore of Sunbeams had come to an end. No book had been written since *Judy and Punch* appeared in 1928; from then till Jean's death in 1930 Ethel was completely preoccupied with her daughter's struggle against tuberculosis, and thereafter, though making brief attempts at major works, she kept nothing going for more than a day or so.

With the completion in August 1931 of Ethel's withdrawal from an active career, there was certainly more time for Herbert, though he was still carrying out his duties as a district court judge, when his precarious health permitted, until he turned 70 in 1939. For their wedding anniversary in 1937 Herbert brought home 'the loveliest basket of flowers, early sweet peas & roses' and Ethel wrote, '41 years married & we grow closer together every year.' On the eve of his retirement the Sunday *Sun* ran a pleasant article, prompting his wife's comment, remembering a piece in the *Daily Telegraph* that had offended him, 'now he is retiring all the papers have uncommonly warm remarks about his personality & power'. Ian accompanied his grandfather to the farewell ceremony 'by command of the officers of the court' as Ethel put it and Herbert sat for the last time in the District Court on 18 August 1939.

At the beginning of Herbert's final year on the bench he suffered a coronary occlusion that put him in bed for a month. Retirement coincided with a further deterioration in health that necessitated the employment of a live-in nursing sister who took from Ethel much of the strain of looking after an extremely difficult patient. He was troubled by dyspepsia, which undermined his appetite, and dropsy, which put an end to the pleasure he'd once had from bushwalking in the Blue Mountains and following the routes of the explorers and road makers.

Cooking for Herbert became a constant source of tension and anxiety for Ethel and a fertile cause of resentment by the domestic staff. Feeling especially bright one morning in 1941, Ethel got up early to cook the bacon 'just as H likes it. And did several very neglected things there. Which giving offence Mrs Grainger gave notice'. On the same day Miss Johnston the maid also left. It would not have been an easy post.

Just as damaging to the happiness of 'Avenel' in Herbert's final few years was the utter loss of a sense of purpose in his life, a closing down of his few remaining interests, even the desire to read books. Ethel wrote in December 1940 of a visit to town, much of the time trying vainly to find some new hobby or activity to fill 'H's long empty hours'.

Almost the only exception to this sense of gathering desolation was the pleasure Herbert still derived from the companionship of his grandson, who seems to have been blessed with a sunny and engaging disposition. The boy was in some danger of being spoilt and according to his mother was only saved from this fate by a miracle. Herbert bought him expensive presents and acceded to his every desire; for Christmas in 1937 he gave Ian, aged only eight, a valuable wrist watch, while for the two children there was a real boat waiting on the 'Avenel' lawn. Soon after, the two families were on holiday at 'Garth' when the rain set in after a dry summer. Since this threatened to block an outing planned for Ian involving a tractor, Herbert 'ran him to Katoomba & bought him a fine oilskin coat & gumboots – he had come without'. Next day he was still busy on a shared project, in Ethel's words, 'happier than the day is long, wet or fine'.

We are all familiar with the saying, 'A prophet is not without honour ... '; it seems from Ethel's experience it is also true of writers. On 8 November, after a visit to her broker to transfer some hundreds of pounds into Defence Loan and Colonial Sugar shares:

Home to Ian whom I presented, at his own request, with 7LA's, writing solemnly in it Ian Curlewis with the author's compliments. He has suddenly developed a great interest in it since a boy at school told him of it.

That interest, fortunately, extended beyond a few small boys at Shore. After years of declining sales of her books, Ward Lock's Australasian representative, C. S. Bligh, came up from Melbourne in February 1937 to spend an afternoon at 'Avenel'. Though most of the time was spent 'talking gardens' they signed a new agreement for a 10 per cent royalty to be paid on half crown editions of her more popular titles. It was hoped that a cheaper edition would generate a greater volume of sales, as indeed proved the case. The following May she saw with satisfaction that her royalties had nearly doubled for the same half year, rising from 56 pounds to 107 pounds, though still remaining at only a tenth of her best results of the previous decade.[2]

In August 1937 the famous George Edwards, pioneer of wireless in Australia, came to see Ethel seeking to buy the broadcast rights for four of her books at 25 pounds each. A week later the offer was increased to 100 pounds for three and although the usually reliable record of the Pen Money Book mentions no such source of income there is evidence in the diary a year later that the project was proceeded with, when Ethel commented approvingly on three sample episodes of *Seven Little Australians* broadcast by station 2UW.

For a time following Neville Chamberlain's ill-conceived mission to Munich in September 1938, Ethel's diary reverberated with fears of a coming war. Japan's annexation of the island of Hainan in February 1939 evoked the simple comment, 'Disturbing' and the rejection by Hitler in late April of American mediation seemed even more alarming. But in mid-May Ethel's personal affairs returned to prominence with an approach by a well-connected group of film makers headed by Sir Benjamin Fuller and the Hollywood director Arthur Collins who had begun negotiating on behalf of O'Brien Productions for the rights to make a movie of *Seven Little Australians*.

It was Adrian who had the first detailed discussions and on 26 May Ethel met the principals at Minter Simpson &

Company, reaching a sufficient level of agreement to warrant her writing to Ward Lock. Up to this point she could have been forgiven for experiencing a sense of déjà vu, for she had started on this road many times in the past twenty years with no tangible results. This time it was different; by 19 July the first batch of script arrived for Ethel's attention from Collins, who had directed such luminaries of the screen as David Niven and Dolores Del Rio.[3]

Ethel's qualities as a businesswoman are nicely revealed by the firmness of her diary entry on 9 August:

Contract for my perusal from Remington, solicitor for Collins – but will have to be altered – tries to grasp too much & too many rights. To Adrian's chambers but he in court.

That obstacle surmounted, filming began on 14 August, 'A very big day in my life' and Ethel was introduced one by one to the cast, of whom she thought very highly, especially the children. Ron Rousel took the role of Bunty, Janet and Nancy Gleeson, recent arrivals with their mother from London, were to play the parts of Nell and Baby, Mary McGowan had the central role of Judy. The *Australian Women's Weekly* had much to say about the making of the film which it reported on 2 December under the headline: THEY ARE SEVEN. ETHEL TURNER'S BELOVED STORY OF AUSTRALIA BECOMES A FILM.

There was much excitement for Ethel during the four weeks of filming. Memorable days were spent on location: at Victoria Barracks, down Oxford Street from the home where Ethel had lived while a student at Sydney Girls High; and for the scene in which Judy was admitted to the boarding school at Mount Victoria, the cameras were moved to Presbyterian Ladies College at Pymble. Once again, for Ethel, a familiar flash of limelight:

Headmistress Miss Knox had the girls all assembled in Great Hall to greet me – 400 of them & then got me on platform & made me make a speech – which I actually did. They also took snapshots of me – This all grows a serious business.

Perhaps there was too much excitement. When the time came for the release of the movie on 1 November, which Ethel described as 'the great event to which my whole creation moved', she was joined by Betty, Ian and Philippa, though not Herbert, who once again had a nursing sister in residence because of a recurrence of his blood clotting problem. Some three weeks later, when Ethel was at last well enough to write up her diary from 31 October 1939, she recalled, 'Doubtless I'm not an unprejudiced critic but it did seem to me very good. Ran so smoothly & lightly. I was able to hear every word. Don't ever remember being so very happy.'

A year earlier, Ethel had accompanied Adrian and Betty when they inspected a large block of land on the high side of Hopetoun Avenue not much more than a stone's throw below 'Avenel', with stunning views of Chinaman's Beach and towards the Heads. 'They have practically decided on it,' Ethel wrote excitedly. Adrian and Betty moved in June to another rented house, in Fairfax Road only five minutes walk from 'Avenel', where they would live until the new place was completed. Ethel arranged to guarantee a loan for 800 pounds from the bank to pay for the land, which came complete with ancient tennis court and tumbledown garage. One Sunday afternoon early in July the whole family went to the land 'which in a fit of zeal the dear lad is starting to clear for himself' and they boiled the billy while enjoying the view and the smell of eucalypts. At the end of the month Lilian's son Eric Thompson brought a model of the intended house for the family to see, complete with its terraced garden and tennis court. He had been an outstanding student of architecture, much influenced by the work of W. G. Waterhouse, well known for his Mosman homes, and designed for the young Curlewises a spectacularly beautiful home in the Art Deco style, with curved external walls of white-painted roughcast brick catching the sun that sparkled also on the harbour below.

Adrian and Betty moved into their new home on 20 March 1939 at a time when Ethel's diary was recording grimly the stages by which the nations slid towards the abyss of another world war. In late July Ethel interviewed a potential new maid whose sister worked for Betty, both refugees from Europe 'come to do our horrid housework for 30/- a week or so'.

The young Curlewises had only six months to enjoy their home at Hopetoun Avenue before the fear of war became a reality, with the announcement of Australia's involvement made by Prime Minister Menzies on 3 September 1939. Adrian and some of his surfing and legal friends had joined the Citizen Military Forces about a year earlier and as early as 6 September we find Ethel's diary recording the work he was doing at night for military intelligence. Frail as he was, Herbert also gave his services, translating letters sent 'home' by members of the Italian community. Upon the collapse of France in May 1940 Adrian indicated his readiness to serve overseas, though at 39 years of age he was exempt from such responsibilities. He joined the 8th Division of the AIF at Rosebery Racecourse, and underwent training as a company commander there and at Duntroon.

From the beginning of 1940 Ethel was preoccupied with the changes in the lives of the family as the war gradually tightened its grip on the Curlewises. At the same time, almost imperceptibly, there was of a growing intimacy between Ethel and her daughter-in-law, which became central to the survival of the family as a warm and mutually supportive unit during the approaching crisis. Writing of the celebration in April 1940 of her 44th wedding anniversary, Ethel noted:

Betty drove me for a 20 minute visit to her garden. She is a very true lover of it which makes one of our closest ties. I am very happy in all four. Adrian is beyond praise.

A month earlier, Philippa as a seven-year-old had taken part in her school's swimming carnival, jumping rather than diving into the water and pleading fervently with her father 'to teach me, and somehow give me the necessary courage, to dive in by the following year'.[4]

No one could have anticipated that Philippa would be twelve before her father attended another of her sports days. During the second half of 1940 Adrian was training at Rosebery and Duntroon. After the fall of France and the rescue of British army survivors from the beaches of Dunkirk Australian movie audiences began to see newsreels showing massive bombing raids on London and other cities. It seemed that a real effort was being made to carry out Hitler's threat that Britain would be swept from the face of the earth if she rejected German terms. It was the sort of news that caused Adrian Curlewis to enlist unconditionally for overseas service at a time when he was 'extracting guineas from an unsuspecting public at the rate of two thousand a year', newly ensconced with his family in a lovely sunny home overlooking Chinaman's Beach and enjoying a satisfying career in public and professional life.[5]

In the spring of 1940 Adrian began a period of intensive training at Duntroon, broken only by a brief period of leave which allowed him to spend Christmas with the family. As Herbert was virtually confined to bed the dinner and present giving were held at 'Avenel'. The next day Ethel wrote:

26 Dec Children & Adrian & Betty at Chinamans & we could

watch them thro' telescope Ian swimming & sailing his model yacht H gave him & all playing water ball.

With the coming of the new year Ethel was delighted to be able to give Adrian a birthday treat by taking Betty and the children to stay for a weekend at the Hotel Canberra. She had been almost housebound for months by Herbert's illness and the shortage of petrol, an abstinence that was not good for the car, 'which gets stiff necked & won't start & has to be sent to the garage'. It was a lovely run of 200 miles, so they enjoyed a wayside picnic lunch and drove past the empty basin of Lake George with its gold and greens, watching rabbits running everywhere, 'oh a delight after so many months shut up'.

At the hotel they had three adjoining rooms. Adrian came in on the Saturday and the family swam in the Olympic Pool at Kingston, marvelling at the opulence of the turquoise bottom and the turquoise sky above and noting the immense growth of the city's trees over the previous twelve years. After dinner that night they spent several hours in the company of Billy Hughes and Dame Mary Gilmore; the old politician knew Ethel from shared occasions at the Journalists' Association lunches during the First World War, when they had been leading campaigners in the divisive and scarifying attempt to introduce conscription for overseas service. He was in fine vein that night and told 'endless entertaining stories'.

Sunday morning saw the family at the Cotter River for a swim and picnic with two of Adrian's officer friends, close to some pastoral land on which Ian Curlewis was eventually to establish his home when he married and set up a legal practice in Canberra. A long phone call that night reassured Ethel that Herbert was being well looked after at 'Avenel'; next morning they deposited Adrian at Duntroon and set off for home in good content.

For her birthday that year, on an extremely hot day, Ethel left a nervy and irritable Herbert in the care of a tiresome nurse to celebrate at a cocktail party at her son's home. News had come two days earlier of the fall of Tobruk to the German army and there was a realization that Adrian was 'going fast'. He embarked with the 8th Division on 3 February in a convoy headed by the Cunard liner *Queen Mary*, bound for the island fortress of Singapore, which was still seen as a firm bulwark denying Japan's assumed ambitions in Southeast Asia.

When Adrian stopped off at 'Avenel' on his way to the wharf he gave his mother a farewell kiss at the gate. At the same time Ethel pressed into his hand a little note on which she had hastily scribbled the words:

Goodbye for a little while my very own beloved son. Remember what ever money you need for anything you only have to ask for. You can't do more than you are doing. Now be happy and steadfast in it.[6]

On the day the convoy sailed, Betty and the children walked to the end of Kirkoswald Avenue to see the ships pass down the harbour. From Adrian's first letter home dated 6 February 1941 they learned that with the help of binoculars he had been able to see them as the ship approached the Heads. A sad threesome returned to Hopetoun Avenue and soon after Philippa heard a sound 'that disturbed me more than anything I could ever remember. My mother was upstairs and she was crying! I didn't know then that mothers ever cried!'

Yet as Philippa realized thirty years later when she compiled her father's diaries and the letters that passed amongst its members during the years of his service and captivity, the family that had begun with the marriage of Ethel and Herbert in April 1896 was sustained by a rare spirit of resilience. As she expressed the point, 'the intimate parts of the letters reveal the tremendous strength that can be gained from a family, and the courage and fortitude that one member can give another'.[7]

Small morsels of news from the war relieved the general gloom. A week after Adrian left in the *Queen Mary*, enjoying as an officer a final taste of luxurious appointments that had made the ship famous on the Atlantic run, the cruiser HMAS *Sydney* returned to its home port with battle honours from service in the Mediterranean. Ethel wrote in her diary of 'Rejoicing over Sydney'. All the schools were given a holiday to enable their students to join the citizens who thronged Macquarie Street and Martin Place to cheer Captain John Collins and his gallant men.

In company with Betty, Ethel went to the Mosman Kinema to see Charles Chauvel's great movie *40,000 Horsemen* dealing with the exploits of the Australian Light Horse in Palestine during the First World War. Ticket sales were in aid of the Children's Library, a project in which Ethel had been interested from the inception. 'By far the best & most powerful film ever done in Australia,' she thought, 'but not for a mother & wife of a man at the front to see – almost beyond endurance.'

For the first time in years Ethel went to the cemetery 'to my little Jean'. It was eleven years to the day since she had died '& in many things the loss is as fresh as if yesterday'. Just seven months earlier she had written to Leo, who had remarried, to congratulate him on a new baby, Leonie Benson Charlton, adding to her diary a cry of continuing anguish, 'May the fates that have dealt so harshly with him keep it safe for him. But it should have been mine.'

April 1941 had brought the most awful news of campaigns involving Australian soldiers in Africa and Greece. Ethel had tried once again to get her pen working, not least in the thought of dealing with a likely 'deficit in Betty's affairs'. Failing in this, she had her niece Marcia drive her to Pymble to Mr Jerrold Nathan, the artist who had painted her portrait some years earlier, thinking to take lessons in painting and so revive a skill that had last been nurtured fifty years earlier. In a spirit almost of desperation, needing a regular activity that took her away from 'Avenel', she wrote in May, 'I *must* have something to do as well as war work & nursing.'

Those painting lessons with Jerrold Nathan gave a real fillip to Ethel's life for several months. One of the projects she embarked on was the painting of a large screen that was destined for Philippa's room with a 'sort of Espalier & Peach blossom design'. Such activity brought Ethel and her granddaughter together, so on 3 June:

I showed P. how to draw freely on a large ground with charcoal that rubs out so easily & she made a quite admirable copy of a branch with peaches on.

In her compilation of *Love and War* Philippa wrote of her

frequent, and often daily, visits to 'Avenel', when my grandmother and I would play together for hours on end. I think the best of all were our puppet plays. First we would write the play, then we would make the puppets, construct a theatre, paint the backdrop and finally both squeeze in behind the stage to perform it. It didn't seem to worry us that there was no applause, because as a rule there was no audience.[8]

The intimacy Philippa recalls with her grandmother, which contributed to her choice of kindergarten teaching as a career and her enjoyment of theatre and public speaking, had its counterpart for Ian in what he remembers as a 'real friendship' with 'Young Erb', as the grandfather was known in the family. In many of Herbert's letters to Adrian in Singapore there is a tendency to say that 'life is just as dull as ever' and the brightest spots are those in which he tells his absent son of the times spent in Ian's company, as in a letter of March 1941:

Directly after school he comes straight here [*Ian's route home from the tram took him down Warringah Road and past 'Avenel'*] polishes off his work in no time and off he goes to swim or sail his boat but always business before pleasure. Our system with maths is he and I do the sums independently. If our results do not agree each of us checks his own work. But if he's wrong I don't help him. He has to find out where he's gone wrong for himself . . .

Of Philippa I see very little. She and her friend rush in after school, make a beeline for the verandah, start playing with Mother's farm, and don't come in to say how do you do till they hear the sound of something to eat.[9]

Fifty years later Ian Curlewis hardly recognises the picture of his grandfather as a bored old man which comes so strongly from Ethel's diaries. Rather he recalls the range and vividness of his interests, the passion for the short wave radio and love of books, the superbly maintained tools in the workshop, where Ian spent hours at a time, both on his own and in company with Herbert, making boats or engaged in other practical tasks. When at 'Garth' Ian commonly accompanied his grandfather on walks that aimed at retracing the routes of the early explorers or road builders, following which they would pore over maps Herbert spread out on the dining room table and worked on with immaculate instruments.[10]

By this time Ethel was quite deaf and utterly reliant on her Aucusticon for any conversation. Ian was conscious of the frustration it caused her to be so dependent on the hearing aid and its heavy clumsy batteries. She became terribly distressed when unable to hear properly and was devastated by the piercing squeal of the instrument when it malfunctioned, which seemed a common experience. Her voice he remembers as having been unusually soft, though with a slightly metallic timbre that he associates with the fact of this grand-mother's deafness. One consequence for Ethel of this disa-bility emerges from a diary entry in 1942 when she had been with Rose by bus and train to Wahroonga to visit Lilian. 'I liked it,' she wrote, 'but the noise of the train & Ro talking to me with my audiphone on was tiring in the extreme.'

By September 1941, after a fortnight when Betty and the children had been away on holiday in the mountains, Ethel was more than usually worn down by Herbert's irritability, a product largely of his constant nausea. It was decided, not without urging from Herbert, that she should have a break in routine by staying for a few days at the Hotel Australia. So, after lunch she was driven into town by her niece Marcia and ensconced in room 622 of the hotel. Having enjoyed dinner in lonely state she walked across the road to the Prince Edward theatre to see 'The Widow of West Point' and felt a surge of hope at watching a newsreel showing the meeting of Roosevelt and Churchill. While in town she called on Mr Cousins at Angus & Robertson's, who were on the point of publishing new editions of her most popular books, no doubt because wartime stringencies prevented Ward Lock from doing so. A month later Cousins told her with satisfac-tion that *Wonder-Child* and *The Secret of the Sea* had each sold over 500 copies in a fortnight.

When Ethel was taken home in the family Chrysler on 25 September after a 'final run about' in the city she reported wistfully to the diary that the breathing space had come to an end, though Herbert was perhaps 'rather improved'.

At the end of spring came 'horrid rumours', shortly con-firmed, that the *Sydney* had been sunk with the loss of all hands in the Indian Ocean. On 8 December 1941 Ethel recorded the bombing of Pearl Harbor and Australia's involvement in war with Japan, realizing a fear that had seen its tentative beginnings at about the time *Seven Little Austra-lians* was published, during the Sino-Japanese War. In the next week or so the news was filled with one disaster after another, reporting the sinking of the battleships *Prince of Wales* and *Repulse*, which had been sent with great fanfare to stiffen the sea defences of Singapore, and mounting evidence of mismanagement in Malaya. Once again, Allied armies were left desperately short of air support.

On Christmas Day in 1941 the family gathered at 'Avenel', with Betty, Ian and Philippa returning from holidays at Palm Beach to share the present giving and the roast dinner as if nothing had changed, a sixth place being set for the absent Adrian. It was a time of drought and severe water restrictions in Sydney, when householders were restricted to a weekly bath and then siphoned the water out to their gardens, taking care not to suck the hose for an instant longer than necessary. Ethel arranged for a 1000 gallon tank to be installed and the whole family was involved in blacking out the house's fifty windows.

Ethel had cancelled the lease of 'Garth' so as to make the cottage available if the family were to be evacuated, a decision that was made on 25 January after news was received of the invasion of Rabaul. A small consignment of luggage was put into storage, mainly linen and silver. The family lawyer came to get instructions for altering Ethel's will, and the house was locked up and vacated by the end of the month. With Betty driving, leaving her children at home with Mrs Jenkins, the Chrysler set off for Leura after lunch on an extremely hot day. Herbert, in pyjamas and dressing gown, remained in lively spirits until Hazelbrook but was fit only for bed when they reached 'Garth'. After helping unload Betty returned to Sydney in the Caves Express leaving Ethel and Herbert 'alone in the stillness'.

Two days after arriving at the peaceful greenness of 'Garth', where the tanks were overflowing with recent rains, Ethel permitted herself a cry from the heart in her diary, 'Malaya news worse & worse – the Japs are within 15 miles of Singapore. Oh where is our boy.' At the same time she wrote a cheerful letter to Adrian, 'My oh so darling boy', telling him of the move to Leura and of Betty's decision to remain in Sydney.[11]

January had brought continuing news of Japanese victories, the landing of a thousand tanks in Malaya, a 'wicked shortage' of allied planes and conflicting reports of General Bennett's death, capture and survival. In mid-February Ethel recorded the surrender of Singapore and wondered if her boy was among the troops who had got away. From the butcher in Katoomba she learned of the first air raid on Darwin so she pressed Betty once again to join her at 'Garth' with the children, a decision that was facilitated on 24th by the evacuation of Ian's school to the Imperial Hotel at Mt Victoria. At the end of the month Ethel noted that Bennett had escaped from Singapore with a small party and was on his way by plane to Sydney. Next day in the boldest of black ink she wrote excitedly that Betty had been in touch with the general's daughter who passed on the news that her father had seen Adrian in good health after the surrender and there were hopes that he also would have got away. Adrian *had* been offered the opportunity of joining the escaping party but had expressed his doubts as to the ethics of the general's leaving his men. The Royal Commission that was held in November 1945 agreed, finding that Bennett was 'not justified' in relinquishing his command and leaving Singapore.[12]

During the weekends in March the whole family was busy at 'Garth', some preparing beds for vegetables 'against famine times', while Ian used his carpentery skills to set up a small fowl yard. But the idea of an extended stay in the mountains was soon abandoned. Encouraging the return to Sydney was the arrival of General Douglas MacArthur, followed by two divisions, planning to use Australia as a base and take command of American and Australian forces in the Pacific. News came early in May of the Coral Sea Battle, which turned back a Japanese invasion force bound for Port Moresby and a month later the Battle of Midway enabled MacArthur to tell Prime Minister Curtin that the security of Australia had been assured.[13]

By July arrangements had been made for the families of Japanese prisoners of war to write through the Red Cross and the letters to Adrian from 'Avenel' and Hopetoun Avenue immediately resumed. On 25 October Betty wrote to her husband to break the news of his father's death on the 11th; 'don't be too miserable', she wrote, 'because his life has not been very happy since he became ill many years ago'. Ethel had 'taken it marvellously, not once have I seen her break down; she really is astounding'.

Ethel wrote a week later summarising for her son the forty-six years of her life with Herbert 'never apart more than a few weeks, never more than the human inevitable frictions and always coming together again closer than ever' ... 'Not half an hour before he died, his hand in mine, he said, "My son".'

Nineteen

*O*n the last day of winter 1942, after a month when the war had brought further disasters to the Allied cause, Ethel's diary recorded 'An amazing change – Australians have won a sweeping victory at Milne Is & Gen MacArthur has practically wiped out the Japs on all the Solomons'. In a mood of returning optimism she went to the Junction for banking and shopping, collected petrol ration tickets and walked home feeling that life might still have sweetness to offer.

A few days earlier Ethel had written a letter to Adrian which began with a quotation from 'The Shropshire Lad' conveying an apt message about self discipline:

When I meet the morning beam
Or lay me down at night to dream
I hear my bones within me say
'Another night – another day.
Therefore they shall do my will
Today while I am master still'.

After reflecting on the utter lack of news about her son Ethel added:

I am writing this very early in the morning at the window seat in my study and when I lift my head I can see the white house you built so happily, and will, *shall*, *must* live in happily again.

There followed detail of the families at 'Avenel' and Hope-toun Avenue and a description of the cherry-coloured bougainvillea and pale pink rondeletia that were blooming on either side of the front gate, which Adrian's family regularly passed on the way home from Spit Road. She closed the letter with an injunction that could equally have come from a Spartan mother, 'keep your heart up my brave and gallant boy'. This letter, like several that followed, was not received by Adrian until after his return in December 1943 to the Changi prison camp in Singapore, following a grim seven months' labour on the notorious Burma-Thailand Railroad.[1]

Yet some scraps of news reached Adrian's loved ones in Mosman, as Ethel recorded excitedly on 6 January 1943:

First news of Adrian! About ten official telegram from Red Cross thro' Geneva to Betty to say 'Capt A Curlewis previously reported missing is now reported interned in a Malayan camp'. B & the children came posting up the hill in the dark all broken up with tears & smiles.

The realization that Adrian was alive restored Ethel's spirits to a high point from which they seldom wavered for the remainder of the war. Even more tangible was the radiogram that came to Betty's hands on 16 June. She had been working since the previous December in a clerical job at the NRMA and telephoned Ethel immediately to say that a message from Adrian had come through the Red Cross, telling the family he was very fit and being well treated. Ethel wrote of her experiences that day in her next letter to Adrian. As she was alone in the house and rarely able to hear the bell of the telephone it seemed something of a miracle that she received the message at all; passing by the instrument in the hall she had put her hand on it and, feeling the vibration, picked up the receiver and listened to Betty's wonderful news.[2]

With Herbert's death removing the partner who had shared 'Avenel' for over forty years Ethel had the home remodelled to meet her changed circumstances, establishing a separate flat upstairs that was let in March for six guineas a week to Mrs Cecelia Knudtson and her two young children. The husband had been interned by the Japanese and Ethel wondered if her tenant would be able to manage after being accustomed in Siam to a staff of eight servants. Finding her own 'minder' proved less easy, especially in view of the wartime restrictions on domestic service, and Ethel had a succession of people occupying the servants' quarters, sometimes trying a husband and wife team with the man driving the car and doing odd jobs and the woman cooking. It was with such a team, the Littles, that Ethel went to 'Garth' in April 1943 for the first visit in a year, feeling 'an intolerable sense of loss' at Herbert's absence and confronting in the garden a 'wilderness of weeds' and grass over a foot high.

This mountain holiday underlined another big change from earlier days, for Ethel had no writing task in hand and kept herself amused by pottering in the garden and reading such books as Webb Miller's *I Found No Peace* and Li Yutang's *My People and My Country*. Wartime restrictions would have inhibited her writing in any case for when she had spoken in March to Mr Cousins of Angus & Robertson's about the new edition of her *Flower o' the Pine* she learned that it had sold out immediately because the print run had been cut to nothing by paper shortages.

A diary entry in mid-August may throw some light on one of the puzzles of Ethel's later years, her failure to resume an active career as a writer:

To town. Bt more comf. shoes & Ald. Huxley's just out book, The Art of Seeing – telling of his miraculous healing of defective sight.

Am going to study it for oh I have a lot of trouble & intolerable weariness with eye strain tho' am getting some sight in the defective eye.

Ethel's novel writing had always occurred in spasmodic bursts that found her working for days at a time till the wee small hours, in her youth often by candlelight. This may well have been the initial cause of the deterioration of vision and an eventual reason for her inability to resume writing when she had adjusted to the loss of her daughter.

Cables from the Pacific front brought heartening news of the destruction in the Bismarck Sea battle of a Japanese invasion force bound for New Guinea. In May Ethel learned with horror of the sinking of the Red Cross hospital ship *Centaur*. Her private response was to applaud Churchill's speech in New York, which seemed to pledge immediate help to the Pacific and that 'the Japs shall be exterminated as soon – or sooner than the Germans'.

Spring came late that year but towards the end of September Ethel wrote of the garden beginning to fill with flowers, peach blossom, wisteria, irises, roses and a few stocks with their heady perfume. She had the family to supper, packed for a holiday at Leura and then wrote a speech to be read for her by Mrs Armitage at the Sydney Girls' High Jubilee Dinner on 'The Abolition of Poverty'.

This speech tells a great deal of Ethel's social conscience as it had developed under the influence of her observations during her travels in Europe thirty years earlier in 1910. She begins by reflecting on the violence of the news coming from Italy and remembers that:

A shadow kept falling again & again across the sunniest hours at the unbelievable poverty & degradation that were continually being glimpsed even in the wealthiest streets & quarters of a city or the outlying districts.

Oh, we knew that there was plenty of poverty in Australia ... but it was a different poverty, a sort of sturdy, independent irascible sort of poverty that you had a notion could be righted as soon as the law-makers of the land really woke up & got to work, forced to it by the same irascible sturdy poor whose powers only wanted direction ...

But the European & even the English poverty I had glimpsed, side by side with luxury, with unbridled spending such as I had never seen before was a thing that gripped the very heart.[3]

During her stay at 'Garth', Ethel went to a Schubert symphony recital where funds were raised for the Red Cross, really her first entertainment since Herbert's death. At the same time she dwelt increasingly on the problem of maintaining the garden at 'Avenel' when able-bodied labour was so scarce. There had been a snake scare in the lower garden, and she had got hold of an ancient gardener and was paying him a guinea a day to hack away at the undergrowth.

May and June 1944 gave promise of a return to happy days. Some friends had heard a broadcast from Singapore in which their officer son had spoken of Adrian and himself being well. In Europe all energies and thoughts were concentrated on the imminent invasion of occupied France and Ethel took Betty and the children to Cahills restaurant as a holiday treat and to occupy the hours of waiting for news. When the story broke on 6 June and the Allied troops landed on the soil of Normandy over which the Curlewises had walked in 1910, Ethel was able to celebrate with a bottle of sherry. It had always been a regular thing on Sundays for Betty and the children to walk up to 'Avenel' for supper and with the prospect of Adrian's release there seems to be a fresh swing to the diary entries, expressed on 2 July with the comment 'My Philippa grows lovelier every week, [in] looks & disposition & intelligence'. Yet even good news had its anxious side and the knowledge that Japan was now being bombed regularly made Ethel exclaim, 'But oh what will become of our prisoners there. No word yet where A is interned'. Betty got the family together for yet another Christmas of the war; soon after, when Adrian's 43rd birthday came around, a broadcast message from Singapore gave the family new hope when it passed on the information that he was a prisoner in Malayan Camp no 1 and was 'feeling fit, happy & well treated'.

By March 1945 Ethel was troubled by arthritis in the shoulder and called in her doctor to ask for a certificate to enable the purchase of a hot water bottle. Condemned to eat 'salads & sich' for weeks and finding that it seemed to make no difference, Ethel broke out at length and took herself to David Jones for a turkey lunch. On the same day she learned that President Roosevelt had died, imparting a 'blow to the civilised world'. Listening to the playing of the 'Star Spangled Banner' on the seven o'clock news upset her as much as if the president had been her father. One regrets the absence of a similar comment on the death of the Australian Prime Minister, John Curtin, whose burden of leadership had brought him to the grave five weeks before the war ended. Ethel, perhaps, was no longer 'a bit of a socialist', as she had claimed to be in 1915.

When the surrender of Germany was announced on the 11 p.m. news a few weeks later Ethel had the frustration of being unable to wake Ian from a deep sleep to share in the joy. Rather against her principles, she agreed to accompany Betty and the children to a thanksgiving service at St Augustine's Church, Neutral Bay, remarking in her diary, 'How can one whole heartedly thank God for his tender mercies while millions are yet broken on the wheel.'

During the final months of the war, when Curlewis hopes were concentrated on the prospect of victory in the Pacific and the return of Adrian, Ethel suffered from a thickening of the arteries and had repeated attacks of sciatica. She was admitted to the Wahroonga Sanitarium just in time to hear that Japan had surrendered after suffering awful casualties and damage from a second atomic bomb. Just before entering hospital Ethel had gone with Rose to see an art show put on by The Sydney Group, where she was glad to encounter Gwen Spencer and the art publisher Sydney Ure Smith, for whom Jean had worked twenty years earlier. Another familiar visitor, and a friend from both Mosman and the Blue Mountains, was Mrs H. V. Evatt, freshly returned from San Francisco, who recalled her childhood visits to 'Avenel' and dressing-up games with Jean.

Even during this illness, a time when most of us become acutely introspective, Ethel's lifetime habit of looking after Lilian remained undiminished. When 'little Lil' came for lunch on 25 July, with the news that she was on the point of giving up her job, Ethel noted in her diary, 'Am fixing up to make a gift of 100 pounds a year for all time; hope to make it more soon'. On 13 August Lilian called to say goodbye to Ethel at the Sanitarium before setting off in the *Mauretania* for a holiday cruise to Africa and Ethel wrote her a cheque for 50 pounds as extra pocket money and promised a further instalment.

Another cheque written from the Wahroonga Sanitarium was intended as a present for Betty's birthday combined with little gifts for Ian and Philippa to help them celebrate the war's end. It was enclosed in a note to Betty which must have come as sweet music to a daughter-in-law:

My little girl, [*Betty stood a head taller*] I can never tell you how I have loved and admired you all these four crashing and heart-twisting years. You have been all things to all and never lost your brightness and poise and steering-skill. I wished Adrian could have seen you today – you never looked younger or sweeter or dearer. Mummie[4]

In the September school vacation that year Betty and the

children filled in the time of waiting by going to Griffith for a holiday on a vineyard belonging to a branch of the McWilliams family. While there Betty was much aware of newspaper stories about men returning to Australia from captivity, often unmet and unsung, so she packed the children into a crowded train and in the middle of the night she received a message from the guard to say that a radio message had been received from Singapore saying 'Curlewis, Barnes, Head and Hackney all alive and well.' On 3 October Ethel learned that her son was a passenger in a Liberator bomber from Darwin bound for Sydney so the family bundled into the car and drove to Mascot:

At last, in the dust, the Liberator, & the doors of it opening & figures running. Someway I got past the constable – Betty & the children had gone another path but the one I had run along was the one that he came running along & caught me up & gave me the first kiss.

When the family reached Mosman at about 8 p.m. a splendid dinner was waiting. Adrian was not looking as thin as everyone feared, for the time at Labuan for some recuperation had set him up, enabling him to get back from a low point of 9 stone to 10 and a half stone, leaving another 3 stone to be regained. On the following Sunday, a 'busy, happy day', Ethel 'made Spanish cream & trifles etc etc for the first supper here since my darling sailed away – over 4 years. All four came – it all seems too good to be true'.

Inevitably Adrian continued to show symptoms of the malaria that had been his constant bane in captivity, so he had a journey by ambulance to the repatriation hospital at Herne Bay. Friends of Adrian's rallied around; one of them arranged for the family to share a cottage perched above the rock pool at Palm Beach of which Ethel had written in January 1926. Philippa and her grandmother slept under the stars on the verandah and by Christmas Day the family was together again.

A significant silence descends on the diary at the start of 1946. On 16 February it is broken by the entry, 'Wet misty & gloomy all day. Am sleeping badly & don't get out to tire myself enough'. Next day, a Sunday, she wrote firmly:

After a week – or weeks of mental turmoil & unhappiness waked very early full of resolve.

Made a charcoal sketch of Adrian – not so bad as a work of art but not in the least like him. Went for a walk. Came back & made a good batch of currant scones. All 4 came to supper. Slept badly so got charcoal stick & made a fair sketch of Ian in the night.

What seems to emerge clearly is that Ethel came to realize that a person of her talent and energy simply could not be satisfied by living vicariously through her family, dear though they were to her. On the Monday she invited friends to morning coffee and after a restless afternoon, 'started to use my pen once again, on a sort of "Diary of a 'leisured' Woman", destined for the Herald possibly. Could use it as a vehicle for many things I'd like to say.' Though nothing seems to have come of this attempt to return to the discipline of the pen the diary entries reflect a far more active turn of mind.

One of the straws in the wind was Ethel's disinclination to put her name down at Admiralty House so as to receive invitations to vice-regal functions. As she put the point in commenting on being left behind when Adrian and Betty had set off for a garden party to the Duke of Gloucester, '[I] definitely think I have done with "all that".' Next day however she wrote a long letter to Eleanor Dark about her 1940 novel *Waterway*, no doubt recalling the times when, thirty years earlier, she had seen her at 'Avenel' in the company of her handsome and engaging father, Dowell

O'Reilly. Almost by return mail came a 'long & quite delightful letter' from Eleanor, inviting Ethel when she was next in the mountains to visit her at 'Varuna', the large and strikingly handsome Art Deco home she and her doctor husband Eric had built just before the war above the falls at Katoomba.

By a nice conjunction of events Ethel was soon able to combine a car trip to Penrith to watch Ian stroke the Shore eight in the Head of the River with a longer journey to Leura, where the trees were 'burning with colour'. 'Garth' seemed even more down at heel than before, an impression that was heightened by the arrival of a wild storm which brought down telegraph lines and marooned them for days. Relief came when a shopkeeper drove down to take an order and came back with the tenderest sirloin and the largest turkey in Leura.

On the following Sunday Ethel was driven down Cascade Street, with its spectacular view of the valley to the south-west, to visit Eleanor and Eric Dark. She wrote later:

Uncommonly interesting visit & lovely home among the burning fires of the autumn coloured trees – maples etc etc House appealed to me as few have done – Pixie's own design – studies for both, lovely landscape windows – calm lounges, dining room with Sheraton furniture – everything I love.

Eric Dark later came to check Ethel's blood pressure and general health, prescribed sedatives and sleeping tablets, and was engaged in conversation about his latest book, *Who are the Reds*.

Somehow this holiday in the mountains turned around Ethel's approach to life. She gained a new vitality and wrote of the 'first return of health' and of showing a new gardener what she wanted done. That Sunday there was a barbecue at Hopetoun Avenue, with Ian in charge of cooking the chops and driving his grandmother home 'tho' he hasn't his licence yet'. Expressing this new spirit of optimism was a period of vigorous and joyous gardening, when Ethel helped George to set out anemomes and prepare a bed for sweet peas, one of her favourite annuals.

Adrian's career at the bar had resumed prosperously at the start of 1946 as did his work as President of the Australian Surf Life Saving Association. Ethel had been reading the diaries he had kept secretly during captivity in defiance of Japanese prohibitions and in late winter he came alone to dine with his mother and sit in front of the fire going through his maps and retracing the campaign, probably a cathartic and useful experience for both of them, Ethel having been absorbed by Rohan Rivett's moving account in *Behind Bamboo* of the building of the Burma railroad.

Meanwhile Ethel had been absorbed in reading a novel that was being serialized in the *Sydney Morning Herald*:

Reading with vivid interest the prize novel; The Harp in the South by Ruth Park – 2000 pounds prize & deserved it. Quite the most sordid tale I ever read but genius without a doubt. Should have a powerful antiseptic effect on Surry Hills slumdom Premier Mc-Kell's constituency for 30 years!!

This diary entry showed no recollection of Ethel's having met Ruth Park when she had come to 'Avenel' a few years earlier to interview her for a Sydney newspaper. Like her, the young New Zealand expatriate had trained for journalism in the hard school of managing children's pages. She still remembers Ethel's beautiful complexion, which she compared in texture to a sweet pea. In clothes and demeanour she was 'like an English gentlewoman with a voice soft and lady-like and a winning smile'.[5]

Two days after writing of *Harp in the South* Ethel met the McKells at a garden party for the Duke and Duchess of Gloucester. She thought Mrs McKell much nicer than her husband, former Premier of New South Wales, 'whom I shd hate to see Gov Genl'. When that appointment was confirmed in February Ethel simply commented 'Language fails!' It was a view the folk of Surry Hills and Redfern would not have shared, especially those members of Sydney's Lebanese community who had found McKell an ever present friend in difficult times.

At this time Ethel's enthusiasm and attention was given largely to the family, attending swimming carnivals where Philippa and Ian distinguished themselves and taking pride in the achievements of their parents, Adrian as a professional and public figure and Betty as a hostess and also as an organiser of the Red Cross Flower Fete which she thought 'beyond praise'. Yet she kept up her own interests too, becoming active again in the garden, where with a heavy heart she supervised the lopping of a giant jacaranda tree whose branches had obstructed the water view of the people in the flats on the high side of Warringah Road. In March she took Philippa to a fine performance at the Children's Theatre which she had been instrumental in forming and wrote to the Town Hall War Memorial Committee recommending the adoption of the Children's Theatre as its principal object.

From money worries, however, Ethel was exempt. In 1947 she began to receive increasingly large royalty payments from her novels, which Ward Lock were bringing out in new editions now that paper was in more abundant supply. A cheque arrived from London for 149 pounds, prompting the comment that 'books must be looking up a little' and twelve months later in October 1948 royalties had risen for the second half of that year to 305 pounds stirling. By now the firm had published five or six of her books in new editions and in May 1949, with the arrival of a bank draft to complete a year's royalties it made a total of 521 pounds, a pleasing sum in view of the fact that there had been no new book for twenty years. To put the figure into perspective it was more than twice the basic wage and about equal to a high school teacher's salary as a top graduate assistant.

Adrian had been offered a district court judgeship in November 1947 and was under strong pressure from Betty and Ethel to accept, though it implied a substantial fall from his salary at the Bar:

But we love the honour better than the wage – about 1650 pounds. He hesitates rather – lots of fight in him & he moans he would have to give up standing on his head on the surf board.

Ethel thought it was practically settled but her son held out till the following July, when he accepted a temporary appointment to the arbitration commission, telling her that he couldn't disappoint her again. A few weeks later he began his first circuit as a District Court judge; it was the beginning of a distinguished career on the bench.

Mid-February 1948 found Ethel with a renewed sense of purpose. Her new Telex hearing aid was working well and she took out the manuscript of 'Two and Two' with the most serious intentions. First however, she cleared her desk of outstanding correspondence and business matters and by the 19th 'Acksherly began to write again', turning out about 4000 words. But progress was now extremely spasmodic, chiefly because there was no longer at her command the driving energy that had made Ethel in her prime an extremely fast writer.

Fresh encouragement to stir herself again professionally came in late October when Ethel was visited by Colonel Shipton, a director of Ward Lock, in company with Mr Avery, the firm's new Melbourne manager. 'They are going to do big things with our books,' she wrote after Adrian had driven the visitors back to the Wentworth Hotel, 'publishing many here in Melbourne as well as London.' First of the local publications was a copy of *Judy and Punch* which arrived in time for Christmas; but it cost 8s 6d and scored no more from the author than, 'Looks quite fair as books look nowadays with good wrapper.' Later on she had the pleasure of seeing two copies of the locally produced *Seven Little Australians*, brought for autograph by Rose's daughter, Mrs Theo Kennard, who had spent much time at 'Avenel' decades earlier.

New Year resolutions in 1949 contributed to Ethel's being able to settle down to a day of writing 'quite in my old style; am feeling so much brighter & better', she wrote enthusiastically. A whole chapter flowed from her pen and soon there came an invitation from Alice Jackson, editor of the *Women's Weekly*, seeking to commit Ethel to publishing 'Two and Two' as a serial, though she was only up to chapter 7. No less encouraging was what she described on 10 February as 'An amazingly nice letter from Dr Evatt in Canberra', following up a letter that he had written to her ten years earlier acknowledging the delight he'd had as a child in getting to know the characters of her novels and 'realising here was the Sydney and the country I knew'. He now stressed the magnitude of the contribution she had made to Australia and to Australian youth. Heady praise indeed for an old lady who had come to feel less and less sure of her place and function and highly encouraging to further efforts as a writer.[6]

Coinciding with this new burst of professional activity was a renewal of Ethel's interest in young people both as a grand-mother and a public figure. With Ian now at university and responding positively to the challenges and pleasures of the new life it was Philippa who carried the family's hopes in her penultimate year at Wenona. She became the school's swimming champion and led her team in the All School's Carnival. Ethel's support for the now well-established concept of a Children's Theatre was expressed in late March by her going to a performance of 'Youth Presents' at Mosman where an audience of 800 gave her a warm welcome. Again in November she joined a Saturday afternoon crowd that had come for the opening of the Children's Library at Bradfield, a 'splendid venture' as she put it, which owed much to the energy of Mrs Matheson. There she was put 'in the seats of the mighty' with Dr Evatt's wife and Dame Mary Gilmore, the Clive Evatts and Dick Windeyer. As she described the occasion:

The rooms are beautiful with lots of bookcases, clever wall decorations etc etc. Mr Evatt made me speak & I did but as badly as ever, tho' they clapped like anything. It is truly a noble dream, nobly (almost) carried out.

Like his mother, Adrian was susceptible to the mood of a new year and to the desire to give energy and talent to public causes. After his birthday in 1950 Ethel wrote proudly:

He had never looked better & happier & fuller of plans – soaring plans for the good of the people. He goes to Canberra in a few days for a big conference. He came to me for all the afternoon.

The conference was in connection with his appointment the previous May as President of the National Fitness Council, an area of public service, like the Surf Lifesaving Movement, to which he gave generously for the rest of his life.

Judges and their families have always been under special pressures, notably those practising in the criminal and family jurisdictions. Two days after expressing her satisfaction at Adrian's new plans, Ethel confided to her diary anxieties she felt at the recent escape of two of the most notorious and violent criminals in our history:

Alone a lot & confess to being nervous. Mears & Dugan are still at large & desperate. As it was A who sentenced them to something like 7 years & then 2 more for escaping they might be inclining to retaliate on our family. One of them wrote A a long letter.

Life was drawing to a close for the youngest of the three little maids who had accompanied Sarah Turner from England seventy years earlier. Rose lived at 139 Middle Head Road, Mosman, so that when her family came to pay their last respects they also visited Ethel nearby. Harold Pockley, whose quest for Rose's hand had seemed to the elder sister both unduly warm and premature, had predeceased his wife. She died in a nursing home on 19 February 1950 after six months of a cruel illness. Lilian was still in good form, occasionally persuading Ethel to join her for an afternoon at Randwick. She had long been a widow and though on the face of it, not badly off, with a house at Lindfield that she sold for 6,500 pounds in May 1951, Ethel continued to supplement her income when she experienced temporary financial reverses.

For her own part, Ethel's spirits remained cheerful, and she was elated mightily by Australia's victory over the United States in the Davis Cup final in August 1950, with a superb team comprising John Bromwich, Frank Sedgman, Ken McGregor and George Worthington. She was still vitally interested in international and domestic affairs, commenting with alarm on revelations of Communist machinations in the unions and the explosion by Russia of an atomic bomb. In June 1949 she had been absorbed for a whole afternoon by the broadcast from Canberra of the fierce debate between Chifley and Menzies at the time of the general strike. She had the odd experience at a Wenona pageant of meeting for the first time in many years Leo Charlton, who now practised medicine at North Sydney and sent his daughter to the same school as Philippa. 'His girl – who should have been my

Jean's & Adrian her uncle.' The hurt of Jean's death was still there.

If there were anxieties about her siblings and the state of the nation, Ethel was able to take comfort from the happiness of her grandchildren. Ian had come to supper and a long talk in front of the fire in November 1949 and seemed to have benefited by the change to university. Philippa in the following year had shown an interest in studying at the Kindergarten Training College at Waverley. Both seemed popular and well adjusted, enjoying the opportunities given to a fortunate generation by time, place and family circumstances.

During 1951, Ethel still displayed an astonishing spirit of optimism, in spite of an underlying difficulty at eighty years of retaining a desired level of independence. The family at Hopetoun Avenue, a few hundred yards away, made it possible for that effort to continue till the last possible moment, sending Ian down to stay the night when Ethel's minders were suddenly unavailable, and providing meals when 'Avenel' lacked its own cook. In those days long before take-aways, Adrian learned the basic skills of a deliverer.

Aptly, in one of the last entries in her diary, Ethel mentions a drive to Leura in Ian's company, when the young man, now 22, had passed on the news that he had been invited by Mr Justice Maxwell to be his assistant. It was a delicious opportunity for a fellow in his final year of Law, offering a salary of about 450 pounds a year, and as his grandmother put it 'just the way Adrian began'.

Ethel's final diary entry was a reminder to take with her to Hornsby Girls High School the usual parcel of three books that were to be presented as annual prizes. Miraculously, on this occasion, her brief speech was captured for posterity and it is the only known recording of her voice.[7]

At 81 she still retained the northern English accent of her childhood, though one can detect the strange timbre of someone who has struggled with deafness for most of her life. The sheer terror of speaking in public hadn't diminished with the passing of the years; in her hand she held a book that she had treasured from soon after her arrival in Sydney, inscribed: 'Ethel S Turner 1881':

I want to send this message to my friends everywhere, many of whom I have never met. I shall not presume to give you any words of my own but want to read to you from Longfellow.

> 'If any thought of mine, or sung or told,
>   Has ever given delight of consolation,
> Ye have repaid me back a thousandfold,
>   By every friendly sign & salutation.
>
> Thanks for the sympathies that ye have shown!
>   Thanks for each kindly word, each silent token,
> That teaches me, when seeming most alone,
>   Friends are around us, though no word be spoken.
>
> Kind messages, that pass from land to land;
>   Kind letters, that betray the heart's deep history,
> In which we feel the pressure of a hand, ...
>   One touch of fire, ... & all the rest is mystery!
>
> Not chance of birth or place has made us friends,
>   Being oftentime of different tongues & nations,
> But the endeavour for the selfsame ends,
>   With the same hopes, and fears, & aspirations.'

Epilogue

*E*thel Turner's public engagements virtually ended with her speech to the students at Hornsby Girls' High School in 1951, marking the close of a career in writing and education that gave pleasure to millions of readers. It was her special achievement to interpret the young people of this country through her first major publication, and this was especially welcome for its brilliant timing. Her friend Banjo Paterson commented that she, like himself, had responded to a singularly favourable opportunity. *Seven Little Australians* had been published in October 1894, while *The Man from Snowy River and other verses* in 1895 and Henry Lawson's collection of stories *While the Billy Boils* appeared in 1896. Among them they had expressed some potent ideas about what it meant to be an Australian. Amazingly, it was a young Englishwoman who helped to effect this.

Two people who enabled Ethel's star to shine were men employed by an English publisher, Ward Lock. William Steele, the firm's Melbourne manager, immediately recognized her talent and made her an offer a week after receiving her manuscript. Coulson Kernahan was the literary adviser in London who reported, 'Here is the Miss Alcott of Australia; here is one of the strongest, simplest, sweetest, sanest and most beautiful child-stories that I have read for years.'

Fifteen years later the same critic wrote a foreword for Ethel's *Birthday Book* which tells us much of her motivation:

She is so possessed by her passion for children that she needs *must* write of them whether she wishes to do so or not. The children of the brain must be brought to the birth no less than the children of the body, and the children born of Ethel Turner's brain are more real and alive, more living flesh and blood, than are many of the very children for whom some of us have bought dolls, toys, or sweetmeats.

Though Ethel's appeal was basically to Australian readers she had a loyal following in Britain, and her books were almost immediately translated and sold in many countries, beginning with *Seven Little Australians* in Sweden, Norway and Holland in 1895 and continuing to the present day. The book has been published in at least eleven languages, including Japanese, and the Spanish paperback edition has been reprinted eight times since 1897. In the Lu Rees Library at Canberra some other foreign titles of Ethel Turner are held, including Dutch and Danish, though Sweden has been the most enthusiastic reprinter of her books.

What of the other media? The ABC was interested in broadcasting Ethel's books from the beginning of radio transmissions in the 1930s. But it was the development of television that ensured the continuing popularity of her work, starting with the BBC black and white production of *Seven Little Australians* in 1953. Quite by co-incidence Ethel's granddaughter Philippa was in London to see the third and final episode and was able to write to Ethel in Sydney with exciting news of this development. It is pleasing to think that this preceded the stroke which incapacitated her for the last few years of her life.

In 1973 the ABC collaborated with the BBC to make a ten-part film for television of *Seven Little Australians*, directed by Ron Way and starring Leonard Teale and Elizabeth Alexander with Jennifer Cluff as Judy. For many Australians the experience of seeing a well-directed and professionally acted series in colour revitalized the story, the timeless quality of which depended on bringing together details of life in Sydney and the Blue Mountains culminating in the famous scene at Yarrahappini Station when Judy died saving her baby brother from a falling tree.

Twenty-seven countries have shown the ABC series in the past twenty years, including Albania, the United States, Cyprus, Japan, Eire, Germany and Namibia and it has been seen several times in Australia.

The musical of *Seven Little Australians* was composed by David Reeves and the lyrics were written by Peter Yeldham and John Palmer. It had its World Premier in Melbourne in 1988 and toured most of the capital cities.

Ethel Turner died on 8 April 1958. On a crisp, clear autumn morning, St Andrew's Cathedral in Sydney was overflowing with those who came to join with her family and give thanks for her life. After the singing of the hymn 'Abide With Me' Dean Pitt referred to the final chapter of *Seven Little Australians*, in which Meg tries to find words to comfort the dying Judy. Floral tributes covered and obscured the chancel steps. Philippa Poole recalls feeling 'totally overwhelmed that so many people were present to honour this tiny grandmother of mine'.

Thirty-six years have passed since that day, and in the centenary year of the publication of *Seven Little Australians*, one wonders what Ethel Turner would have thought had she known that her simple tale was still being read, and re-read, and loved by children not only in Australia but all over the world.

PROLOGUE:

1. Ethel Turner, open letter to the *Journal of the Junior Literary Society*, vol. 1, no. 1, 1 June 1927, q. by Lesley Heath, 'The Junior Literary Society', p. 7.
2. A doctoral student, history department, Uni. NSW.
3. *Parthenon*, vol. 1, no. 1, 1 January 1889.
4. Ruth Park, *A Fence Around the Cuckoo*, pp. 248–9.
5. Brenda Niall, *Seven Little Billabongs*, p. 26.
6. Zora Cross, cited by Margaret Trask, 'Early Australian Children's Writers', I, p. 17.

CHAPTER 1:

1. *Three Little Maids*, p. 19.
2. Sarah Cope to Rose Pockley, 19 February 1912, q. Poole, *The Diaries of Ethel Turner*, pp. 280–1.

CHAPTER 2:

1. *Sydney Morning Herald*, 6–7 October, 14 October, 1933.
2. Lilith Norman, *The Brown and Yellow*, p. 24.
3. Ibid., pp. 23, 31.
4. Ibid., pp. 25–6.
5. Ibid., pp. 20–1.

6. Philippa Poole, *The Diaries of Ethel Turner*, p. 12; Sydney Girls' High School *Gazette*, No. 8, August 1888, p. 6.

CHAPTER 3:

1. Graeme Davison and others (eds), Sydney 1987, *Australians 1888*, pp. 5–13.
2. Details of Herbert Curlewis at Newington courtesy of the archivist, Dr Peter Swain.
3. *Sydney Morning Herald*, 6 December 1889.
4. Mary Ann Cope's last will, Sup. Ct. NSW, 34949. Mary left 12 472 pounds in 1905. Joseph Cope died in 1862, leaving 31 100 pounds, Sup. Ct. Will 5464.
5. Courtesy of Annette Butterfield, 7 January 1992.
6. William Astley Papers, ML, A/72/2, 655-73b.

CHAPTER 4:

1. *Sands Directory*, Paddington, 1885; Newtown, 1891.
2. From the Poole Collection.
3. Dowell O'Reilly Papers, ML MSS 231/11.

CHAPTER 5:

1. Article on 'Inglewood' (later 'Woodlands') in *North Shore Times* compiled by Kuringai Historical Society, Poole Collection.
2. Herbert Curlewis to Turner, 25 October 1891, Poole Collection.
3. Russell Ward, *The Australian Legend*, 1978, p. 42.
4. Joseph Cope's will, sworn at 31 100 pounds, NSW Supreme Court, Will 5464.
5. Nancy Phelan, *Louise Mack*, p. 43.
6. Turner to William Astley, 6 January 1892, William Astley papers, ML, A72, vol. 2, p. 65.
7. Turner to O'Reilly, 1 December 1891, Dowell O'Reilly Papers, ML MSS 231/11, pp. 173–5.
8. Ibid., 31 May 1892, pp. 177–80.
9. *Illustrated Sydney News*, 4 February 1893.

CHAPTER 6:

1. ANL MS 749, Item 104, Article, 'Why I Wrote 7 Little Australians'.
2. Manning Clark, *A History of Australia*, vol. 5, p. 97.
3. William Steele to Turner, 20 November 1893, ML MSS 667/5, pp. 1–4.
4. Steele to Turner, 4 December 1893, ML MSS 667/5.

CHAPTER 7:

1. Niall, *Seven Little Billabongs*, p. 15.
2. Phelan, *Louise Mack*, pp. 84–5.
3. Steele to Turner, 11 June 1894, Poole Collection, Box 4.
4. ML MSS 667/9, p. 29, 16 October 1902. (Author's italics)
5. Poole Collection, Box 4.
6. Ethel Turner, *The Little Larrikin*, p. 30.
7. Ibid., p. 121.
8. Kerry White, 'Blooming with Childhood's Fragrance', *Australian Feminist Studies*, 7 & 8, Summer 1988, p. 57.
9. Niall, op.cit., p. 102.
10. *Sydney Morning Herald*, 25 July 1894.
11. *Bulletin*, 29 October 1894, p. 9.
12. *Daily Telegraph*, 27 October 1894.
13. Steele to Turner, 28 November 1894, Poole Collection, Box 4.
14. *Town and Country Journal*, 21 December 1895, pp. 26–30.
15. George Meredith to Turner, 18 April 1895, ML MSS 667/12.
16. Steele to Turner, 20 and 25 May 1895, ML MSS 667/5, pp. 31–3, 35.
17. Steele to Turner, 10 and 14 May 1895, ibid., pp. 13–16.
18. Steele to Turner, 29 July and 2 August 1895, ibid., pp. 53, 55.
19. ML MSS 667/5, p. 81.
20. Frances Hodgson Burnett to Turner, no date but noted in Diary, 22 September 1895, ML MSS 667/12, pp. 205–9.
21. Steele to Turner, 13 October 1895, ML MSS 667/5, p. 94.
22. Steele to Turner, 27 August 1901, enclosing H. H. Driver's letter of 20 July, ML MSS 667/5, pp. 37, 51b.

CHAPTER 8:

1. Steele to Turner, 15 April 1896, enclosing extract from James Bowden's letter of 17 January, ML MSS 667/5, pp. 173–9.
2. *Windsor Magazine*, vol. 1, January 1895; Steele to Turner, 3 March 1896, ML MSS 667/5, pp. 159–60.
3. Steele to Turner, 10 August 1896, ML MSS 667/5; *Windsor Magazine*, vol. 5, December 1896, pp. 392–402.
4. Steele to Turner, 9 October and 1 September 1896, ML MSS 667/5, pp. 197, 203–4.
5. Steele to Turner, ibid., ML MSS 667/5, p. 196.
6. Information on the Boards given by Eric Pollard of Orange, a descendant, 8 December 1992.
7. A. B. Paterson to Turner, 7 December 1895, ML MSS 667/12, pp. 29–32.
8. Phelan, *Louise Mack*, pp. 72–7.
9. For the point about the Brontës the author is indebted to Peter Radford.
10. Turner to Stephens, 17 June 1897, A. G. Stephens Papers, ML MSS 4937 2(30), pp. 149–55.

CHAPTER 9:

1. Manning Clark, *In Search of Henry Lawson*, p. 86.
2. James Bowden to Steele, 3 December 1895, ML MSS 667/5, p. 251.
3. Carol Mills, 'Illustrators: D. H. Souter', Lu Rees Archives Jnl. no 7, 1986, p. 20.
4. Henry Lawson to Turner, 12 April 1900, ML MSS 667/12, p. 79; Clark, op.cit., pp. 86–8.
5. Pen Money and Accounts Books, Poole Collection.

CHAPTER 10:

1. Poems of Ethel Turner, Book II, Poole Collection.
2. Correspondence with theatre companies, 1900–21, ML MSS 667/11.
3. *McClure's*, New York, May 1905.
4. Baby Book, Christmas 1902, Poole Collection.
5. J. C. Williamson to Turner, 16 February 1903, ML MSS 667/11, p. 45.

6. Charles Arnold to Turner, 13 November 1900, 30 March 1903; Williamson to Turner, 19 December 1903, ML MSS 667/11, pp. 1–4, 21–2, 55–8, 59.

7. *Daily Telegraph*, 6 January 1903.

8. Pen Money Book, Poole Collection.

9. Niall, *Seven Little Billabongs*, p. 26.

10. George Lock to Turner, 9 September 1904, ML MSS 667/6, pp. 117–8.

11. Information from Mrs Jenny Priestley, September 1992.

12. Williamson to Turner, 16 and 31 January 1905, ML MSS 667/11, pp. 69, 75.

13. *Life*, 15 March 1904; *Daily Telegraph*, 24 December 1904.

14. Personal communication, Philippa Poole, 5 September 1991; Ian Curlewis, 18 August 1992.

15. On Cullen see esp. J. M. Bennett, 'Sir William Porteous Cullen – Scholar and Judge', *Canberra Historical Journal*, September 1977.

16. Poems of Ethel Turner, Book I, Poole Collection.

17. Turner to 'My dear Winnie', 17 and 28 January, 18 May 1905, courtesy Dr P. J. Millard, Narrabeen, 3 March 1992.

CHAPTER 11:

1. For account of Girls' Realm Guild see *Sydney Mail*, 23 August 1911.

2. Contract details in Poole Collection.

3. Cassell to Turner, 17 September 1909, ML MSS 667/8, p. 77; Curtis Brown & Massie to Turner, 27 January 1911. ML MSS 667/9, p. 281.

4. Turner to Lock, 9 December 1909, ML MSS 667/3.

5. Lock to Turner, 15 July 1909; Steele to Turner, 2 September 1909; ML MSS 667/6, pp. 283–4, 295–8.

6. Turner to Hodder & Stoughton, 9 December 1909, ML MSS 667/3.

7. Massie to Turner, 15 June 1910; ML MSS 667/9, pp. 213–5, 30 August 1911; ibid., p. 289.

8. For the birth certificate the author is indebted to Mr Peter Radford.

9. *Sydney Morning Herald*, 27 and 28 September 1910.

CHAPTER 12:

1. Hughes Massie to Turner, 19 July 1910, ML MSS 667/9, p. 229.
2. Turner to Massie, 12 November 1910, ML MSS 667/3.
3. Massie to Turner, 13 January 1911, ML MSS 667/9, pp. 273–4.
4. Turner to Massie, 20 February 1911, ML MSS 667/3.
5. Turner to Hodder Williams, 20 March 1911, ML MSS 667/3.
6. Curtis Brown to Turner, 30 August 1911, ML MSS 667/9, p. 289.
7. Desiree Bertram's scrapbook, kindly lent by Maurice Keane, Director of the New South Wales Aboriginal Land Council.
8. Niall, *Australia Through the Looking-Glass*, p. 107.
9. Turner to Henry Irving, 25 November 1911, ML MSS 667/3.
10. *Daily Telegraph*, 17 December 1913.
11. Helen Brown of Sussex to P. Poole, 21 January 1982, Poole Collection.
12. C. Warne, *Pictorial Memories, Lower North Shore*, 1984, pp. 16–17.
13. Poems by Ethel Turner, Book II, P. Poole (ed.), Poole Collection.
14. Turner to Hodder Williams and Northern Newspaper Syndicate, 18 April 1914, ML MSS 667/4, pp. 33, 27; Hodder to Turner, 9 July 1914, ML MSS 667/9, p. 203; Turner to Cassell & Co., 24 March 1916, ML MSS 667/4, p. 155.
15. Pen Money Book, 1914, Poole Collection.
16. *Sydney Morning Herald*, 22 August 1914.
17. Ibid., 12 August 1914.
18. Poems by Ethel Turner, Book II, P. Poole (ed.), Poole Collection.
19. Niall, *Seven Little Billabongs*, p. 135.
20. Ibid., p. 136.
21. Bartholemew to Turner, 16 June 1911, ML MSS 667/10, pp. 1–3.
22. Turner to Steele, 16 October 1911, ML MSS 667/3.
23. Turner to Steele, 18 October 1913, ML MSS 667/4, p. 7; Steele to Turner, 28 July 1914, ML MSS 667/7, p. 97.
24. Turner to Hodder Williams, 1 August 1914, ML MSS 667/4, p. 51.
25. Turner to Hodder Williams, 25 July 1912, ML MSS 667/3; Steele to Turner, 18 November, 14 December 1914, ML MSS 667/7, pp. 121, 129.
26. Steele to Turner, 22 November 1915, ML MSS 667/7, pp. 195–6.
27. Turner to Steele, 11 November 1915, ML MSS 667/4, p. 131.

CHAPTER 13:

1. Poems of Ethel Turner, Book II, P. Poole (ed.), Poole Collection.
2. Ibid., *Sydney Morning Herald*, 10 July 1915.
3. *Sydney Morning Herald*, 5 July 1915.
4. *Lone Hand*, 1 November 1915, p. 357.
5. Ibid.
6. Ibid.
7. 'The Edith Cavell Memorial Home', newspaper cuttings, ML QA823/T945/1.
8. *Sydney Morning Herald*, *Daily Telegraph*, 25 September 1915.
9. *Australian Soldiers' Gift Book*, p. 16.
10. Niall, *Australia Through the Looking-Glass*, p. 106.
11. *Sydney Morning Herald*, 4 October 1916.
12. *Sydney Morning Herald*, 21 October 1916.
13. Turner to Adrian Curlewis, 'Arrankamp', Bowral, 6 November 1916, Poole Collection.
14. Turner to Steele, 16 November 1916, ML MSS 667/4, p. 161.
15. Niall, *Seven Little Billabongs*, pp. 36–42.
16. Steele to Turner, 26 September 1917, ML MSS 667/7, p. 265.
17. Turner to Little, Brown & Co., 16 February 1918, ML MSS 67/4, p. 205.
18. Dowell O'Reilly Papers, ML MSS 231/10, pp. 217–8.
19. Interview with 'Elizabethans' at Sydney Girls' High School Old Girls lunch, 30 November 1991.

CHAPTER 14:

1. C. S. Bligh to Turner, 11 September 1918; Morris to Turner, 16 September 1918; ML MSS 667/8, pp. 5, 7–11.
2. *Smith's Weekly*, 31 January 1920.
3. 'Behind That Brilliant Proscenium', *Sydney Morning Herald*, 20 November 1912.
4. Newspaper cuttings, ML QA823/T945/1.
5. *Smith's Weekly*, 13 March 1920.
6. Turner to *Sun*, 18 July 1919, ML MSS 667/4, pp. 231–3.
7. Turner, undated manuscript in Poole Collection.

8. Account Book 1922, Pen Money Book 1914–24, Poole Collection.
9. Harold Copping to Ward Lock, 1 June 1922, ML MSS 667/8, p. 65.

CHAPTER 15:
1. *Daily Telegraph*, 13 December 1922.
2. Ward Lock to Turner, 17 April 1924, ML MSS 667/8, p. 85.
3. *Bulletin*, 1 November 1923.
4. Interview in *Daily Telegraph*, 17 December 1913.
5. Wills of Joseph Cope, d. 5/7/1862 Supreme Court 1862, series 1, 5464 (£31,100); Mary Ann Cope, d. 20/7/1905 (£12,472), 34949; Jean Cope, d. 21/10/23, (£1040), 129468; Charles Cope, d. 30/5/25, £13,047), 133595.

CHAPTER 16:
1. *Sydney Morning Herald*, 9 January 1926.
2. Poole Collection.
3. Turner to Rose Pockley, no date [5 May 1926], Connery Collection; D & J Pope, *North Island Travel Guide*, 1984.
4. Turner to Rose Pockley, 9, 10 and 13 May 1926, Connery Collection.
5. Turner to Rose Pockley, 20 May 1926, Connery Collection.
6. Interview with Lady Curlewis, 25 June 1992.
7. Poole Collection, Poems of Ethel Turner.
8. Turner to Rose Pockley, undated, 1925.
9. Pen Money Book.

CHAPTER 17:
1. *Lux*, 1930, pp. 41–2.
2. Crowley, *Modern Australia in Documents*, I, 461–81.
3. Poems of Ethel Turner, Book II, P. Poole (ed.), Poole Collection.

CHAPTER 18:
1. Interview with Lady Curlewis, 6 August 1992.
2. Pen Money Book, Poole Collection.
3. *Australian Women's Weekly*, 2 December 1939.
4. Philippa Poole, *Of Love and War*, p. 20.
5. Adrian Curlewis to family, 5 December 1941; *Of Love and War*, p. 87.

6. Poole, *Of Love and War*, p. 23.

7. Ibid., p. 6.

8. Ibid., pp. 19–20.

9. Ibid., p. 34.

10. Interview with Ian Curlewis, 18 August 1992.

11. Poole, *Of Love and War*, pp. 105–6.

12. Ibid., pp. 123–5.

13. *Australians, Events and Places*, pp. 157–8.

CHAPTER 19:

1. Poole, *Of Love and War*, pp. 147–8.

2. Turner to Adrian Curlewis, 20 June 1943; *Of Love and War*, p. 198.

3. Turner, manuscript of speech for Jubilee Dinner, Historical Resources Centre, Sydney Girls' High School.

4. Turner to Betty Curlewis, 15 August 1945, *Of Love and War*, pp. 258–9.

5. Interview with Ruth Park, September 1992.

6. Niall, *Seven Little Billabongs*, pp. 3–4.

7. Turner manuscript, Poole Collection.

The life of Ethel Turner was the subject of one of the great literary diaries in Australia. She began writing it in January 1889, and apart from breaks occasioned by ill health she continued until the end of 1951. The complete diaries are available in microfilm at the Mitchell Library for study by authorised students.

PRIMARY SOURCES:
Manuscripts
Ethel Turner Diaries ML, Microfilm FM 4/6539–6541.
Papers of Ethel Turner, 1888–1948 ML MS 667 including correspondence with publishers and theatre companies; also a collection of letters received from Jimmy Bancks, H. V. Evatt, Miles Franklin and Henry Lawson.
Papers of Ethel Turner, ML MSS 4525 (including MS of The Sundowner, a play in three acts).
Papers of Curlewis Family 1881–1966, ML MS 2159.
Ethel Turner Papers ANL MS 749.
Angus & Robertson Correspondence, ML MS CY 1612.
A. G. Stephens Papers 1859–1933, ML MS 4937.

Published Diaries
Poole, Philippa, (compiler), *The Diaries of Ethel Turner*, Sydney, 1979.
Poole, Philippa, *Of Love and War: The letters and diaries of Captain Adrian Curlewis and his family 1939–1945*, Sydney, 1985.

Official Records

Certificates of birth, marriage and death used in the United Kingdom and Sydney.

New South Wales Archives Office, Shipping Master's Office, Passenger List, Sydney 24 March 1880, details of Turner party.

Books by Ethel Turner

Exact dates of publication are rarely known, since the London premises of Ward, Lock & Bowden (who soon after became Ward Lock) were destroyed by bombing during WWII. Approximate dates were determined by the time of arrival in Australia, by reference to Ethel's diary and to her Pen Money Book, in which she recorded her earnings (Poole Collection).

Seven Little Australians, illustrated by A. J. Johnson, Ward, Lock & Bowden, London, 1894.

The Story of a Baby, illustrated by St Clair Simmons, Ward, Lock & Bowden, London, 1895.

The Family at Misrule, illustrated by A. J. Johnson, Ward, Lock & Bowden, London, 1895.

The Little Duchess, short stories, illustrated by Sydney Cowell, Ward, Lock & Bowden, London, 1896.

The Little Larrikin, illustrated by A. J. Johnson, Ward Lock, London, 1896.

Miss Bobbie, illustrated by Harold Copping, Ward Lock, London, 1897.

The Camp at Wandinong, illustrated by Frances Ewan and others, Ward Lock, London, 1898.

Three Little Maids, illustrated by A. J. Johnson, Ward Lock, London, 1900.

Gum Leaves, stories and poems, illustrated by D. H. Souter, William Brooks, Sydney, 1900.

The Wonder-Child: an Australian Story, illustrated by Gordon Browne, Religious Tract Society, London, 1901.

Little Mother Meg, illustrated by A. J. Johnson, Ward Lock, London, 1902.

Betty & Co, illustrated by Arthur Buckland and others, Ward Lock, London, 1903.

Mother's Little Girl, illustrated by A. J. Johnson, Ward Lock, London, 1904.

A White Roof-Tree, illustrated by A. J. Johnson and others, Ward Lock, London, 1905.

In the Mist of the Mountains, illustrated by J. Macfarlane, Ward Lock, London, 1906.

The Stolen Voyage, illustrated by R. Hawcridge and others, Ward Lock, London, 1907.

Happy Hearts: a Picture Book for Boys and Girls, illustrated by D. H. Souter and others, Ward Lock, London, 1908.

That Girl, illustrated by Frances Ewan, T. Fisher Unwin, London, 1908.

Ethel Turner Birthday Book: a Selection of Passages from the Books of Ethel Turner, arranged by Lilian Turner Thompson, illustrated, Ward Lock, London, 1909.

Fugitives from Fortune, short stories, illustrated by J. Macfarlane, Ward Lock, London, 1910.

Fair Ines, illustrated, Hodder & Stoughton, London, 1910.

The Raft in the Bush, short stories, illustrated by H. C. Sandy and D. H. Souter, Ward Lock, London, 1910.

The Tiny House and Other Verses, Ward Lock, London, 1911.

Fifteen and Fair, verse, Hodder & Stoughton, London, 1911.

The Apple of Happiness, illustrated by A. N. Gough, Hodder & Stoughton, London, 1911.

An Ogre Up-to-date, short stories and verses, illustrated by H. C. Sandy and D. H. Souter, Ward Lock, London, 1911.

Ports and Happy Havens, travel, illustrated, Hodder & Stoughton, London, 1912.

The Secret of the Sea, illustrated, Hodder & Stoughton, London, 1913.

Oh, Boys in Brown, verse, Sydney, 1914.

Flower o' the Pine, illustrated by J. H. Hartley, Hodder & Stoughton, London, 1914.

The Cub: Six Months in His Life: A Story in War-time, illustrated by Harold Copping, Ward Lock, London, 1915.

John of Daunt, illustrated by Harold Copping, Ward Lock, London, 1916.

Captain Cub, illustrated by Harold Copping, Ward Lock, London, 1917.

Australian Soldiers' Gift Book, edited by Ethel Turner and Bertram Stevens, Voluntary Workers' Association, Sydney, 1918.

St. Tom and the Dragon, illustrated by Harold Copping, Ward Lock, London, 1918.

Brigid and the Cub, illustrated by Harold Copping, Ward Lock, London, 1919.

Laughing Water, illustrated by Harold Copping, Ward Lock, London, 1920.

King Anne, illustrated by Harold Copping, Ward Lock, London, 1921.

Jennifer, J., illustrated by Harold Copping, Ward Lock, London, 1922.

The Sunshine Family: a Book of Nonsense for Girls and Boys, by Ethel Turner & Jean Curlewis, illustrated by D. H. Souter and others, Ward Lock, London, 1923.

Nicola Silver, illustrated by Harold Copping, Ward Lock, London, 1924.

The Ungardeners, illustrated, Ward Lock, London, 1925.

Funny, illustrated by W. E. Wightman, Ward Lock, London, 1926.

Judy and Punch, illustrated by Harold Copping, Ward Lock, London, 1928.

Other Writings by Ethel Turner

Parthenon, edited by Ethel and Lilian Turner, January 1889 to March 1892.

7 December 1889, engaged by Mr Astley to write the Ladies' Letter for the *Tasmanian Mail*.

'The Altar of Examdomania', poem, *Hermes*, 4 December 1889, pp. 8–9.

'A Mutable Maiden', *Illustrated Sydney News*, 13 August 1892, pp. 4–6.

'Between Ourselves' (extracts from the letters of a Sydney girl 'Yum Yum', to her friend in the bush,) beginning in *Illustrated Sydney News*, 22 October 1892, p. 7.

'The Children's Corner', beginning in *Illustrated Sydney News*, 26 November 1892, p. 17. The first issue of 'The Children's Corner' included the start of a serial story, 'Laddie', by Ethel G. Turner [*sic*].

'On the Manly Rocks. A Sweet Small Tragedy', *Illustrated Sydney News*, 22 April 1893, p. 12.

'It was a dream', *Illustrated Sydney News*, 7 March 1893.

'Sweetheart', *Bulletin*, 8 March 1893.

'Wilkes of Waterloo, A Suburban Sketch', *Daily Telegraph*, 24 June 1893, p. 9.

'Toychild, A Potts Point Sketch', *Daily Telegraph*, 1 July 1893.

'Told in the Wattle Scrub', *Town and Country Journal*, 16 December 1893, p. 14.

'A Modern Achilles', *Town and Country Journal*, 16 December 1893, pp. 21–2.

'The Little Duchess', *Bulletin*, 16 December 1893, p. 20.

'At a street corner', *Bulletin*, 20 January 1894, p. 24.

'To the City of Raspberry Jam', article, *Town and Country Journal*, 3 March 1894, pp. 28–9.

'Ananias and Sapphira', *Bulletin*, 12 May 1894, p. 21.

'A Canvas', poem, *Bulletin*, 19 May 1894, p. 14.

The Wig, (play) performed by SUDS 24 July 1894.

'For half a day', poem, *Cosmos*, 31 January 1895, p. 273.

Seven Little Australians, 10 July 1895, a play based on the book.

'Shabby Shoes', and 'Orphaned by the Sea', verses, *Bulletin*, 26 October 1895.

'A Saucepan Sketch', *Windsor Magazine*, December 1895, vol. ii, pp. 632–7.

'A Story of Strange Sights', *Town and Country Journal*, 21 December 1895, pp. 26–30.

'An Ogre Up-to-date', *Sunday Times*, 22 December 1895, p. 13.

'Almost an Idyll', *Bulletin*, December 1895.

'The Doing Of It', *Windsor Magazine*, July–November 1896, vol. iv, pp. 92–8.

'Between a Sleep and a Sleep', *Sunday Times*, 20 December 1896, p. 9.

'School at Jimbaree', *Windsor Magazine*, December 1896, vol. v, pp. 56–64.

'A Champion in Ankle-Straps', *Windsor Magazine*, December 1896, vol. v, pp. 392–402.

'The Gloves of Gregan McAlister', *Windsor Magazine*, December 1896, vol. v, pp. 749–56 (first published in *Cosmos*, December 1895).

'The Child of the Children', *Windsor Magazine*, 1897, vol. vii, pp. 144–53.

'The Argonautic Expedition', *Town and Country Journal*, 18 December 1897, pp. 38–40.

'A Suburban Terrace', *Windsor Magazine*, June 1898, vol. viii, pp. 101–6.

'Second Nature', *Windsor Magazine*, June 1898, vol. viii, pp. 549–57.

'What the Postman Brought', *Windsor Magazine*, June 1898, vol. viii, pp. 332–39.

Interview by A. G. Stephens in *Bookfellow*, 25 March 1899, pp. 23–5, publishing Ethel's poem 'A Trembling Star'.

'A Vagabond Day', *Windsor Magazine*, December 1900, vol. xiii, pp. 265–74.

'Early Morning at Brown's', *Windsor Magazine*, June 1901, vol. xiv, pp. 37–42.

Two school songs, commissioned by Angus & Robertson, Pen Money Book, October 1902.

'A Woman's Appeal', letter to editor, *Daily Telegraph*, 7 February 1903, p. 9.

Interview by J. A. Hampshire in *New Idea*, 1 April 1903, pp. 704–8.

'A Day at the Zoo', *Evening News*, 18 October 1903.

'The Going Forth of Tod', *Town and Country Journal*, 9 December 1903, pp. 71–2.

'How I Wrote "Seven Little Australians" ', article in *Life*, March 1904, pp. 284–6.

'In the Silence of the Sleep-Time', *Windsor Magazine*, June 1904, vol. xiv, pp. 94–8.

'At a Little Xmas party', verse, *Town and Country Journal*, August 1904.

'At Concert', [Paderewski], *Evening News*, August 1904.

'Snails: and incidentally Christmas', *Sydney Morning Herald*, 24 December 1904, p. 9.

'Taylor Trainguard', *Australasian*, 12 March 1905.

'The Marriage Morn', *McClure's Magazine*, New York, May 1905, vol. 25, pp. 104–8. First published in *Idler*.

'Mr Jessop's Experiment', *Windsor Magazine*, June 1905, vol. xxii, pp. 569–78.

'The Tale of the Tiny House', poem, *Windsor Magazine*, June 1905, vol. xxii, pp. 678–80.

'Fifteen and her Literature', *Sydney Morning Herald*, September 1905.

'The Light of a Star', *Town and Country Journal*, 13 December 1905, pp. 44–5.

'Before My Bookshelves', article, *Daily Telegraph*, 23 December 1905, p. 6.

'An Afternoon Call', *Lone Hand*, 30 May 1907.

'A day of small things', *Red Funnel*, 1 June 1907.

'Widening the Horizon', *Lone Hand*, June 1907, pp. 134–9.

'The Broken Siesta', *Lone Hand*, 1 October 1907, pp. 622–30.

'Some Notable Nonsense', article, *Town and Country Journal*, 11 December 1907, pp. 48–9.

'The Revolving Bookcase', article, *Town and Country Journal*, 25 December 1907, p. 32.

'The Angels' Peril', poem, *Lone Hand*, 1 February 1908, p. 352.

'The Railway Journey', *Australian Star*, 27 August 1907.

'But Where Does the Winter Go?', poem, *Lone Hand*, 2 November 1908, p. 103.

'Reading without tears', article, *Sydney Morning Herald*, 11 November 1908, p. 5.

'A World without a Flower', article, *Amateur Gardener*, p. 130, 31 May 1909.

'The Christ-Child Day in Australia', poem, *Lone Hand*, 1 January 1910, pp. 233–5.

'Walking to School', poem, *Windsor Magazine*, June 1910, vol. xxxii, p. 418.

'Is the world growing better', and 'Surplus of women', verse, *Sydney Morning Herald*, 11 September 1911.

'The Passing Book', article, *Sydney Morning Herald*, 9 December 1911, p. 7.

'Behind that Brilliant Proscenium', article, *Sydney Morning Herald*, 20 November 1912, Woman's Page.

'Big Browne and Little Browne', *Windsor Magazine*, December 1912, vol. xxxiii, pp. 443–48.

'Girl of 35', *Girls' Realm*, mentioned in Diary 26 April 1913.

'The Books that I Remember', article, *Lone Hand*, April 1913, pp. 525–9.

'The Pink Elixir', *Lone Hand*, 1 October 1914, pp. 337–40.

'Women and Wartime', three articles in *Sydney Morning Herald*, 8, 12, 14 August 1914.

'War Orphans', article, *Sydney Morning Herald*, 14 October 1914, p. 10.

Seven Little Australians, as a four-act play, shown at the Palace Theatre, Pitt Street, Sydney. Final performance in Sydney 6 February 1915.

'Belgium, Our Tears', poem, recited by Lawrence Campbell for the

National Belgium Relief Fund of NSW on 29 May 1915.

'Oh, Boys In Brown', poem, *Sydney Morning Herald*, 10 July 1915, p. 12.

Letter, *Sydney Morning Herald* and *Daily Telegraph*, 25 September 1915, urging early closing of hotels to aid the war effort.

Letter, *Sydney Morning Herald* and *Daily Telegraph*, 29 September 1915, explaining her use of the phrase 'soured temperance reformer'.

'The Gallant Risk', article in *Daily Telegraph*, 15 October 1915, p. 6, urging government action on early closing of hotels.

Interview by Bertram Stevens in *Lone Hand*, 1 November 1915, pp. 355–8.

'War! And Our Weapons Not All In Use!', article in *Sydney Morning Herald*, 13 November 1915, p. 8.

'Not Beer Gardens. Music Gardens with Light Beer', article in *Sydney Morning Herald*, 20 November 1915, p. 16.

'His Wonders to Perform', *Windsor Magazine*, 20 March 1916.

'Magic Moment', verse, *Sydney Morning Herald*, 1 June 1916.

'*Sed Miles, Sed Pro Patria*', poem in memory of Captain Arthur Ferguson, *Sydney Morning Herald*, 5 July 1916, p. 12.

'Getting Dressed', *Windsor Magazine*, August 1916, vol. xxxxiv, pp. 213–16.

'Yes!', poem in *Sydney Morning Herald*, 4 October 1916, to accompany a leader written by C. Brunsdon Fletcher, 'The Great Issue'.

'Hostels', *Sydney Morning Herald*, 3 December 1917.

'The Things of Youth', poem, Joan of Arc Gift Day Souvenir Programme, 15 December 1917.

'The Someone or Something', poem, *Hermes*, August 1918, p. 225.

'From a Woman in a Valley. Bits of a Real Life', article, *Daily Telegraph*, 5 March 1919, p. 6.

'The Sun is on the Hill', article, *Sydney Morning Herald*, 14 June 1919, p. 9.

'Spring Cleaning. And the Business in our Midst', *Sydney Morning Herald*, 29 October 1919, p. 9.

'Silk Stockings. Keeping up the Cost of Living. Women's Responsibility', article, *Daily Telegraph*, 28 January 1920, p. 9.

'Paradise', *Smith's Weekly*, 31 January 1920, p. 3.

'The Seeing Eye', *Smith's Weekly*, 13 March 1920, p. 4.

'A Great Gift. An Autumn Race Meeting', article, *Sydney Morning Herald*, 6 March 1920, p. 7.

'A Woman in a Valley', article, *Daily Telegraph*, 17 August 1921, p. 8.

Sydney *Sun*, begins Children's Page, titled 'Sunbeams', 9 October 1921.

'Popular Australian Writer. A Chat with Ethel Turner', interview, *Daily Telegraph*, 10 June 1922, p. 13.

'Too Much to do. School Drudgery', speech at Sydney Girls' High School, *Daily Telegraph*, 13 December 1922.

Interview by Carlotta Smith, *Woman's World*, 1 February 1923, p. 99.

'A Prophet's Honour', *Smith's Weekly*, 8 December 1923, p. 13.

'John Hunter', poem in memory of Professor John Hunter, *Sydney Morning Herald*, 12 December, p. 13.

'The Power and the Glory', *Wentworth Magazine*, July 1925, p. 4ff.

'The Orange Frock', *Wentworth Magazine*, October 1925, pp. 4, 10, 38.

'The Salad', *Wentworth Magazine*, 3 December 1925.

'Palm Beach', poem, *Sydney Morning Herald*, 16 March 1926.

'Across the Creek. A Visit to New Zealand', a series of articles in the *Sydney Morning Herald* from July to September 1926.

'Paradise Valley', story, *Sun*, 26 December 1926, p. 5.

'Waters of Wellington, poem, c. 1926.

Interview by Nora Cooper, photographs by Cazneaux, 'The Home of an Australian Authoress', *Australian Home Beautiful*, 2 July 1928, pp. 13–17.

'Mrs Billington', *Home Magazine*, December 1928.

'Lady Cullen. Some Memories', obituary, *Sydney Morning Herald*, 17 June 1931, p. 10.

'Girlhood Memories', article in Women's Supplement, *Sydney Morning Herald*, 23 November 1933.

'Book at Midnight', verse, (Burns Philp), 24 September 1934, pp. 52–3.

'There was a Cherry Tree', verse, *Sydney Morning Herald*, December 1934.

Interview by Margot Kinnear, 'Ethel Turner at Home', *Woman*, 14 February 1935.

'At the Roots of the Mountains', *Sydney Mail*, 10 April 1935, pp. 10–12 (a composite story).

'The Death Ride', *Murder Pie*, Angus & Robertson, 1936.

'Ethel Turner's Achievements. Recognition by Fellow Writers', *Sydney Morning Herald*, 11 June 1936, p. 19.

'A Good-Bye to Redgum', obituary of Mr Lockley who had written a nature column for many years, *Sydney Morning Herald*, 29 May 1937, p. 12.

'They are Seven. Ethel Turner's Beloved Story of Australia Becomes a Film', *Women's Weekly*, 2 December 1939.

'The Broken Siesta', and 'An Afternoon Call', *Some Stories by Ten Famous Writers*, New Century Press, Sydney, 1940, pp. 229–46, 247–65. Ethel's contributions were probably the last stories she published.

Interview by Margaret Adams in *Christian Science Monitor*, 18 April 1941.

'Ethel Turner Writes New Book at 75. Little Australians have read her stories for fifty years', interview by Joan Powe, *Women's Weekly*, 6 November 1948, pp. 17–18.

Interview by M.K., in 'Outstanding Women of our Time', *A.B.C. Weekly*, 13 August 1949, p. 4.

Interview by Marie J. Fanning, 'An Authoress at Home', *NZ Women's Weekly*, 10 November 1949.

'She's Read by Millions', interview in *People*, 28 February 1951, pp. 13–15.

SECONDARY SOURCES:
Books
Ackerman, Jessie, *Australia from a Woman's Point of View*, London, 1913.

Barker, A. W., *Letters to an Australian Publisher: Dear Robertson*, Sydney, 1982.

Bloomfield, Lin (ed.), *The World of Norman Lindsay*, Melbourne, 1979.

Clark, Axel, *Christopher Brennan: A Critical Biography*, Carlton, 1980.

Clark, Rosemary, *Literary Legends of the 1890s*, Melbourne, 1991.

Clarke, Patricia, *Pen Portraits, Women Writers and Journalists in Nineteenth Century Australia*, Sydney, 1988;

Docker, John and Modjeska, Drusilla (eds), *Nellie Melba*; *Ginger Meggs and Friends: Essays in Australian Cultural History*, Malmsbury, 1982.

Ferrier, Carole (ed.), *As Good as a Yarn with you: Letters between Miles*

Franklin, Katharine Susannah Prichard, Jean Devanny, Marjorie Barnard, Flora Eldershaw and Eleanor Dark, Cambridge, 1992.

Green, H. M., *A History of Australian Literature*, 2 vols, Sydney, 1961.

Howley, Adrienne, *My Heart, My Country*, Brisbane, 1989.

Kramer, Leonie (ed.), *The Oxford History of Australia*, Melbourne, 1981.

Lawson, Sylvia, *The Archibald Paradox: a stange case of authorship*, Melbourne, 1971.

Lindsay, Norman, *Bohemians of the Bulletin*, Sydney, 1965.

Margarey, Susan, *Unbridling the Tongues of Women: A Biography of Catherine Helen Spence*, Sydney, 1985.

Miller, E. Morris, *Australian Literature 1795–1928*, 2 vols, Sydney, 1975.

Modjeska, Drusilla, *Exiles at Home: Australian Women Writers, 1925–45*, Melbourne, 1981.

Niall, Brenda, *Australia through the Looking-Glass: Children's Fiction 1830–1980*, Melbourne, 1980.

Niall, Brenda, *Seven Little Billabongs*, Melbourne, 1982.

Norman, Lilith, *The Brown and Yellow, Sydney Girls' High School 1883–1983*, Melbourne, 1983.

Palmer, Vance, *A. G. Stephens: His Life and Work*, Melbourne, 1941.

Palmer, Vance, *The Legend of the Nineties*, Melbourne, 1954.

Park, Ruth, *A Fence around the Cuckoo*, 1992; *Fishing in the Styx*, 1993, Ringwood.

Roberts, Jan, *Maybanke Anderson: Sex, Suffrage & Social Reform*, Sydney, 1993.

Roderick, Colin, *Henry Lawson: Poet and Short Story Writer*, Sydney, 1966.

Roe, Jill (ed.), *My Congenials: Miles Franklin & Friends in Letters, 1879–1954*, 2 vols, Sydney, 1993.

Saxby, Maurice, *A History of Australian Children's Literature 1841–1970*, 2 vols, Sydney, 1969–1971.

Saxby, Maurice, *The Proof of the Puddin': Australian Children's Literature 1970–1990*, Gosford, 1993.

Tate, Audrey, *Ada Cambridge: Her Life and Work 1844–1926*, Melbourne, 1991.

Thorne, L. G., *A History of North Shore Sydney from 1788 to Today*, Sydney, 1968.

Wilde, William H., Hooton, Joy and Andrews, Barry, *Oxford Dictionary of Australian Literature*, Melbourne, 1985.

Wilde, W. H. and Moore, T. Inglis (eds), *Letters of Mary Gilmore*, Melbourne, 1980.

Articles

Coupe, Sheena, 'All the World ought to be Respectably Comfortable: Aspects of the Social Philosophy of Ethel Turner', *Orana*, vol. 15, no. 1, February 1979, pp. 15–19.

Mills, Carol, 'Illustrators: D. H. Souter (1862–1935)', *Lu Rees Archives*, Issue 7, 1986, pp. 17–21.

Niall, Brenda, 'Mythmakers of Australian Childhood', *This Australia*, Summer 1881–2, pp. 64–72.

Nimon, Maureen, 'Ethel Turner. A re-assessment of some aspects of her work', *Orana*, February 1987, pp. 17–22.

Rossiter, Richard, 'Australian Children's Literature: A Question of Values', *Orana*, February 1991, pp. 6–17.

Ryan, J. S., 'The Ongoing Significance of Ethel Turner', *Orana*, November 1980, pp. 141–7.

Walker, David, 'War, Women and the Bush: The Novels of Mary Grant Bruce and Ethel Turner', *Historical Studies*, vol. 18, no. 71, 1978, pp. 297–315.

White, Kerry M., 'Blooming with Childhood Fragrance: Sweet Words and Tough Times for Women Writers in the 1890s', *Australian Feminist Studies*, Summer 1988, pp. 49–63.

Yarwood, A. T., 'Ethel Turner and the Concept of "Two Kinds of Australian Patriotism"', *Magpies*, no. 3, July 1993, pp. 13–14.

Two names stand out. Philippa Poole kept the memory of her grandmother green in the minds of millions and created, in *The Diaries of Ethel Turner*, a collection to which I constantly resorted, for Ethel left one of the great Australian literary diaries. And I pay tribute to an English friend, Peter Radford, a former Chief Superintendent of Scotland Yard, who unravelled Ethel's background in England.

Many illustrations came from the Poole Collection, to which my debt is sincerely acknowledged. The Mitchell Library has been generous in its help largely through Paul Brunton and the manuscript and photographic collections. Access to the rich store of maps and photographs at the Sydney Water Board made a huge difference to the task of finding illustrations. Important also was the assistance given by Kay Clarke and my friends at the Mosman Library. Ruth Park and Jyoti Brunsdon made available formerly unpublished photographs of some of Ethel's associates.

Archivists at Sydney Girls' High School and Newington were immensely helpful, and also the owners of homes where the Cope family lived, including Dr Bremer, Mr Mouratidis and Mrs Patricia Mills. I spent a month at 'Varuna', courtesy of the Eleanor Dark Foundation, which gave leisure and stimulus for writing and enabled me to visit 'Yanalla' and 'Garth', Ethel's homes in Leura.

Several people lent copies of Ethel's many novels, including Geoffrey King, Vanessa Lowe and Lady Curlewis, while scores recalled the pleasure they had had as readers, of whom the late D'Arcy Niland, Helen Kenny and Patti Miller were outstanding. My friends Rosemary Parle and Marianne Payten helped with the proofs while Ann Carr-Boyd gave much support and encouragement.

Sandy Yarwood, Sydney.

Index

338–9; and charity work 352; and
first home 329-30; on HC's death
340; marriage of 308; and
relationship with ET 347;
Curlewis, Billy 124
Curlewis, Dolly 129, 167, 271
Curlewis, Ethel *see* Turner, Ethel
Curlewis, Frederick 40, 169
Curlewis, Georgiana 40, 53, 61, 116,
271
Curlewis, Herbert Raine 1; and
bicycling 225, 153; and Charles
Cope 167; and career 41, 65, 67, 77,
111, 245, 320; as contributor to
Parthenon 25; and contribution to
ET's work 129; and courtship of
ET 29, 32–3, 40, 42, 43, 44–5,
48–9, 50–1, 52, 66–7, 94; death of
339–340; education of 25; in
England 197–205; family
background 40–41, 76; health of
180, 194–5, 253–4, 277, 278, 318,
325–6, 329, 337; marriage of 116,
118–9, 277; at Newington 152; on
religion 59; and WWII 330; as
writer 43–4, 94, 104, 126, 151, 183,
203
Curlewis, Ian 332; birth of 311;
childhood of 309, 313, 317, 324,
335, 336, 350; education of 354; as
lawyer 357
Curlewis, Jean 167–8, 347; birth of
141; as bridesmaid 162, 192;
childhood of 150, 169–70, 174, 212;
and Christian Science 309; death of
310, 324; education of 168, 184,
188, 195, 224, 245–6; and family
entertainment 163; health of 269,
285, 293, 300–1, 305, 308–9;
marriage of 284, 286; as writer 157,

245, 253, 263, 276, 277, 290, 295,
299, 300, 334
Curlewis, Philippa birth of 318;
childhood of 335, 331, 323, 345; on
ET's death 361; and family
relationships 333; and swimming
354
Curtis Brown 202, 209, 210–11 *see also*
literary agents

Daily Telegraph, 81, 91, 104–5, 171,
172, 179–80, 212, 276; and ET's
speech at SGHS 278; and HC's
serial 203; and temperance 241
'Dame Durden' ET writing as 71, 80,
95, 129, 136, 164, 218; *see also*
pseudonyms
Dark, Eleanor 195, 349–50; *see also*
O'Reilly, Pixie
Dark, Eric 195, 350
'Daveney Daunt' ET writing as 223;
see also pseudonyms
Depression, the 78, 313–14
Diary of a Dairy Farm (ET) 193
diaries of ET, 1 and *passim*
Drought Relief Committee 171
Drought Relief Fund 172

English Comedy Company 165
'Erang' 17, 21
Ethel Turner Annual 190
Ethel Turner Birthday Book (LT) 195–6
Ethel Turner Prize for Literature 12
Evans, Wynifred 168–9, 184–5
Fair Ines (ET) 193–4, 195, 198, 201,
209, 210, 230
Fairy (LT) 199; *see also* Turner, Lilian
as writer
Family at Misrule, The (ET) 86, 96,
111, 124; and translation of 113

Thompson, Lilian *see* Turner, Lilian; *see also* Burwell, Lilian

Three Little Maids (ET) 7, 11, 17, 121, 133, 139, 140, 149, 152, 204

Titanic sinking of 205, 216, 217

Town and Country Journal 2, 72, 79, 80, 86, 91, 125, 126, 159, 179, 183, 195, 213, 218; *see also* Jeffery, Walter

Turner, Annie 10

Turner, Ethel childhood of 3, 10, 11–15, 18, 67–8, 177, 204, 258, 279; as business woman 17, 25, 85, 96, 98, 111, 126–7, 210, 221–2, 257–8, 304, 319, 323, 327; courtship by Herbert 1, 32–3, 40, 42, 43, 44–5, 48–9, 50–1, 52, 66, 90; diary of 1, 2, 22, and *passim*; death of 361; on education 22, 169, 181, 217, 218, 277–8; on exercise 28, 147, 153, 187, 190, 219; and family relationships 7, 79, 80–1, 105, 126, 148, 168, 178, 244–5, 276, 286–7, 298–8, 347; finances of 77–8, 155, 161, 179, 191, 268, 281, 352; as gardener 58, 182, 214–5, 275, 344–5, 351; health of 76, 102, 131, 132–3, 139, 141, 143–4, 147, 152, 157, 187, 205, 246, 291, 302, 321, 336, 342, 343–4, 346–7, 353; and literary circles 125, 164, 203, 245; on marriage 1, 22, 33, 92–3, 99, 112, 116, 118–19, 128–9, 130–31, 149, 181, 325, 340; as playwright 82, 156, 165, 170–11, 178, 190, 202, 216, 223, 239, 288; as poet 32, 151, 154, 179, 182–3, 188–9, 206–7, 228, 237–8, 247; and politics 78, 171, 181, 221, 235, 246–7, 314; overseas sales 4, 124, 177–8, 209, 210, 232; pseudonyms of, *see individual entries for* 'Aunt Elgitha', 'Chief Sunbeamer', 'Dame Durden', 'Daveney Daunt', 'Princess Ida', 'Sheila Shaw', 'Yum Yum'; as public speaker 195, 207, 277–8, 344, 357; and religious beliefs 13, 14, 28, 37, 38–9, 58–9, 111, 145, 237; self-education of 31, 46–7, 63, 91, as song writer 164–5, 220, 303; on temperance 149, 240–2; translations of 113, 124, 151, 321; and travel 92–4, 192–205, 297–9; and war(s) 224–5, 226–7, 327, 333, 334, 338–9, 341–2, 345–6; on women's role 55, 81, 89, 108, 135, 137, 173, 202, 261–2; on writing for adults 88, 156, 177, 223.

Turner, Henry 8, 9, 204

Turner, Lilian 178, 287, 356; and ambitions 34; attitude to HC 67–8, 73; education of 14; relationship with ET 7, 126; as writer 17, 23, 47, 64, 103, 106, 127, 195, 199, 201, 244–5, 299, 307; *see also* Burwell, Lilian

Turner, Lucy 10, 11, 12; *see also* Board, Lucy

Turner, Jeanie Rose 33, 47, 80, 105; birth of 9, 204; marriage of 162; *see also* Pockley, Rose 165

Turner, Sarah 8, 9, 10, 11; *see also* Cope, Sarah

Two and Two (ET) 353, 354

Ungardeners (ET) 288, 289

'Under God's Sky' (ET) 166

University Dramatic Society 83, 102

University of Sydney 14; ET social ties with 39; open to women 18